Architects of Delusion

To John Broderick —

With appreciation for

his leadership, and

with friendship —

Simon —

Architects of Delusion

Europe, America, and the Iraq War

Simon Serfaty

PENN

University of Pennsylvania Press

Philadelphia

PUBLISHED BY

UNIVERSITY OF PENNSYLVANIA PRESS

PHILADELPHIA, PENNSYLVANIA 19104−4112

Printed in the United States of America on acid-free paper

10 9 8 7 6 5 4 3 2 1

A Cataloging-in-Publication record is available from the
Library of Congress

ISBN-13: 978-0-8122-4060-3
ISBN-10: 0-8122-4060-X

For my students, past and present—with appreciation

CONTENTS

Introduction

THE ALLEGED FACTS of "power and weakness" that characterized the transatlantic debate over the use of force in Iraq were theoretically flawed and historically misleading. Theoretically, the "facts" of American power appeared to reduce the concept of power to its military dimension at the expense of, or over, anything that might expose U.S. weakness. Historically, the "facts" of European weakness neglected the postwar transformation of Europe into a union that gives its members the nonmilitary power they lack individually. All together, the argument conveyed a sense of lasting American omnipotence for what was no more than passing preponderance, while providing a caricature of Europe as an avid consumer of American capabilities and a demanding producer of additional security responsibilities for the United States.

A conversation that starts with a cursory "Me Tarzan, you Jane" is not conducive to a dialogue. Absent a dialogue, there is little room for consultation, and without consultation there is no alliance of sovereign countries but, at best, coalitions: one coalition per mission, one mission per coalition, organized by the preponderant power—the "sheriff" in the posse—with states that are willing to join for reasons of their own, even if they are not sufficiently capable for, or directly relevant to, the mission.[1]

This book is not about America's power and the weakness of its main European allies—Britain, France, and Germany—but about the power and the weaknesses of both, the United States in its prevailing condition of preponderance, and the states of Europe in their new but unfinished incarnation as a European Union (EU).

The facts of American power are not in doubt. At home, knowledge of these facts sharpened citizen anger at the horrific events of September 11, 2001, which could not be allowed to stand unanswered, and led most Americans to rebel against like-minded allies who grew unwilling to stand with their senior partner after the broad consensus achieved in Afghanistan collapsed over Iraq. Without a doubt, much that has been learned over the years has weakened the U.S. case for war in Iraq, as it was initially presented by the Bush administration and embraced by much of the country. By now the nation's anger is aimed no less at the decision proper than at its execution: more specifically, an incapacity to prepare for the aftermath of the war, on the basis of what was known at the time, and an unwillingness to acknowledge mistakes and make related tactical adjustments until it proved too late. After a relatively easy, and remarkably effective, military campaign in Iraq in the spring of 2003, the U.S. failure grew out of a devastating combination of an inept postwar strategy for peacekeeping and an ill-prepared civilian management for peacemaking. Nearly four years into the war, the former was confirmed at the highest levels of the Bush administration in the days and weeks that followed Secretary Donald Rumsfeld's replacement in early November 2006, after the latter had been demonstrated repeatedly on the ground during the previous years.

The decision to wage war on Saddam Hussein—after the arithmetic of risk taking had been seemingly modified by the attacks on New York City and the Pentagon—was made by George W. Bush on behalf of America and with the nonpartisan support of Americans. In its immediate post-September 11 context, the war was widely viewed as the extension of the existential war that had begun with the earlier intervention in Afghanistan. Only subsequently did the mounting evidence of failure help turn it progressively into an "imagination war"—a war of choice rather than a necessary war.[2] The progression is not without significance: this was an American war that received the near unanimous support of the U.S. Senate before it became Bush's war at home and a civil war in Iraq. Conditions were different in Europe, where the case for war never proved convincing, even in the countries that joined the coalition and as other acts of terror took place—Madrid on March 11, 2004, and London on July 7, 2005, among other such targets. Indeed, after a short-lived moment of collective mourning, the post-September 11 debate in Europe was an intra-European debate over American power before it became a Euro-Atlantic debate over Iraq; and even when it became the latter, the debate was narrowly limited to the war in Iraq rather than extended to its broader context of "the long war" of September 11.

The pages that follow, however, are not designed as a historical narrative of this multidimensional debate, both within Europe and with the United States, and its consequences. Rather, they present a historical interpretation of how and why the decision to wage war in Iraq came to be endorsed by some of America's main European allies (especially Britain) and opposed by others (especially France and Germany).

Written into that interpretation is the assumption that there was not much the allies could do unless they acted together, which, of course, they did not do. Bush and his administration understood that basic fact of transatlantic relations better than their interlocutors: no single European state can effectively derail, deflect, or assist an American decision deemed to be of vital significance to U.S. security interests because none can show enough weight to act decisively as an effective counterpart to U.S. leadership, let alone an adversarial counterweight of American power. That ability to influence America for the better can only be exerted by Europe as a union: it is that ability that was squandered by Tony Blair, Jacques Chirac, and Gerhard Schroeder, as their divisions left them with little tangible influence on the United States and, accordingly, on the war that became the centerpiece of the post-September 11 security agenda.

The heads of state and government that are at the center of this book were the architects of the most serious crisis in transatlantic relations since the mid-1950s, when an agonizing debate over the terms of Germany's rearmament, soon followed by a dramatic clash over an Anglo-French attempt to reassert their status and influence in the Middle East, threatened to derail the Atlantic Alliance and kill any serious prospect of European integration. Each of these men, however, was an agent of his country's traditions, interests, attitudes, and policies. They were all, therefore, the victims not only of their own delusions but also of their nations' illusions.

To be sure, more than any of his predecessors, a domineering and righteous George W. Bush gave his critics in Europe a target that proved particularly conducive to hostility and even bellicosity. Surfacing after Europe's pledges of "total solidarity" that were extended over the attacks of September 11, Bush found such an antagonistic tone understandably offensive, first coming from Schroeder during the German elections of September 2002 and next coming from Chirac during the weeks of confrontation in early 2003. Yet reducing the crisis that followed to issues of personalities would neglect a more decisive element—the fact that neither Bush and Blair nor Chirac and Schroeder changed the established terms of their countries' relations with one another: "terms of estrangement" between France and either the United States or Britain, "terms of endearment" between the United States and either Britain or Germany, "terms of disparagement" between Britain and either Germany or France, and "terms of entanglement" between them all. As a result, all four men played the hand that their countries had handed them—the forceful hand of preponderance for a righteous America, the principled hand of acquiescence for a faithful Britain, the determined hand of intransigence for a quarrelsome France, and the ambiguous *deutscher Weg* of a recast Germany that cannot yet provide a convincing explanation of what is precisely the new "German way."

That hand, however, was not well played by any one of these four heads of state and government, especially because it proved to be weaker than each one of them seemed to assume.

* * *

Unlike the situation for U.S. allies in Europe, territorial vulnerability to external attacks is not a condition that history has taught America well, and it is not one, therefore, that Americans can feel comfortable with for long. After September 11, any other president of the United States would have taken the same position as George W. Bush and would have been deemed equally right by an overwhelming majority of the populace: the position, that is, that America was at war. But having said that with the appropriate tones of inner fortitude and external confidence, Bush was wrong, by his own admission, to swagger his way into inviting America's new adversaries to "bring it on," hatred and all, and he was ill-advised to follow them in a world that was changed further by the scope and inefficacy of American power after the world had rebelled against the horror and criminality of the acts of terror that inspired its use.[3] It is unto that world that neither Chirac nor Schroeder dared to venture.

Blair understood the risks, but better than anyone outside the United States he also understood and shared Bush's anguish. Like Winston Churchill, whom he sought to emulate, Blair assumed a "blood right to speak" on behalf of "the all-conquering alliance of the English-speaking people" that had been so dramatically challenged in the New World. As had also been the case between Churchill and Roosevelt after America's entry into World War II in December 1941, the events of September 11 brought Bush and Blair together into a genuine and warm friendship based on a mutual appreciation of the truth they had uncovered and now shared to the fullest: Blair's tones were passionate because he personally felt the emotions of that somber moment.[4] Like Bush, Blair reasoned that "we have to act not react" because, as

Vice President Dick Cheney put it, "the risks of inaction are far greater now than the risks of action," including, Blair insisted, a requirement for "preemptive and not simply reactive response[s]" that would be decided "on the basis of prediction not certainty."[5]

Thus Bush and Blair were genuine comrades-in-arms. Strategically, they were both the stepchildren of the 1930s, and the images of appeasement they had of that decade colored their shared vision of the future, Blair admittedly more deeply and more coherently than Bush, and Bush admittedly more spontaneously and more passionately than Blair. Politically, they both belonged to the 1980s and hoped to duplicate the pictures of strength and resolve left by their respective predecessors, Ronald Reagan and Margaret Thatcher, who had most influenced them and who had also shared a similar intimacy at the close of the Cold War as Bush and Blair would share at the start of a new global war.

That in opposition to Blair or Bush, Chirac took the lead in organizing Europe's anti-Anglo-Saxon brigade should not come as a surprise, but, however predictable, that did not help moderate the conflict that followed. Over the years, France has been America's most outspoken, most reluctant, and most frustrating ally—and, by French standards, so was America to them. Paradoxically, each, as will be shown, has also been the other's most rewarding and effective partner. Yet, even in the context of such a history of bilateral discord and cooperation, and notwithstanding the clichés that either country uses to define the other, the French and Chirac bashing, as well as the anti-American and anti-Bush discourse, that erupted in 2003 were unprecedented and troubling: a display of ill will, hostility, and even anger that paradoxically unveiled the passion that the United States and France feel for and about each other when either fails to live up to expectations. No less than America's relationship with Britain, France's relationship with the United States is therefore "special," although clearly with opposite consequences.

In the midst of this public quarrel, the French kept their sight on America's power, but Americans seemed to lose sight of their interlocutor's. Yet, and as had been apparent throughout the Cold War, the nature of French influence should have been obvious. France, as a middle-size to small power, matters to the United States to the extent that France matters to Europe, whose elevation to an integrated union in turn matters to the United States as a like-minded ally of choice. Subsequently, Robert Kagan, the godfather of the power-and-weakness argument, also discovered an "embraceable EU" and, in a belated afterword written for his earlier work, insisted that "to address today's global threats Americans will need the legitimacy that Europe can provide."[6] That came late, however, though it is not without a touch of irony that by early 2007 the architects of such grand intellectual constructs as the famous conversion of "French fries" into "freedom fries"—designed to reflect the U.S. bitterness over France's obstructionism at the United Nations—were deserting their own party to vote against President Bush's decision to increase the number of U.S. forces deployed in Iraq.[7]

Even though the U.S. need went beyond the vague idea of "legitimacy" to include the more tangible but nonmilitary dimensions of EU power and influence, renewed concern in the United States that "Europeans may well fail to provide" that power, however defined, is justified. As a matter of historical fact, Europe's capacity to do so is highly dependent on France, whose relations with the United States thus determines, to a significant extent, the future of U.S. relations with the European Union. In other words, while France can act most decisively if and when it speaks with and on behalf of Europe, the United States can also best depend on Europe when the European allies act collectively as a union that includes France, as well as Britain, but also Germany. In short, without Europe, France may not count for much, but without France, it may not be possible to count on Europe for much.

* * *

Years later, a main regret written into this book is not, or not only, that Chirac and Schroeder, unlike Blair, openly attempted to stand in the way of Bush's decision. Nor is it that Blair, unlike his two main counterparts across the English Channel, was an uncritical follower of Bush for too long. The regret instead is that neither the opposition of Chirac et al. nor the support of Blair et al. produced much effect. However directed, a common European position would have had more influence in helping the United States avoid or correct mistakes heavy with consequences for all. But Chirac or Schroeder's opposition was no better stated to, and no more readily understood by, Bush than the latter's decision was communicated to, or acknowledged in, Paris or Berlin. As to Blair, he neither gained enough influence in Washington nor showed sufficient motivation relative to Paris and Berlin to convince either side otherwise: not enough influence, that is, to convince Bush that Chirac and Schroeder were not wrong in seeking a postponement of the war, but not enough motivation in convincing Chirac and Schroeder that Bush was not wrong in wanting a war that would at last topple the "evil regime" in Iraq.

Ironically, each of these men had previously anticipated a different policy course aimed at reversing the paths taken by their respective predecessors: Chirac, who had hoped to make of France America's best ally; Blair, who had planned to restore Britain's leadership in Europe; Schroeder, who had wanted to reduce Germany's dependence on France by achieving unprecedented intimacy with Britain; and even Bush, who had spoken of ending the false divisions that remained after the Cold War both within Europe and with the United States. Whose fault it is that each man ended at the opposite end of the spectrum from his initial goal can be debated. The contention here is that, as none was entirely right, none was entirely wrong either in his approach to the others but also to the issues, before and during the war as well as after the war's major combat operations in the spring of 2003. More important, however, and most specifically, their conflict over Iraq confirmed that political unity in Europe now depends on effective cooperation between Britain and France no less than it does on France's cooperation with Germany. Absent Anglo-French cooperation, Europe's ability to influence the United States—or, to put it more bluntly, to constrain America's preponderance while asserting Europe's own relevance—is weakened.

* * *

As an intra-European debate over the use of American power in and beyond Iraq, the debate over Iraq was also an Anglo-French debate about Europe. "Should England and France agree to act together," de Gaulle told Churchill as he was urging an Anglo-French alliance in November 1944, "they will wield enough power to prevent anything being done which they themselves have not accepted or decided."[8] However wishful that sort of thinking may seem, it persisted: after September 11, no less than after the Cold War and as had been the case after World War II, bilateral relations between France and Britain have continued to define largely the sort of future available for the European Union and its relations with the United States. Like Josephine Baker in the old postwar days, Blair had *deux amours—mon pays* (and Britain's privileged relationship with the United States) *et Paris* (meaning, the making of an integrated Europe that he knew he could influence only by endearing himself to the French). The fault for Blair, for which history will hold him especially responsible, was to allow Bush's conviction and faith to prevail over his own judgment and related concerns. Only Blair could have influenced Bush enough to modify the course of U.S. policies. Although the British prime minister understood that influence, he stubbornly refused to make use of it. The price for him was not insignificant: not only a loss for Britain but also for Europe—the former because of the leadership Britain failed to gain and the latter because of the cohesion Europe failed to achieve.

For Blair to follow Bush, both in his policies in Iraq and over his broader vision of the post-September 11 security normalcy, was no more surprising than for Chirac to resist him. Aside from Anthony Eden in 1956, whose premiership barely lasted the time of the Suez crisis, this is what Britain's prime ministers have done since Churchill: a choice of the New World across the Atlantic over the Old World across the channel. There were moments of doubt, to be sure, from Macmillan, who seemed ready to give up on President Kennedy and embrace de Gaulle in December 1962, to Blair, who seemed tempted to distance himself from President Clinton and embrace Chirac in December 1998. Even Thatcher, who did not like Bush as much as she loved Reagan, had her moments of ambivalence about the desirability of Britain's close partnership with the United States, over Germany's unification, for example, as did her successor, John Major, who was not averse to showing that he had liked Bush better than he did Clinton. But on the whole, Britain remained faithful, because as a rule, the French were no more trusted in London than the sort of Europe they wanted to build.

When persuading the stronger, which is the better way for the weaker: going alone or going along? When listening to the weaker, which way is better for the stronger: hearing the voice of the faithful or listening to the quarrelsome words of the critic?

Britain and France each had their own question to which they both had different answers. "There is no more dangerous policy in international politics," observed Blair in June 2003, "than that we need to balance the power of America with other competitive powers; different poles around which nations gather."[9] Blair's point was not about the need for balance in an emerging multipolar age: instead, his point was about the need for solidarity in an age of U.S. preponderance. For the French, conversely, the strong "can only lean on something that offers resistance," which, in de Gaulle's view, demanded from France an intransigence that grew out of its character no less than out of its capabilities.[10] Bridging the gap between these two views was made even more difficult during a unipolar moment when accommodation was viewed as an unnecessary sign of weakness by the strong and an undesirable sign of subservience by the weak.

* * *

In any case, and just in case, with the United States estranged from France and not always in unison with Britain, the United States could always view Germany as its fallback position of choice—as an ally that could be tempted by a special partnership with the United States, the only country that fully embraces rather than disparages signs of a renewed Germany, united and strong. Blair's personalized embrace of Bush and Iraq was a matter of national tradition but also one of personal conviction; for Chirac, opposition to America and Iraq was not only a matter of tradition—France's "instinctive fear of giants"—but also a matter of geopolitical convictions. As to Schroeder, his opposition to Bush, America, and Iraq, while occasionally experienced during the short postwar life of the new Germany, was also a matter of personal dislike and political opportunism.

Throughout the Cold War, the Germans said little about their own future; after the Cold War, they thought little about their past. Their allies did, though—especially Britain and France, whose constant disparagement of a German nation said to have brought shame to Europe and the world did not quite end when a divided Germany joined its two victorious powers in the West. As Germany was thus recast within the North Atlantic Treaty Organization (NATO) and the emerging European community—a winner at last, for the first time in the twentieth century, marveled Chancellor Helmut Kohl—it gained a voice that, notwithstanding a distinctive French accent, was nonetheless encouraged by the United States. After the Cold War, Bush and Clinton both wanted to make Germany America's new privileged partner—a copartner in peace. But power over, rather than with, Europe—and against, rather than with, France—is neither what Germany wants nor what Europe needs. Instead, Germany's new postwar(s) normality responds to a logic of minimal appropriateness and maximal adaptability: the lesser the better.[11]

Schroeder's objections to Bush—his insubordination and betrayal, deplored his critics—were also motivated by his understanding of September 11 in the context of Germany's changed appreciation of force as a legitimate tool of action in the world. For Germans of all persuasions, the events of September 11, 2001, were not those of a *global war* of such unprecedented nature as to demand a radical preemptive strategy of regime change—meaning, in Iraq. Rather, this was a *specific crime* whose direct perpetrators had to be punished—meaning, in Afghanistan.[12] Seemingly Bush neither understood nor welcomed Schroeder's new Germany, born during the Cold War, matured since reunification, and now eager to show how to use and respect its power and its institutions within the limits set by its new traditions and commitments. Chirac did. As a result, bilateral relations between France and Germany grew closer while the gap between Germany and both Britain and the United States grew wider. Yet, in each of these cases, Schroeder enjoyed an autonomy that none of his predecessors had dared assume: this was Schroeder's hidden battle. Compared to those who had preceded him and whom Schroeder viewed disdainfully as trained parrots, the German chancellor viewed himself as a true patriot—now at last, a "partner without restrictions," explained his chief diplomatic adviser during Schroeder's initial encounter with a newly elected President Bush.[13]

* * *

Schroeder is gone, as are Chirac and Blair, both of whom left long past their time. Surprisingly, it is Schroeder who was able to leave office most honorably in the fall of 2005, a near winner in an early election that he had been reportedly sure to lose. By comparison, Chirac and Blair fared quite poorly during their closing political lap in 2006. Apparently, dissenting from Bush did not serve the French president at home any better than following him served the British prime minister's political fortunes. In 2007, Chirac could not run for a third presidential term, as he had hoped, and Blair could not complete his own third term, as he had wished. Yet it is on the U.S. president that instant historians render their harshest verdict. The charge of incompetence is heard, with unusual bipartisan tone and no longer from Europe, where the Chirac-Schroeder coalition of the discontented has overwhelmed the Bush-Blair coalition of the willing, but in the United States, where the ranks of the discontented have also swollen to include three-fifths of the public. "The thing I know now that I did not know then," noted an especially competent military historian whose writing had earlier provided an education for Bush and his most senior advisers, "is just how incredibly incompetent we [Americans] would be." And another neocon figure added, notwithstanding a known and long-standing friendship with Cheney, Rumsfeld et al.: "what I considered to be the most competent national-security team since Truman . . . turned out to be among the most incompetent teams in the postwar era."[14]

Like Reagan, but unlike Blair and Chirac, Bush did not conceive all of the American policy on Iraq, but no policy could have been conceived without him leading the way. But unlike Ronald Reagan, who did not know much but knew enough "to find his way from an ideological instinct to a practical course of action," George W. Bush did not know enough to respond to the changing exigencies of the war because too many of his key advisers, who did all of the policy making, surprisingly showed that they did not know enough themselves.[15] Whether upon their election or after the horrific events of September 11, there was neither a plot nor a plan for Iraq—only an attitude that sought out the facts to the extent that these facts might confirm their assumptions. In short, the new mandarins of the post–Cold War era of U.S. preponderance had grown so very comfortable on an ideological level with the idea of intervention as the fulfillment of the American role in the world—as "a nation uniquely trusted by others . . . a superpower with a conscience"—that they allowed their strategic responsibilities, of which they were fully aware, to be overwhelmed by their moral convictions, to which they were fully committed.[16]

Still, why stop with the United States? There is plenty of blame to go around. Not only Bush and senior members of his administration but also all of his European interlocutors qualify collectively for such a harsh assessment—and sharing the blame, too, are all those who chose to follow or to object, meaning Blair and Chirac and Schroeder and others, too many to be reviewed in this book. The significance of the war in Iraq is such, and the fluidity of new security conditions in the world is such, that there will be ample opportunity for history to pass a more comprehensive and conclusive judgment—and pass it anew and differently when another generation of historians, dubbed revisionist, revisit the issue, as will surely be done many times in the future. For the war in Iraq was not a small event. Its consequences, already evident in 2007 even before the war has run its course, will linger for a generation to come, most directly attributable to a U.S. president who had the time and the fortitude to change the world before his critics, in Europe and at home, were able to change him.

What may remain the same, however, is the tale about Europe and its relations with the United States: That for America and Europe to work together, the United States and France must end their estrangement; that for Europe to work together as a union, France and Britain must resolve their differences; that for the European Union to act as a world power, Germany must carry its weight relative to both France and Britain; and that for the European Union and NATO to resurrect a strong and cohesive West in the emerging new multipolarity that lurches ahead, the United States must exert the same visionary and bold leadership for the twenty-first century that it showed during its rise to preeminence in the twentieth century.

CHAPTER ONE

Terms of Estrangement

"With no other country [in Europe] except France . . . do we feel that
we have to deal with such antipathy," complained Secretary of
State James Baker shortly before the first Gulf War and after a NATO
meeting where the French ambassador had been reportedly told "not to
agree on anything." Baker's counterpart, Roland Dumas, acknowledged,
in a different context, "There is in our attitude a measure of misplaced
pride, a feeling that the United States imposes things on France."

Asked whether he thought the French disliked the Americans, Charles de
Gaulle claimed surprise. "I don't think such a thing [anti-Americanism]
exists. . . . The French people, like most other nations, are xenophobic in
this sense. They want to do things themselves. And they regret it very
much when they cannot. . . . They don't like to resign themselves to
letting others do things for them." [1]

OVER THE YEARS, France has been America's most difficult ally in Europe.
When asserting its leadership in and beyond Europe, the United States repeatedly found France to be an obstacle—the first ally to raise objections,
however marginal, and often the last to join the consensus. So it was after
1945 during the immediate postwar years over the related issues of Germany,
the defeated state whose recovery France wanted to stifle or at least to control;
the Soviet Union, the ascending state whose power France wanted to engage
no less than contain; and the Third World, where France hoped to sustain

its influence even in the midst of its collapsing empire. But so it was, too, after the Cold War over the same related issues of Germany, whose unification the French hoped to delay; the Soviet Union, whose collapse was feared; and the Third World, where U.S. primary influence was not welcomed. During each of these periods, the terms of U.S.-French estrangement often defined the most significant crises that opposed America and its European allies, not only over traditional security issues but also over economic, monetary, and political issues: relations with the Left, trade tensions and the role of the U.S. dollar relative to other national currencies, and even cultural differences.

Paradoxically, in the past six decades, France has also been America's most constructive ally in Europe. That such would be the case can be explained succinctly. After 1945, the much-maligned French Fourth Republic was the main architect of the united Europe that was central to the U.S. postwar vision for the Old World. From the start, the essence of this bold and extravagant idea was understood in the United States: Europe's unity could be neither sought nor achieved without France, whose lead role was therefore both sought and welcomed by the Truman administration, on occasion at the cost of or even because of its relations with other leading European states, including Great Britain and Germany. "The key to progress towards integration is in French hands," noted Secretary of State Dean Acheson in the fall of 1949 as he reasserted America's preference for "some merger of sovereignty" as the most effective tool for the organization of a new security system in Europe.[2]

The irony is there for everyone to see. A Europe that would be strong again but united at last was the cornerstone of the French vision of its future in Europe, even though there were good reasons to question its commitment to enforcing that vision, but it was also the cornerstone of the U.S. vision of its future with Europe, even though its ability to live with that vision after it had been fulfilled could also be questioned. Admittedly, the very idea of a united and strong Europe was especially bold—so bold, indeed, that only the French could dare entertain it under conditions of wartime humiliation and postwar decline. But there was enough pragmatism in the idea for it to be endorsed in, and even adopted by, the United States, thus making it also an American idea.

In subsequent years, within or outside the emerging European institutional structure whose blueprint had been provided by the narrowly construed European Coal and Steel Community, France also proved to be a reliable and proactive partner whenever crises reached a dangerous point:

with Harry Truman in Korea; with Dwight D. Eisenhower over Hungary; with John F. Kennedy during the Cuban missile crisis; with Ronald Reagan over the then-defining issue of further Soviet deployment of strategic forces in Europe; with George Herbert Walker Bush in the Persian Gulf; and with William Jefferson Clinton in Bosnia and Kosovo—not because of an underlying French interest in helping its senior partner but on more elementary grounds of self-interest. In short, however ambivalent the U.S. perception of France is, circumstances and issues have sustained the U.S.-French relationship as one that matters greatly and possibly decisively for the totality of transatlantic relations, including America's relations with other leading European countries within the Atlantic Alliance and relations among European countries within their emerging community, now a union.[3]

The same patterns of estrangement apply on both sides of this complex and passionate bilateral relationship: over the years, America too has been France's most frustrating *and* most rewarding partner, often the source of what France needed to gain most urgently (including security, but also economic prosperity and political stability), as well as an obstacle to what it wanted to preserve most adamantly (including rank and status in the world but also relative to its European partners within the Atlantic Alliance). As former foreign minister Hubert Védrine noted, France's relations with the United States "always seem to reflect a mixture of fascination, sympathy, admiration and exasperation"—a condition that Védrine, unlike his U.S. counterparts, found to be "normal."[4] That such would be the case may well be that on the whole, Paris's reluctant followership of the United States served France rather well and at little cost. The Fifth Republic enjoyed an influence in and beyond Europe that exceeded its power and could be exerted without any fear of U.S. retribution precisely because of its central place in the emerging Euro-Atlantic institutional order. As de Gaulle once noted, and as his successors often felt, for France to be in apparent control of the conditions that controlled it was not unpleasant (*"pas désagréable"*).[5] By the end of the Cold War, France was arguably more stable as a state, more affluent as a nation, and safer as a country than it had been at any time before—and so was Europe, whose expanding community of states also grew exponentially more stable, more affluent, and safer within a cohesive and triumphant Atlantic Alliance with the United States.

Because the French views on any issue of bilateral concern are hardly unique among EU countries, recurring tensions in U.S.-French relations have consequences that are significant and can occasionally be serious.[6] Their repetitiveness should not, therefore, be an invitation to complacency. Nor can they be dismissed as a secondary matter of process over substance, and personalities over issues, at the expense of reality and facts, power and principles. To many of their proponents, these representations suggest a bilateral relationship that may no longer be necessary, relevant, or even desirable. Sensitive to political pressures exerted in either country from the bottom up, but occasionally manipulated by political leaders from the top down, each side is prone to blame the other for faulty leadership or insufficient followership. The cumulative impact of these crises in turn encourages Francophobic and anti-American sentiments that make it even more difficult to address constructively the differences that exist between the United States and France, and thus damage both the alliance that defines the terms of entanglement across the Atlantic and the European Union that defines the terms of state-to-state engagement within Europe. All of these tendencies found their way in the bilateral clash over Iraq that followed the horrific events of September 11, 2001.

Quarrelsome France

"France," it has been said, "is what the French make of it, but the French are what we make of them."[7] Being French does not come easily, or even naturally: it is a full-time commitment—an attitude that defines an identity rather than the other way around. Once the commitment to the idea of France has been made, acting accordingly is all consuming, and becoming un-French is simply not possible, for there is no distinction between the country and the idea it embodies. Abroad especially, living up to the idea (image or cliché) that others have of the French can become a heavy burden. This is not a mission for the weak or the fainthearted. "Obscurely," wrote political scientist Stanley Hoffmann in an autobiographical essay, "I seemed to know that it would be easier for me to be French abroad than in France." Admittedly, Hoffmann, who was taken to prewar France by his Austrian mother as a young boy, had his reasons for this comment. Although his sensibility was "largely French," he acknowledged a "social sensibility" that resisted "the French hardness, style of authority and of human relations." "Teaching" France to Americans, and even "speaking French" to American power was therefore to define his professional life.[8] His lifetime journey in

America was more a discovery of his own Frenchness than it was an unveiling of his emerging Americanness.

Yet even Hoffmann's dedication and considerable intellect were tested. Although (and because) there is no spatially defined or culturally conscious French-born community in the United States, comparable to other groups readily identified and "forgiven" for their Italian, Irish, or Polish origins, for example, Americans will not easily let go of the Frenchness they see and, most of all, hear in anyone or anything. It is not a *death* sentence, to be sure: many an American citizen of immediate French origin or related French background has done well in most areas. But it is a *life* sentence that provides for no parole and is to be simultaneously endured and enjoyed because such Frenchness is itself conducive, among Americans, to the most diverse, but also the most passionate, sentiments—admiration and exasperation, emulation and denunciation, but never indifference and neglect.[9] "Why can't they be like us," asked George Bernard Shaw's Henry Higgins, allegedly puzzled by the behavior of women. To America, France is not a fair lady—which may well be a reason why the early French immigrants who entered the United States from Canada and Arcadia showed a desire and a capacity for assimilation perhaps stronger than for any other national group of immigrants from Europe.[10]

Such tensions were not always apparent. After Americans gave birth to a nation, they developed a personality that was initially molded in opposition to Great Britain and in association with France. A sense of revolutionary affinity, even convergence, linked France and the United States together not only politically but also emotionally and even intellectually.[11] Most Founding Fathers often sounded enthralled with France's "politeness, elegance, softness, delicacy" and other "innumerable" delights—including, according to Benjamin Franklin, "some frivolities" that were gently dismissed as "harmless" by the U.S. ambassador to a country whose capital, Paris, reportedly had more prostitutes than there were soldiers in the American revolutionary army.[12] "Stern and haughty republican as I am," confessed John Quincy Adams in 1778, "I cannot help loving these people." Adams noted approvingly of "the universal opinion of the people here . . . that a friendship between France and America is in the interest of both countries."[13] According to Thomas Jefferson, "Ask the traveled inhabitant of any nation in what country on earth would you rather live? Certainly in my own . . . Which would be your second choice? France."[14]

Yet, over the years, outside the bonds of friendship and mutual feelings of admiration, history steadily drove the two countries apart—though never against each other. For the French, and for others in Europe, history is tragedy, and the ability to survive it, shape it, and, ultimately, master it is evidence of a people's character and greatness.[15] As a result, the nation's feelings about itself, as well as the nation's sense of the world and its own role in the world, are not limited to allegedly "primitive" considerations of force and money, especially when these appear to fall short of other great powers in or beyond Europe. "*Regarder loin et viser haut*," as Charles de Gaulle learned to say during the war years of exile and decadence in London, is a claim—to look far and aim high—that the French comprehend as a mission that must be assumed on behalf (and often in spite) of others;[16] but it is also a mission that must be enforced by the French no less for than in spite of themselves.[17] It is this self-serving idea that defines the French understanding of *droit*—not a mere question of "law," meaning a set of codified obligations and the consequences of not respecting the discipline thus assumed. It is also, and possibly above all, a question of rights, as in *j'ai mes droits*, and an obligation (*devoir*, which is more than a task-oriented duty and nearly a principle-based assignment). Indeed, to insist on these rights even when they are of no immediate consequence or could raise questions of *fair play* (an English phrase that offers, pointedly enough, no appropriate French translation) is itself an obligation.

The idea that Americans have of their nation and themselves offers comparable universal pretensions. Unlike the French, however, Americans have lived a much safer (and shorter) history—one that, according to Védrine, "inspires dreams" among those who had to endure a more dangerous and painful past that cannot be understood, let alone felt, by their privileged partners across the Atlantic.[18] Where the French might remind themselves of what they overcame to achieve greatness and justify the status they still claim, Americans tend to view their God-endowed history as a manmade story of growth that ought to inspire others.[19] In other words, compared to the dangerous and often tragic history traveled by France (and other countries in Europe), America was able to travel light. Its history proved to be mainly an extended exercise in regional cartography, and the ability to conquer, endure, and tame territorial space as a matter of "destiny" was the decisive test of America's character as a people, and its greatness as a nation.

At first, there was little that was unusual in the American journey. Based very openly and confidently on power realities, the U.S. "free ride" to its preeminent status was eased by the protection of the British navy and, until late in the nineteenth century, a stable balance of power in Europe. Thus placed in a geopolitical context that provided for security on the cheap, American diplomats seemed to be seized by a "romantic spirit" that convinced them of the unique role they were called to play in the world.[20] Not just to be good but also to do good (and well); not just to be something but also to change a few things; not just to defeat the enemy in war but also to defeat war itself. The spirit eventually took America back to the continent Americans had left and away from which they had wanted to live. While it was still deemed possible for America to return home after witnessing the aberrant atrocities of World War I and in opposition to the unsustainable peace that followed the war, withdrawal was not an option in 1945, when U.S. statesmen refused to abandon Europe to the Europeans and devised policies that proved to be visionary not only for the goals they sought but also for the methods they favored.

Back in Old Europe after two world wars it had won but had not started, the United States found France to be its most skeptical ally. Already in 1919, no other country had been more willing to oppose or just ignore U.S. leadership, as the French government insisted on enforcing a misbegotten peace that was the source of much trouble afterward. Watching from a distance, Americans were alarmed by the bitterness of French policies toward Germany, especially on the decisive question of wartime reparations. But Paris's stubborn objections to a more lenient policy, which proved especially consequential over the invasion and occupation of the Ruhr barely four years after the Armistice of November 1918, were not helped by the U.S. refusal to write off Europe's war debts: genuinely (and legitimately) appalled, the French led the defaulters in 1933 just as they had led the enforcers ten years earlier.[21] Hence the trauma of defeat in June 1940, when "a certain idea of France" collapsed and a profoundly proud and civilized nation became "a nation of refugees" during four years of German occupation.[22] After that experience, there could no longer be either dependence or surrender, and even the new limits of French power would not be allowed to stand in the way of France's traditional claims for rank and independence as psychological primers for the state's rehabilitation and the nation's renewal.[23] Where other countries might follow either superpower, the ever-quarrelsome French would stand as Europe's proud exception: claiming and asserting France's right to participate in all decisions that might affect its security and well-being, but also attending to the duty of the French state to protect and defend the nation's independence relative to its adversaries and, perhaps most of all, vis-à-vis its allies, including especially the United States, whose postwar and interwar policies were said to have contributed decisively to the calamities that followed.[24]

When Benjamin Franklin was ambassador to Paris, it has been noted, he "quickly mastered the French art of accomplishing much while appearing to accomplish little."[25] That feature was especially in evidence after 1945, when France's reluctance to follow the American leadership did not look like much but still helped produce ideas and initiatives that effectively restored a rank otherwise questioned by U.S. statesmen who remembered the French surrender in June 1940 rather than the huge casualties suffered during the fighting that had preceded it that spring. But despite, or because of, this reluctance, France's ideas, which often were developed in response to or in anticipation of U.S. ideas, helped gain the united and strong Europe, à l'américaine, envisioned by the Truman administration after World War II. Admittedly, Britain stood as a plausible alternative to the leadership eagerly assumed by a weak and politically divided France. But widely viewed in the United States as "the constant stumbling block in the economic organization of Europe," Britain was also heard in the United States as the leading voice for a pervasive anti-American chorus in the Old World, one to which Americans were all the more sensitive as it was articulated in a language they could readily understand.[26]

The French, it often seems, like to make everything difficult for themselves no less than for everyone else.[27] With de Gaulle's Fifth Republic finally putting an end to the constitutional conflicts that had characterized the nation's history since its unfinished revolution of 1789, they could now make things a bit less difficult for themselves at home. But when it comes to others, including especially Britain and, most of all, the United States, the French capacity to be difficult remains relentless. As John F. Kennedy reportedly observed prior to his first meeting with de Gaulle in June 1961, the French seem "to prefer tensions instead of intimacy in [their] relations with the United States as a matter of pride and independence."[28] Their sensitivity is said to stand in the way, as if any disagreement with them demands some sort of apology—indeed, as if allies are expected to apologize for not being French.[29] It is not that the French never do the right thing. But too often, even as they do the right thing, they say the wrong things seemingly for the sheer pleasure to say *something*, especially if it is said well. As a result, bilateral differences are repeatedly most visible in theory—"between the bureaucrats and the officials," noted President George H. W. Bush—notwithstanding the convergences that might exist in practice between the two countries.[30]

In 1919 and during the interwar years, but also after 1945 and throughout the Cold War, it is thus argued, the exercise of American leadership would have been much easier had it not been for the French unwillingness to follow and cooperate. Making of France the source and inspiration of every objection to U.S. policies conveniently implies that were it not for the French there would be no objection to the United States in Europe. *Cherchez la France*: It is more than a bad habit but a reflex, and more than a reflex but nearly a vice. As a matter of fact, no other country in the world endures a comparable discourse of estrangement, suffers the same kind of cultural bashing, lends itself to the same measure of personal disparagement, and faces the same system of demeaning and even outright hostile "clichés, prejudices, obsessions, sensitivities or allergies."[31] Read James Baker, who served as secretary of state during the George H. W. Bush presidency. When negotiating "to get Germany unified . . . it was [unfortunately] business as usual for the French, as [they] objected to almost everything." When preparing for war in the Persian Gulf, writes Baker, the "congenitally difficult" French were, "*as usual* . . . a labor-intensive proposition." When dealing with China over the Tiananmen massacre, "we felt the French were being French"—which, Baker assumes, says it all, as he adds nothing further to describe their attitude.[32] So much for George Bush's praise for François Mitterrand, the "sage French leader . . . , a dependable ally and friend" who presided over France during nearly all the Reagan and Bush presidencies, as well as part of the first Clinton presidency.

Like their anti-American equivalent in France, anti-French attitudes in the United States can be mildly entertaining though fundamentally disturbing and ultimately exasperating—like a harmless but attention-grabbing facial tic. Thus, the instinctive U.S. response to any French idea is initially one of concern, mistrust, and rejection, not because of its merits but because of its origin.[33] But after 1991, and especially after September 11, 2001, the tone became disturbingly vindictive and confrontational. "Can America trust the French?" Baker asked before the first Gulf War; twelve years later, on the eve of the second such war, Vice President Dick Cheney was even blunter when he asked whether "France was an ally or an adversary of the United States."[34] For former senior defense official Richard Perle, the answer was self-evident. "To be blunt about it," he said, "French policy [is] to diminish American influence in Europe, and indeed in the world." *New York Times* columnist Thomas Friedman declared France "at war" with the United States and urged voting France off the UN Security Council and replacing it with

India.[35] The notion—why bother calling it an idea—appeals to a neoconservative intelligentsia that finds the French short on the two central issues of power (and the will to use it) and principles (and a willingness to enforce them). "Why should France keep those unearned privileges [inherent in a central role at the United Nations] when she grows more neo-Vichy all the time . . . ? Tight with the Germans, hostile to England, intensely wary of the United States, no friend of the Jews, contemptuous of Eastern Europe, thoroughly defeatist and desirous above all of avoiding trouble."[36]

Research need not stand in the way of such writing, nor competence stand as an obstacle to such grand characterizations. At their most extreme, these Francophobic exaggerations accomplish a miracle of logic. They tie the abstract of French weaknesses and cowardice with the concrete of France's ability to block and even derail an all-powerful and resolute America. The leading question asked in an abusive book on *The Arrogance of the French* is an example among many. Moving relentlessly from misleading to offensive caricatures, the author finds easy answers to "why they can't stand us—and why the feeling is mutual" with the conclusion that "the shameful vision of France blocking the Anglo-American position at the United Nations convinced Saddam Hussein that he had nothing to fear from ignoring UN calls to come clean."[37]

It is when such diatribes make a historic detour that they become especially gross. "I always marveled at the Europeans' ability to praise Hitler as a man of peace, and get terribly annoyed at Czechoslovakia for . . . existing in his Lebensraum," wrote Michael Ledeen, a leading neocon author. "Needless to say," adds a neocon sympathizer from Britain, when war finally came in 1940, "the French went down with scarcely a fight: mortality amounted to less than 1 percent of the prewar population."[38] How odd. As the war was about to start in September 1939, nearly 5 million Frenchmen were mobilized, many of them fortunate survivors of the mass slaughters that had defined another such war twenty years earlier. The German offensive actually began on May 10, 1940, and German forces entered Paris on June 14. During those horrific six weeks, more than one hundred thousand French citizens died, and nearly two hundred thousand were wounded. After the defeat, nearly 2 million French citizens were sent to prisoners' camps in Germany. Notwithstanding such curious criteria of patriotism, these losses amount to more than "scarcely a fight," even if they did not reach a 1 percent standard that would have required close to 2 million dead to confirm the patriotism of Americans during World War II. Nonetheless, the myth of a cowardly French surrender has taken hold, leaving behind the questionable conclusion that it is France's defeat in June 1940 that precipitated the Western debacle and therefore was the catalyst for America's forced entry in the war (notwithstanding the fact that, sadly enough, it had to be Hitler who declared war on the United States after the Japanese attack on December 7, 1941).

"Thank God for not being French," wrote one of the leaders of the Francophobic brigade in the United States, Canadian-born Charles Krauthammer, who singles out the French as the vanguard of modern anti-Semitism. Conservative columnist George Will adds that this anti-Semitism is so creative as to exist even "without Jews." More than any other feature, anti-Semitism stands as a pillar of what then-defense secretary Donald Rumsfeld dismissed as "Old Europe"—"the release," insists Krauthammer, "of a millennium old urge that powerfully infected and shaped European history."[39] Anti-Semitism, which pointedly links up with pervasive charges of appeasement and cowardice associated with June 1940, complements a pattern of anti-Americanism, to which Germany is insidiously linked, and against which stands a "New Europe" that suffered from the Old Europe and anti-Semitism no less than from Soviet brutality and communism and appreciates, therefore, the benefits of U.S. leadership.

The anti-French case thus rests on a troika of charges that was used conveniently to explain the French "betrayal" in Iraq: a visceral anti-Semitism that serves well the French mercantilist courting of the Arabs at the expense of the Jews; a penchant for appeasement, bound, to use Paul Wolfowitz's reported warning, "to pay some consequences, not just with us, but with other countries who view it this way"; and a bastion of anti-Americanism as the moving force for the construction of Europe as an adversarial counterweight to U.S. power and influence. In 2003, this characterization painted the image of a "French blackmailer" loosely charged with "hypocrisy," "cowardice," and "thuggery."[40] But unlike the burst of anti-Americanism that erupted in France at the expense of Bush more than in the name of America, these passionate U.S. outbursts of Francophobic sentiments explicitly targeted France and its people—no less who they are than what they do or fail to do, not only in Iraq and now but everywhere else and at any time.

Such doubts about French policies and intentions would not be significant if it were not for their consequences for U.S. relations with the totality of Europe and, most of all, for the U.S. perceptions of Europe's transformation into a European Union. With France understood to have played a central role in launching and nurturing the European Community fifty years ago, questions about French intentions in, and related vision of, Europe are cause for ambivalence or worse in the United States. The French, it is said, mainly await the U.S. withdrawal from Europe that they have deemed imminent, and have wished, for decades. As viewed after the Cold War by an American diplomat who knew France well, "So convinced do the French seem that the U.S. will rapidly withdraw its forces from Europe that they are thinking, and at times acting, as if we were already gone."[41] Indeed, complained Senator Gordon Smith, "a belief that NATO and the United States are barriers to be overcome" is central to French thinking and their related plans for Europe.[42] Thus, the case against Europe starts with a case about France—a *procès d'intentions* that goes to the core of U.S. interests, as the French final intent is perceived to be the removal of Europe from its Atlantic context.

This "tale of two new Europes"[43] evokes one Europe that is allegedly Atlanticist and another that is reportedly Gaullist. The tale is told in languages that are fundamentally incompatible: in translation, Europe's Gaullist dimension seems simplistically anti-American while its Atlanticist dimension sounds simplistically anti-European. Evoking this tale in the United States provokes warnings of agonizing reappraisal and transatlantic divorce that have been meant to respond to French challenges over a wide range of issues: the calls for an illusory third force in the late 1940s, the determined opposition to Germany's rearmament early in the 1950s, the strategic objections to the U.S. nuclear deterrent, and the role of the dollar in the 1960s—not to mention, for the balance of the Cold War, France's recurring concerns over every facet of U.S. influence, including its preponderant power, its malign role in the Third World, its pervasive cultural intrusiveness, and much more.

To mute these challenges and to heal the resulting tensions, the United States often relied on a linkage strategy that was designed to isolate the French from their favorite partner of the moment—Great Britain at first, then Germany—even though in so doing Europe's ability to move on with its institutional integration was inevitably affected. Embrace Britain, assuage Germany, and isolate France: Even if France could not be forced back into the Atlantic fold, at least its perceived intent to move Europe away from America would be frustrated by the political counterweights thus built within the European institutions. It is after one of these clashes—over the nuclear deterrent—that a frustrated de Gaulle took France out of NATO, and NATO out of France, in March 1966. To this day, the withdrawal from NATO remains the symbol of French distance from, and occasional hostility to, the

United States, notwithstanding periodic attempts at reconciliation with hints of a French return to NATO—whether from Mitterrand at the Williamsburg Summit in May 1983 or through Chirac's address to the U.S. Congress in February 1996.

During the Cold War, however, bilateral crises between France and the United States never had serious or lasting consequences. The Cold War was won and Europe continued to be built. But after the Cold War seemed to unglue the Atlantic Alliance, and with a European Union moving closer to institutional finality, too much bilateral tension over one or more critical issues could now be truly significant and lastingly prejudicial to all, as it might move Europe behind France because of the United States, and America away from Europe because of France. That concern alone should motivate French and Americans to seek cures for the ailments that keep them separate even when history has sentenced them both to remain inseparable by temperament as well as by interests.

Righteous America

Long before Henry James described and bemoaned the complexities of being American, and even before Alexis de Tocqueville's classical description of *Democracy in America*, it was up to another Frenchman who had left his native Normandy for a new life in New England to uncover the appealing simplicity of America—"this great asylum" where "the poor of Europe have met together" as "Western pilgrims . . . whose labors and posterity will one day cause great changes in the world."[44] Much later, Hubert Védrine, still his country's foreign minister at the time, also acknowledged the "unprecedented domination" of the United States in equally sympathetic terms, as possibly "the result of a project" though certainly not "the result of a plot."[45]

Most Americans share Védrine's benign view of their "preponderant" status in the world. There was a project in 1945—the vision thing—but its hegemonic dimensions were unwanted, mainly the result of Europe's insistent "invitation" to America to extend its stay after the war.[46] Beyond helping win a war or two against Germany, and besides avoiding a war or two with Russia, the American project was to shape a durable European peace structure that would make an ever larger piece of Europe more democratically stable, more economically affluent, and more regionally safe than at any time in its history. That project, which had not been possible after World War I, began after World War II and was sufficiently developed during the Cold War to make of President George H. W. Bush's call for a "whole and free" Europe no more than the completion of Truman's initial postwar vision of a new security order in and beyond Europe.

There is a *mal américain* in France, and its most visible symptom is to deny the many good results of the original U.S. "project" and to fear instead a "plot" that can at last be exposed and defeated in the aftermath of the Cold War. It is this perception of the U.S. intent that helps explain every setback for France in Europe, as well as for Europe and its role in the world, as a consequence of U.S. policies. The cure is said to be self-evident: absent the United States, there would be more Europe, meaning not only more unity in Europe but also more French leadership for Europe. During the Cold War, this flawed logic was anti-Americanism light—the ability, that is, to make an explicit distinction between America and the United States: to respect the original American societal model but not wish to emulate what became of the American Union, to admire America's achievements but not U.S. policies, to like Americans but not the presidents they elect, and to respect American power but not its use.[47] Thus understood, anti-Americanism in France and elsewhere in Europe remained benign because it never raised obstacles that could not be ignored or, at least, quickly overcome. It came and went like the seasons—something for Americans to expect periodically and endure for a moment. It is as if the French fears of, and disappointments with those "baffling Americans" paralleled their own fears and disappointments, as if they deplored America's inability to meet the very standards of perfection that the French themselves were no longer capable of meeting, however hard they tried.[48]

In short, the French mythical idea of France, dear to de Gaulle, mirrors an idea of America, and anti-Americanism in France (and, usually, elsewhere in Europe) is about what America does (or is said to be doing) relative to what it ought to be (or is perceived to be) doing—a proposition that is often shared by almost one-half of the Americans who disagree with their government's policies at any given moment. That is why Americans are usually much more liked in France for who they are than America is for what it does—a broad view that has been reinforced in recent years and stands in opposition to conditions in the United States where France is usually liked more than the French.

In the spring of 2003, however, the debate over Iraq proved to be a perfect storm that moved the traditional terms of U.S.-French estrangement beyond the known terms of exasperation and soothing neglect and toward unprecedented levels of mutual anger and even hostility. Yet earlier the French had reacted to the horrific events of September 11 with a spontaneous display of concern and support, all the more remarkable as it was inspired from the bottom up and confirmed from the top down. That reaction should have been expected. However difficult the French may be, they have been reliable partners during the most demanding and most dangerous moments of the Cold War. The 1962 Cuban missile crisis is a case in point: at the time, de Gaulle's support was unconditional, despite the enormous risks to which President Kennedy's determination to deny the Soviet nuclear foray in the Caribbean was exposing France and the other European allies.[49] Much later, in the fall of 1990, Prime Minister Margaret Thatcher perceived that trait in French policies especially well as she pointedly reminded President Bush, on the eve of the first Gulf War, that faithful to their commitment, the French would be there[50]—and they were there, too, during the war in Bosnia, viewed by many as the first true test of post–Cold War Euro-Atlantic solidarity, and also during the war in Kosovo, the first and possibly last war waged by NATO without even the legitimacy of a UN mandate.

In 2002, however, the French rejected the U.S. thesis that Iraq and September 11 were the defining parts of a common security edifice based on the twin pillars of weapons of mass destruction (WMD) and global terrorism, Afghanistan and Iraq, and Saddam Hussein and Osama bin Laden. That Saddam's Iraq was cause for concern and possibly a central dimension of the "new security normalcy" feared by Vice President Cheney raised little doubt. Undoubtedly, too, international terrorism was a primary security concern that left no country safe. But a link between Saddam and September 11, and between terrorism and WMD, was deemed to be speculative at best. Even if Iraq had significant quantities of WMD, the French argued, the Iraqi regime would not make them available to terrorist groups over which Saddam had little control and which therefore might engage in actions that would place his regime at risk for reasons that were of limited concern to him. To that extent, the French were puzzled by President Bush's unveiling of an "axis of evil" that extended the common front against terror into a "war" against a number of regimes with which the United States still had unfinished business inherited from the Cold War: North Korea, Iran, and Iraq since 1953, 1981, and 1991, respectively—not to mention Cuba since the fall of 1962.

Yet after Bush chose to go to the United Nations for the multilateral endorsement of a military intervention in Iraq, the French government worked closely with the United States to write a Security Council Resolution for which Chirac helped gain unanimous support by overcoming Syria's opposition and by providing the reassurances needed to overcome China's and Russia's ambivalence over U.S. intentions. Indeed, in early November 2002, on the day when UN Security Council Resolution 1441 was adopted, U.S.-French bilateral relations had gained an intimacy that had been missing during most of the twentieth century. Even Tony Blair, the most willing of the willing allies, seemed left on the sidelines as France was making a bid as America's privileged partner on the Continent—possibly the most convincing such bid since the Revolutionary Wars.

There was no French intent to deceive then, and in the months that followed there was no betrayal of the United States either. The French government understood the broad implications of the UN resolution to which it had subscribed, and it actively prepared to join the military action that President Bush had begun to organize soon after the end of combat operations in Afghanistan. The French, however, made two assumptions that proved to be flawed. First, like the British government (as will be discussed), the French government assumed that Saddam's response to UN Security Council Resolution 1441 would be so defiant as to make automatic the adoption of a second resolution that would confirm and authorize the use of force. Instead, Saddam, eager to placate the United Nations, made enough concessions to permit a new round of inspections, especially after the terse response of the Iraqi dictator's initial rebuttal of the UN declaration as "a defective and mendacious re-hash of earlier declarations . . . [that] played into the hands of the hawks."[51] Still, because of the lingering concern with Saddam's access to those weapons, the French continued to anticipate a military action because they also assumed that U.S. intelligence had enough evidence to tie Iraq to September 11, or at the very least, to confirm Saddam's illegal possession of WMD and their location.

That, of course, was not the case. As it was confirmed subsequently, such intelligence was not available because the Iraqis, in the words of chief U.S. weapons inspector David Kay, "were telling the truth" when denying the existence of these weapons.[52] Absent that evidence, the French found no "imminent" threat and therefore refused to endorse, let alone join, the U.S. preemptive action. The inspectors' invasion of Iraq, coupled with the military buildup outside Iraq, had placed Saddam back in a cage within which he could no longer act with impunity. Lacking urgency, military action could now be postponed pending further inspection of suspected WMD development and deployment sites in Iraq.[53]

Historians will be surprised by the global consequences of this bilateral debate, and notwithstanding the established patterns of U.S.-French relations, they will conclude that the dispute did not have to escalate into the full-fledged transatlantic and intra-European crisis it became. But as French doubts increased, the Bush administration made two serious political mistakes. In late November 2002, at the otherwise highly successful NATO Summit held in Prague, President Bush stubbornly refused to engage his German counterpart, Gerhard Schroeder. On personal grounds alone, Bush's reasons were understandable: Schroeder's reelection in September had been based on an unprecedented anti-American, anti-Bush discourse that the U.S. president found not only inexcusable but also plainly unforgivable. We will return to Bush's anger with Schroeder, but his stubborn resistance to approaching the German chancellor ignored a basic procedure followed by each of his predecessors: when in doubt about France, keep its government isolated from its main European ally—from Great Britain in 1956 and again in 1963, or from Germany in 1967 and again in 1974—because once isolated, the French government can no longer exert the same influence in and beyond Europe.

Having thus failed to deny France the privileged ally it needed, and its only remaining option given Britain's firm choices over the issue, the Bush administration then neglected the public dimensions of its diplomacy. During the crucial week of March 11, prior to the ultimatum to Saddam on March 17, Blair, who reportedly spoke to thirty heads of state or government, was the voice of the U.S. president, who only spoke to his key advisers. Meanwhile, Secretary of State Colin Powell, who persisted in staying home, neglected the diplomatic trips that his counterpart in Paris, de Villepin, was making in anticipation of a decision to which the French objected. Surely, America's inability to gain support from countries in Latin America that happened to be in the Security Council at the time, including Chile, could not be attributed merely to the sort of French pressures that de Villepin was exerting on, say, Cameroon, also a Security Council member at the time. Nor was Turkey's resistance to U.S. enticements to join the coalition of the willing only attributable to French obstruction in NATO: when courting the Turkish government in late 1990, prior to the first Gulf War, Powell's predecessor, James Baker, had gone to Turkey on three different occasions— "one of twenty countries he would visit during the crisis"—and President Bush had reportedly called his counterpart in Ankara dozens of times as, in

Baker's words, "pragmatic manifestations of political realities." Powell did not travel much that winter, and George W. Bush called three times.[54] And, to make matters worse, the U.S. administration's promises could hardly be guaranteed to a Turkish government that had learned the hard way over the years that the U.S. Congress can dispose all too easily of what the White House merely proposes.

Seemingly, Bush assumed that a world that had been outraged by the horrific events of September 11, 2001, and openly supportive of the subsequent war in Afghanistan would remain equally responsive to the U.S. determination to change the Iraqi regime. That, however, failed to be the case. Even though the support of a majority of European heads of state and government justified Bush's claim that he was acting in unison with Europe, the antiwar mood that spread throughout all of Europe enabled Chirac to insist that he was speaking on behalf of the Europeans. In sum, Chirac and Bush both adopted an adversarial, dismissive, and disdainful tone that exacerbated two unusually serious postwar crises in transatlantic and intra-European relations—arguably the most serious crisis within NATO since the French rejection of the European Defense Community in August 1954, and within the European Union since the initial French refusal to open the door of the European Community to Great Britain in January 1963.

Even as the transatlantic crisis within and about NATO began to recede after Bush's reelection to a second four-year presidential term in November 2004, its lasting impact was being felt in France and elsewhere in Europe. In the spring of 2005, over four-fifths of the French were convinced that Bush had lied about Iraq, and a mere one-fourth (26 percent) believed that the United States could solve the world's problems. Outside France, two-thirds of all people in Europe (and three-fifths around the world) still believed that it was a good thing for the United States to feel vulnerable like it had since September 11, 2001—but also like everyone else ever had.[55] In other words, perceptions, issues, and circumstances had succeeded in extending France's image of the United States to much of Europe, rather than the other way around, meaning the implantation in Europe of America's image of France. After that, as conditions in Iraq continued to deteriorate, America's image continued to worsen.[56]

Limits of Unilateralism

Tensions between France and the United States over Iraq were extreme, but they still embodied well the parallel systems of stereotypes, biases, and misplaced sensitivities that affect each country's vision of the other.[57] Americans tend to like France but not the French, or at least the caricature they have drawn of that people and their history and the perception that Americans have of their policies and their motives. As to the French, they tend to like Americans more than they do the United States, or at least the representation they make of what its government does and why.[58] These visions are reciprocal. Each holds the other as a mirror that reflects what it likes least about itself, with the French as well as the Americans better at defining what is worst about the other than about themselves. To that extent, France's nearly obsessive concern with anything that is American often singles out issues that also raise deep concerns among many Americans still in search of their Founding Fathers' "more perfect Union." Similarly, American sentiments about France repeat those held by a large proportion of the French people as well—which helps explain why both sides are most aware of their Frenchness or Americanness abroad, where they stubbornly deny such caricatures, than at home, where they willingly contribute to them.[59]

However French policies may be (mis)represented in the United States, and whatever may be thought of U.S. policies in France, understanding them for what they are, and why—and what they do, and how—would be more constructive than the oversimplified, and occasionally offensive, characterizations that have become commonplace on both sides of the Atlantic. France is France, and Europe is its power: each of these propositions deserves some qualification. The French have come to resemble other Europeans in terms of not only who they are but also what they do; Europe has come to absorb, and resemble, France in terms of not only what it becomes but also what it wants. In late 2005 the ghosts of France's past were sighted anew first in the suburbs and next, in early 2006, in the streets of Paris—"Paris which is Paris only when it tears its cobblestones," as it used to be described by the French communist poet Aragon. Only thus can the French periodically reassert their revolutionary commitment to solidarity—la *fraternité* of 1789—but such moments never last long, as the anarchy that is thus unleashed is such as to require more rigor to restore the order that the French ultimately favor. That is le *mal français*: It is, as another French writer observed, like the life of a sleeping cat: "from time to time . . . a leap, a claw scratching, a yawn that has the air of being action; then everything draws into its fur and sleeps again."[60]

At home in France, this recurring pattern—which moves from rebellion to repression to stasis—traditionally defined the nation's gap between democracy and monarchy, at least until de Gaulle's semipresidential regime helped bridge it.[61] Abroad and in and beyond the United States, this pattern takes the form of repeated attempts to assert French leadership with very public voices of disapproval followed by discreet actions of support.

Acts of civil violence and disobedience in November 2005, when thousands of young and darker Frenchmen unleashed their anger at a society alleged to deny them their identity, and, a few months later, when millions of Frenchmen aimed their anger more explicitly at a government that was no longer representing them, seemed to renew this pattern after two decades of relative stability. But notwithstanding intense media coverage in the United States, these bursts of public anger were hardly limited to France. The malaise was no less real in most other EU countries, or even in the United States where, in early spring 2006, immigrant workers from the South were burning the American flag in California or where American schools were flying the Mexican flag in Texas. That, in the end, is why those riotous French events should have mattered: not because they were happening in France but because they were also happening elsewhere in the Euro-Atlantic West.

Similarly, what mattered in the spring of 2003 was less the specifically French opposition to Bush's intention to go to war in Iraq than the broader European context within which that opposition was articulated. That alone should have been enough to get the attention of the Bush administration, not because a French-led Europe knows better but because it is with a Europe that includes France that America can do better. In other words, a deepening European mood of growing alienation from the United States mattered more than the national context of French estrangement, meaning that what the French say must be heard especially attentively when the French use a European voice that carries a weight, and hence an influence, that they do not have when left on their own. Admittedly, Chirac's attempts to sound like de Gaulle were not convincing, neither in France, where the former could hardly be assimilated to the latter, nor in the United States, where memories of de Gaulle are all but enticing. Where the founding father of the Fifth Republic embodied "une idée de la France," as de Gaulle liked to put it, Chirac embraced separate ideas for each moment—hardly a vision but rather a "rampart" against the weaknesses he had conveniently attributed, at any point in time, to his political rivals at home and diplomatic adversaries abroad, including, in either case, some who were known to have been his friends.[62]

That there was no love lost between the French and the American heads of state should have been of little significance. Chirac needed Bush for his money—meaning U.S. capabilities without which the French ideas seemed of little consequence—and Bush wanted Chirac on his side to provide a presence that would have given the U.S. policies a legitimacy they clearly lacked in Europe's absence: especially in the political realm, this sort of trade-off has defined many lasting relationships. Notwithstanding the prevailing opinion of most people in France and many in the United States, subsequent events in Iraq therefore did not make Chirac's earlier opposition to the war right: to make that argument would be to deny relevance for France and Europe, as it implicitly assumes that their participation in the war would not have helped the United States and its willing coalition to address postwar conditions more effectively than was the case in their absence.

As has been said many times, name-calling is not a policy, but, as it has often been shown, it is an attitude that stands in the way of policy. The temptation in the United States to reduce the terms of bilateral estrangement over Iraq to Chirac and Foreign Minister de Villepin, or to France's deliberate anti-American instinct and lingering reminiscences of past grandeur, was no more serious than the French parallel tendency to reduce U.S. policies to Bush and his vice president, or to an alleged disdain for France and irresistible ambitions of imperial expansion. During the crisis over Iraq, the Bush administration and the French government underestimated each other's determination while overestimating their own strength—the strength that might have permitted Washington to ignore its allies' objections or might have enabled Paris to block America's action. In any case, the widespread public opposition to the use of force found even among the "pro-American" governments in Europe (including Britain and, at the time, Spain), and the subsequent rise of that opposition everywhere, suggests that bottom-up aversion to the war exacerbated Europe's "anti-American" sentiments rather than caused them.[63] In France, but also for a majority of Europeans, a war with Saddam Hussein was deemed more dangerous than Saddam himself; for most Americans, it is Saddam who was deemed more dangerous than war. Perhaps that is why the Europeans remained far more concerned about postwar conditions than did the Americans—and, accordingly, that is why the Bush administration was in far more of a hurry than its allies in and outside Europe. The fact, however, is that both the war and its aftermath were equally dangerous. To this day, none of the war critics has argued convincingly that absent Saddam's removal, conditions in the region would be better than they became after the U.S. military intervention in March 2003. What has been demonstrated conclusively is that too many of the decisions that were made by either party in 2003 were made in the absence of sufficient consultation and that too much of the consultation that took place occurred after the decisions had been made. Had it been otherwise, even the same decisions might have produced better outcomes.

In the end, the French were wrong in fearing the war (though not its aftermath), but the Bush administration was also mistaken in neglecting the war after the war (though not the war proper). Chirac's opposition to Bush was not the issue, although that is what the perception became in the United States and in some of the countries that joined the coalition in Iraq. The issue was how, and how strongly, France's opposition to the United States was asserted, both within Europe and at the United Nations. Nor was Bush's resentment of Chirac the issue, although that is how it evolved; the issue was how publicly that resentment was stated at all senior levels of the U.S. administration and how long it lasted. To put it plainly, both sides overdid it even though both sides knew or should have known better. Admittedly, Iraq was what it had become because of Saddam, whose removal was therefore a precondition for security from that country; but to a certain extent, Saddam was the way he was in part because of Iraq, whose stability was hence a precondition for his removal. Yet notwithstanding the many warnings the Bush administration received from its own intelligence, a righteous U.S. administration never wavered.[64]

Had both the United States and France called a time-out from their quarrel to engage in a moment of reflection over the existential crisis at hand, they would have concluded, on the basis of the information that was available at the time, that a forceful regime change was only the first (and arguably the easiest) of several "missions," because after the regime had been changed and Saddam removed, Iraq's reconstruction would be a prerequisite for the rehabilitation of its government and for reconciliation among its communities. To this extent, the interests of France would have been better served had Chirac followed the U.S. lead after it had been shown that Bush would not be convinced of any other way, and the interests of the United States would have been enhanced had Bush made room for the French in a coalition that would need some serious rethinking after it had completed its military mission.

Even before the war had begun, Chirac outlined the limits of his objections to U.S. policies with an explicit warning to Saddam Hussein against any "preposterous initiative" that "would change [France's] position"—an initiative that the French ambassador to Washington quickly clarified as the use of chemical and biological weapons.[65] As soon as the war was over, Chirac again seemed to understand the postwar context more clearly than his main counterpart across the Atlantic. Maybe it is because, like Schroeder, Chirac was more pragmatic—less principled, according to his U.S. critics—than Bush, or even Blair, and therefore did not need a "decent interval" to return to life as usual. At Evian, France, where the Group of Eight (G-8) met in late May 2003, and subsequently in New York during the UN General Assembly, Chirac hoped to return to a diplomatic normalcy that Bush was still reluctant to accept. That the French president met with little response from a triumphant U.S. president who had just announced the painless end of "major combat operations" and was merely waiting for Saddam's capture to complete Iraq's liberation in 2003 is another example of Bush's overplay of a weak hand. But in 2004, Chirac too seemed to overdo it as he passively watched Bush's travails in Iraq, where the insurgency quickly gained the momentum that the French president had feared in the first place: his apparent complacency was not justified by his country's exposure to the consequences of America's failure. As sentiments grew in France and all over Europe that the war in Iraq had left Europe more exposed to the threats of global terrorism, the fault was not limited to what Bush had done in spite of the warnings he had refused to hear in 2003, but also to what some of his key allies had failed to do despite his repeated calls for help in 2005.

The postwar debates over the prewar debates left little time for a more significant debate over the gross insufficiencies that conditioned the prewar preparation for postwar conditions in Iraq. Absolving the Bush administration for the former in light of what was known or presumed at the time need not entail absolution for the latter in light of what was known or should have been known at the time as well. After September 11, 2001, there was a forceful case to be made by Bush on behalf of prevention in Iraq; instead, Bush chose to make a much more difficult case for preemption. In either case, and for Bush as well as for Blair or their followers (including, most of all, Spain's José María Aznar), to err is not to lie: the misrepresentation of Saddam's capabilities—the insistence, that is, that he had significant stockpiles of WMD and even that their location was known—was a matter of self-deception before it was possibly turned into one of outright deception. Chirac was not willing to listen to a case for preemption, which implied an imminent threat, but he understood the case for prevention, which entailed less urgency.

To make matters worse, Bush next argued in the even larger context of an "axis of evil" that obfuscated the case further and hinted that the will to follow Bush in Iraq would make a refusal to condone similar actions elsewhere along this ever-extending axis even more difficult. As events eventually confirmed, there was no need for preemption because there was no imminent threat. In not looking for ways to assuage Chirac's concerns and enroll him in the coalition he wanted to build, Bush lost sight of the U.S. needs for the postwar nonmilitary missions that awaited the coalition and thus did not find it necessary to make Paris (and Berlin) obligatory stops on the way to Baghdad.

As a result, Bush's attempt to open up in mid-2004, like Chirac's own attempts twelve months earlier, was met with some indifference. Apparently France and others in Europe assumed that the upcoming U.S. elections would bring a new president, better suited for, and more readily responsive to, "Old Europe." Seemingly, the French president, who liked to boast of his knowledge of America, where he had briefly studied and worked as a young man, had little understanding of post–September 11 Americans: his wistful calls for the better America he had known clashed with a new and more pagan outlook that had run out of compassion and feared to be running out of time after the attacks of September 11. In the words used by President Bush, but ready to be adopted by Senator John Kerry had he been elected in November 2004, this was not an "impotent America . . . a flaccid, you know, kind of technologically competent but not very tough country, . . . so materialistic . . . , almost hedonistic, . . . that we wouldn't fight back."[66] But that misunderstanding and underappreciation of post–September 11 America was hardly Chirac's alone and persist to this day as the French and others in Europe continue to reduce the strategic dimensions of the Euro-American clash to issues of personalities or political alignments.

"It is not too much to say," wrote Saul Bellow, "that another America was formed" by the experiences of the Great Depression and under the influence of Franklin D. Roosevelt's eight years in office prior to the U.S. entry into World War II.[67] Nor is it too much to say now that another America appeared to be emerging after September 11 and under the influence of Bush's decisions during the years that followed—an America wary of entangling commitments and eager, like Gulliver, to loosen the ties that constrain its action. In 2004, America stood not only as a country challenged by its enemies but also as a nation prepared to challenge its allies and assume the new missions, in Iraq and elsewhere, needed to defeat the security conditions inherited since the Cold War and started after September 11, 2001. Like Truman and his administration after 1945, Bush intuitively felt that "only the

United States had the power to grab hold of history and make it conform."[68] Admittedly, the missions at hand might be broadly comparable to the postwar missions assumed by Truman—reconstruction, rehabilitation, and reconciliation. But, clearly, the "coalition of the willing" that agreed to follow Bush for the military tasks of regime change in Iraq was unable to attend to subsequent nonmilitary missions, for lack of capabilities and even relevance, as was learned during and after 2004.

However disturbing such a "lesson" may have been for Bush and in the United States, it was an invitation to move the debate beyond the realm of personalities and place the bilateral relationship with Chirac's France (or Schroeder's Germany and even Blair's Britain) within the larger framework of the transatlantic partnership between the United States and Europe. That conclusion followed logically from the broad terms of the Iraq crisis. What mattered then was not the French resistance to U.S. policies—a predictable occurrence given the history of France's relations with the United States. What mattered instead was the French president's unprecedented ability to speak in the name of a majority of Europeans whose mistrust of the United States and its president grew during the march to war and did not recede even after Bush attempted to renew his partnership with Europe.[69]

But the need to transcend the confining context of bilateral, U.S.-French relations also followed logically from the postwar history of Europe's relations with the United States: no single European country, or even small group of countries within Europe, is enough to derail U.S. policies that find support from one or more Atlanticist state within the European institutions. In other words, France can act most decisively when it speaks on behalf of Europe, and the United States can best depend on Europe when the European allies act collectively as a union. For only then can the states of Europe show the reach and the capabilities they need to influence their senior partner across the Atlantic and help the United States resist a unilateralist temptation that results from the post–Cold War preponderance of its power and the urgency of the post–September 11 moment.[70] That is true for France, but it is also equally true, as shall be seen next, for Britain and Germany—and it is true most of all for the United States.

Terms of Endearment

For the past six decades, France and the United States have viewed each other with an ambivalence deepened by their mutual refusal to acknowledge their limits, and even their errors. As a result, they have remained unwilling, or unable, to move beyond the perceptions they have of each other— perceptions that motivate their reactions to each other irrespective of issues and circumstances. This can be expected from two distant countries that history has shaped distinctively. But is there an arrangement to this pattern that has remained so substantively persistent even as it often proved to be so very personal? Can either country and its leaders learn to see the other for what it is—a demanding but reliable ally, difficult to accommodate when available and willing, and even more difficult to replace when absent and confrontational? Can either country see the other for what it has become— surprisingly closer to what each wanted the other to be? There are three conclusions that emerge from this recent display of bad temper, bad decisions, and bad policies over Iraq, which apply to conditions that are bound to reemerge and test, again and again, the will and the vision of leaders in both national capitals.

The first of these conclusions is for the United States and France to stop pretending that life without each other would be easier or better than life together.

To so believe *n'est pas du wishful*, and it is time for the French but also the Americans to "re-understand" and accommodate their respective inability to go it alone, or almost, in new coalitions they might try to form or enter without each other.[71] However separated both countries remain as a matter of perceptions and even preferences, they are no longer separable as a matter of facts or even as a matter of needs. That neither can afford the risks of rupture reflects the mature closeness of an older couple whose comfort with each other (and whose shared wealth built during a lifetime spent together) has come to take precedence over romance. Even as the terms of endearment between the United States and France have faded, there is between them a new intimacy born of combined assets, a converging identity, and shared interests. For that couple at last, divorce is no longer a credible option despite how exasperating and unsatisfying the relationship seems to be at any time.

The new intimacy between France and the United States is a central part of the economic entanglement that has ended the fragmentation of space and, from one side of the Atlantic to the other, literally moved over here the over there of yesteryear, to form an entangling economic relationship worth more than $1 billion of commercial transactions a day. The numbers speak for themselves. Notwithstanding the clichés, Americans find France a good place to work and do business in, and notwithstanding the prejudices, the

French think the same of the United States. In 2004, total French foreign direct investments (FDI) in the United States amounted to $143 billion, two and a half times the total U.S. investments in France ($60 billion)—itself a remarkable reversal of the asymmetry that used to characterize the "American challenge" of the 1960s, when U.S. capital seemed poised to acquire Europe, to the public horror of de Gaulle's France.[72] The nearly 2,500 French-owned companies operating in the United States, which held $600 billion in assets (2004), contributed $43 billion to the U.S. gross domestic product (GDP) in 2004, slightly less than the $47 billion contributed to France's GDP by the more than 1,300 U.S.-owned companies operating there. All together, these businesses employ about 1 million "in-source" workers in good, high-wage jobs in each of the two countries. With regard to merchandise trade, France has become the ninth-largest trading partner for the United States, which in turn stands as France's largest trading partner outside the European Union. With much of that trade concentrated in similar industries and sectors, restrictions placed by one country on the other would hurt domestic production and employment of the country initiating the restrictions. This condition in turn helps explain why most of this bilateral wealth is depoliticized, meaning that it is oblivious to spats of bad humor from either country or to competitive clashes in third countries.

In other words, neither politics nor policy suffices to stand in the way. At the highest point of the bilateral clash over Iraq in 2003, French new investments in the United States remained especially strong (at $4.2 billion), and U.S. investment flows to France rose by more than 10 percent to $2.3 billion. Similarly, U.S. imports from France increased each of the three years 2003 to 2005 relative to the previous year, with an overall 20 percent growth from 2002 ($28.2 billion) to 2005 ($33.5 billion).

Nor is such intimacy a matter of economic reality only. Charges of a societal drift fail to show the retroactive perspective that can best help measure the transformation of France à l'américaine. American travelers who used to go to France with some trepidation due to the alien and even inhospitable character of the country and the continent they entered, now view the crossing of the Atlantic as a ritual that moves them from one family residence to another rather than from one planet to another.[73] Even language, France's weapon of choice, has ceased to keep both countries apart: like their European partners, the French, too, now make English their common second language, ahead of German, just as the study of English in Germany has also come to take precedence over the study of French.

Admittedly, demographic and cultural changes may loosen this intimacy and create enough "metamorphosis" on each side of the Atlantic to end the synthesis of the past fifty years—with an America that will stay young and populous but become less Anglo-Saxon, meaning less "European," while France becomes a bit smaller, much older, and somewhat darker, meaning less "Western."[74] That, however, is not a reality yet, and pretending otherwise makes it even more difficult to address real differences between the United States and France but also, through France, between the United States and Europe, thereby denying both Americans and Europeans the benefits of the partnership they have forged over the past fifty years.[75]

Finally, and no less substantively, there is the matter of shared interests. Although the United States is the most complete power in the world, France stands with Great Britain as one of the two most complete powers in Europe. Like Britain, but more than any other EU country, France seeks to maintain significant military capabilities that it remains willing to use, alone or together with others; offers a view of the world served by a global strategy that may occasionally exceed available capabilities but always reflects a sense of the national self not readily found elsewhere in Europe; enjoys a saliency that is rooted in its history and traditions; and sustains an influence that repeatedly seems second to none, depending on the region, the issue, and the institutional venue.

While these traits can often be causes for tension with the United States, they need not be causes for concerns for the United States. Over such system-shaping issues as the relevance of military force and the future of nuclear weapons, for example, France and the United States are often closer to each other than they are to their respective partners of choice, respectively, Germany (where there is little taste for anything that is military) and Britain (where there is little taste for anything that is nuclear). That, to be sure, does not mean future policy convergence—over, say, the use of force in Iran, tactical decisions concerning the most effective approaches to radical Islamic groups and their states sponsors, or the specific circumstances of a hypothetical first use of nuclear weapons—but it does suggest a potential for enough bilateral coordination to produce at least compatible and even complementary policies.

In other words, it is wrong to ask what France can do for the United States, and vice versa, but it is useful, and even necessary, to seek what France can do with the United States, and vice versa. As a result, a second conclusion is for both the United States and France to acknowledge their respective contributions and learn from these contributions not only what to ask from each other and how but also when to stop asking and why.[76]

A characteristic of the Germans, it used to be said, is that it is difficult to be entirely wrong about them—presumably because they are never entirely right. That being the case, it is similarly characteristic of both the French and the Americans that it is difficult to be entirely right about them—because they never seem to be entirely wrong. Thus reviewed, the tone of Bush's and Chirac's joust over whether force should be used in Iraq, on whose authority and when, was hardly unusual, but it did help each man overlook the better half of what the other had to say, one while asking for action and the other while urging caution. Bush's swagger encouraged Chirac's intransigence (or even arrogance), and, in turn, Chirac's perceived arrogance reinforced Bush's intransigence in a vicious circle of mutual righteousness from which neither man would demur.

Both sides need to refurbish their message in ways that make room for the other's exasperation over the tone and implications it needlessly carries. The French and Americans understand the need to speak to one another, and they can surely hear each other, but they do not seem to know, culturally and specifically, how to listen to the other and, as the French would say, *faire la part des choses* (another one of those French phrases that are all the more frustrating for non-French-speaking Americans, as the French themselves find it difficult to explain its meaning, either verbally or through their own actions). Instead, people on both sides of the Atlantic would rather hear the wrong part of half-baked arguments that make of France or the United States an explanation, an alibi, or an outright scapegoat for what is missing or goes wrong in the United States or France.

In and after 2003, Bush and Chirac's joint exercises in self-delusion were not new in the broad context of U.S.-French relations, but they proved especially harmful to their respective interests. A case in point is the exchange that took place between the two men on the eve of the war with Iraq and as a final push was under way to get a new UN resolution that might have avoided a rupture that neither the Americans nor the French actually wanted. "We really don't need the UN approval" to act, boasted Bush in his news conference of March 6, in answer to a question that was designed to help him reassure his European allies that he was not "defiant of the United Nations." And in case he might not be understood, he added: "when it comes to our security, we really don't need anybody's permission." Thus having been reminded of the irrelevance of France's efforts at the United Nations—

and, by implication, his own—Chirac lost no time in shooting back: "France will oppose [a] resolution [authorizing war]," he asserted, no longer willing to read it first since his U.S. interlocutor had seemingly declared his intention to dismiss the UN vote unless it matched his own preferences.[77]

The irony of this exchange is that the French government had insisted earlier that further UN approval prior to a U.S.-led military action was not needed: the decision to seek that approval nonetheless responded mainly to Tony Blair's political need for a multilateral cover that only the United Nations could provide. Lost in the exchange was also the fact that the two countries were otherwise cooperating on intelligence matters with unparalleled intimacy and unprecedented effectiveness, as later acknowledged by Vice President Cheney and others in the U.S. administration. And lost in the exchange, too, was the wider dimension of the dialogue—Chirac's ability to represent a majority of Europeans who were increasingly concerned over Bush's use of America's preponderant power, relative to America's ability to rely on a majority of his European counterparts sensitive to the intensity of Americans' feelings about the existential war that had been declared upon them on September 11, 2001. By denying their relative advantages, Bush and Chirac denied the other room for accommodation, as if neither country had any alternative to making the concessions needed lest one country be left alone after it had been abandoned by the other.

The idea of arrogance, which is commonly associated with the French personality, applies no less well to the facts of American power. That de Gaulle did not like Roosevelt much may well have been true, but he understood quite well his reliance on U.S. power to end the war against Germany and to avoid a war with the Soviet Union. "I know you are ready to help [France] materially," de Gaulle told Roosevelt at the White House in the fall of 1944, but "it is in the political sphere that she must regain her vigor, her self-confidence, and therefore her role."[78] De Gaulle's lack of tact in explaining his country's needs matched Roosevelt's lack of empathy in insisting on his country's contributions. When persuading the stronger, which is the better way for the weaker: going alone or going along; when listening to the weaker, which is the better way for the stronger: hearing the voice of the faithful or listening to the quarrelsome words of the critic? When at variance with U.S. policies, the French often seem to be asking many more questions than they can answer, but there have been occasions too when the answers provided by the Americans were so rigid or obtuse as to demand those questions—not to offend the senior partner but to assist him, and not to disrupt a sound policy but to redirect it. The wars in Vietnam and in Iraq are cases in point, as Chirac's warnings about the latter in 2003 echo de Gaulle's warnings about the former nearly forty years earlier. Those warnings deserved at least a hearing, as did U.S. warnings to France over, say, its wars in Indochina and Algeria.

For the United States, consultation is one thing, readily agreed to on the presumption that the cooperation that must follow will confirm its leadership; for France, however, cooperation is something else, grudgingly agreed to on the assumption that the consultation that must precede it will help share that leadership. In anticipation of the action, the French ask the Americans "Do you know what you're doing?" and Americans are left all the more exasperated as, in the midst of the action, the French lack the capabilities to make it right even when they do have the experience to know better.[79] The onus, however, is on the Americans to make the needed correction because what they *do* or can do matter more—much more—than what the French *say* or might say.

Undoubtedly, France's behavior in early 2003 was disruptive—arguably more than at any other moment in the history of U.S.-French relations since 1945. But on many of the issues the French raised, and with many of the arguments they made, in anticipation of and after the initial phase of the war, officials should have kept their minds open to the possibility that Chirac might have been right—which is what a majority of Europeans concluded even before the failures of Bush's postwar planning began to accumulate. In the end, however, the U.S. dismissal of, and anger with, France's objections was not because France was wrong (a proposition that senior members of the administration took for granted) but because it did not matter enough for those objections to be of consequence even if they proved to be right— because France did not need to be taken into account since its government was as usual acting for parochial French interests, or according to senseless French prejudices, and not in support of Europe, whose name the French president evoked so easily. As events later confirmed, such a dismissal of the French objections exaggerated France's weakness in prewar Europe no less than it exaggerated America's power in postwar Iraq.

A third conclusion is that the state of U.S.-European relations depends, to a significant extent, on U.S. relations with a quarrelsome France, but the state of Europe also depends, to a significant extent, on French relations with a righteous United States.

The U.S. case against France is easiest to make in combination with a

case against Europe. In other words, France would be less significant to the
United States if it were of lesser significance to Europe. At the close of World
War II, this compelling dimension of bilateral cooperation was implicitly understood: a stronger Europe would not weaken America, but a weaker Europe
did; a weaker France might not strengthen America's influence in Europe, but
it would weaken Europe. These two principles alone should have sufficed to
contain either side's instinctive tendency to overreact toward the other and,
instead, to encourage closer cooperation between them. Thus, after 1945, concerns over the French role in Europe conditioned many of the decisions made
by the Truman administration: not only the decision to assume a leadership
role in postwar Europe, which could clearly no longer be left on its own, but
also the decision to rely on a privileged European partner that would add
legitimacy to emerging U.S. policies for a new security order in Europe.

Ironically, it is Britain's postwar objections to moving in, and becoming
a part of, Europe, which, in the late 1940s, left France as America's most
indispensable partner. In the specific context of the U.S. commitment to a
strong and united Europe, this assessment of the French contribution was
confirmed in subsequent decades when French politics and policies distinctively shaped the transformation of Europe and the U.S. concern with, and
response to, such transformation often originated with, and were shaped
by, the U.S. perceptions of France's own transformation. Political changes
that the United States might otherwise have deplored because of their possible impact on U.S. interests were applauded. In May 1958, for example, de
Gaulle's return to power amid the institutional debris of the Fourth Republic
was celebrated, notwithstanding the challenges President Eisenhower knew
he could expect from a French president whose "unwavering" will he had
learned to know during the war.[80] The same reaction emerged in the aftermath of the socialist victory in May 1981, when the return of the Communist
Party in the French government might have been viewed by the Reagan
administration as a good cause for rupture but was instead ignored as further
evidence of France's new political stability.

Similarly, instances of lesser French interest in Europe were met with
concern in the United States. Thus, in August 1954, rejection of the European
Defense Community by a divided France, weakened further by the humiliating defeat in Indochina a few months earlier, threatened to kill the infant idea
of Europe and even, by association, the Atlantic idea faced with a potentially
"agonizing" reappraisal of the U.S. commitment. But it was then that the
United States, together with Great Britain, put the final touches on NATO

with the Treaty of Paris that fall and the entry of West Germany into NATO the following spring—two decisions that helped finalize the Western architecture for the Cold War. A few years later, both Kennedy and Johnson found de Gaulle politically difficult and diplomatically frustrating. But they recognized the power of de Gaulle's voice in and over Europe and usually tried to limit their disagreement with his policies—especially as Europe's security dependence on the United States during the Cold War made it difficult for the French to gain broad support for their periodic challenges to U.S. leadership.[81] Similar U.S. concern prevailed again when François Mitterrand seemed tempted by a so-called Albanian option that would have taken France out of Europe and Europe out of the U.S. vision for a security order that seemed to be faced with its moment of greatest danger.[82] Finally, a bit more than twenty years later, in May 2005, France's rejection of the constitutional treaty, another major initiative encouraged and scuttled by France, strengthened Bush's decision to reassert his unequivocal commitment to an ever-closer Europe, which many in Europe had pointedly questioned. In each case, the U.S. goal was not to take advantage of France's (and Europe's) disarray but to help both France and Europe regain their balance with a confident display of U.S. power and influence for the *relance* that was required after France's serious political misstep.

While there is ample evidence that this mutual ambivalence between America and France can periodically be overcome over specific issues, a normalization of the U.S.-French relationship—meaning a shared willingness to avoid making every bilateral difference a test of each other's reliability and even good faith—remains difficult and even doubtful. Even the highly personal tone of disparagement that shaped the quarrel over Iraq was not new: every previous U.S. president, as well as his French counterpart, had also had their moments of disparagement in the past. It is truly puzzling: both countries are so far away and yet, in innumerable ways, they are so much alike. If *mission civilisatrice* were not a French phrase, it would be an American sentence reflective of America's own sense of a civilizing mission for which it was preordained. If "manifest destiny" were not an intrinsic part of America's history, it would outline the history of France, whose faith in its *destin* was never shattered by any of the wars it lost or any of the revolutions it failed to complete. Each country has always had a certain idea of itself—and of the other. There is no cure: neither nation adheres to any ideology because each of them embodies one; neither nation approves of the other because neither can quite respond to the ideals it has paradoxically imagined for the other.

CHAPTER TWO

Terms of Endearment

> Though [Franklin D. Roosevelt and Winston Churchill] had their dif-
> ferences . . . they cared passionately about the same overarching truth:
> breaking the Axis. They also shared the conviction that they were des-
> tined to play these roles. A friendship like Roosevelt and Churchill's is
> rightly understood as a fond relationship in which two people have an
> interest not just in each other . . . but also . . . in a shared external truth
> or mission.

> "The primary duty of a British prime minister is to get on with the U.S.
> president," Margaret Thatcher told Tony Blair at their first meeting
> following his election. "The British-US relationship is unique," said
> President George W. Bush in January 2006, "and I'm convinced it will
> be unique in the future, for the good of the world."[1]

THROUGHOUT THE PREWAR debate over Iraq, the clash between George
W. Bush and Jacques Chirac—between the United States and France—
provided for the most significant crisis in transatlantic relations since the
debates over Germany's rearmament and the Suez crisis fifty years earlier.
That was not all, however. Britain and Prime Minister Tony Blair were
equally central to that debate—a country whose identity was fundamentally
built away from Europe and a prime minister whose decisions were influenced by the close personal relationship he developed with the president of
the United States.

By comparison, no such levels of intimacy or even cooperation could ever be achieved between France and Britain, or between their respective leaders. Mitterrand, wrote Margaret Thatcher, "was really not quite sure whether it was easier to deal with [her] when she was difficult or when she was cheerful." Thatcher claims she "liked both" Mitterrand and Chirac, but her portraits of either man make this claim hardly convincing, which may be why Thatcher herself found her fondness for them somewhat "odd."[2] So it has always been, whether with de Gaulle during and after World War II, or with Raymond Poincaré during and after World War I.[3] Repeatedly, it seems, the Anglo-French rivalry defined the history of Europe even after they signed a supposedly "cordial" alliance, which they modestly (and realistically) dubbed an *entente*, early in the twentieth century. The divide exacerbates France's estrangement from the United States as its supposedly "European" view of Europe (also labeled, presumably distastefully, Gaullist) clashes with a view that de Gaulle used to describe dismissively as Anglo-Saxon, meaning, principally, Anglo-American.

The contrast between these views is exaggerated. As we have seen, there is less divergence in U.S.-French relations than meets the ear, and as will be seen, there is more convergence in Anglo-French relations than meets the eye. Yet there is truth in the idea that Britain traditionally has sought to *influence* while France has wanted to *induce* and that Britain's influence has relied on an ability to convince or even manipulate while France's inducement has depended on its ability to coerce or merely obstruct. The British attitude is firmly entrenched in a long-standing belief in the role of *médiateur*: an assumption that "jaw-jaw is better than war-war," as Winston Churchill liked to put it. By comparison, the French attitude is deeply rooted in an aversion to the role of *demandeur*; a position that is reflective of a weakness that invites dependence and prevents the needed renewal.[4] Where the French tend to argue forcefully—in bold characters and with exclamation marks— the British tend to reason more gently, in italics and with question marks. In attempting to manage their quarrelsome people, the French government's attempts to assert leadership forcefully from the top down often degenerate into endless theological arguments. The lingering clichés of the country's history provide a shortcut to France's rationality: one Frenchman shall produce a king; two Frenchmen, an argument; and three Frenchmen, a revolution. For Britain, the reverse is true. In London, as a matter of tradition but in the absence of constitutional matter, there is a willingness to follow, before there can be a will to compete or a demonstrable capacity to lead. The cliché is predictably different: one Englishman, it is expected, will produce a model of courtesy; two Englishmen, a model of fair play; and three Englishmen, an imperial model.[5]

Such characterizations are admittedly simplistic and even a bit tasteless, but they can nonetheless help explain the differences that have kept Britain and the United States separate from France and relatively close to each other. These are perhaps most vividly differences between a culture of action, about which Britain has traditionally excelled and for which it gained its taste for facts over ideas, and a more introspective French culture that prefers thought over action and is more likely to respond to ideas than to submit to facts.

After the end of World War II, relations with the United States became the central focus of this culture clash between two European powers that had lost their sway and were looking for ways to regain their rank on the cheap. To be sure, both Britain and France often shared the same doubts over, and even the same differences with, their senior partner across the Atlantic. But their reactions to these doubts and their responses to these differences were markedly distinct. While governments in London patiently endured, cajoled, and outlasted their respective U.S. interlocutors, successive French governments seemed more willing to outwit, ignore, and confront them. This odd Anglo-French ballet thus featured a *pas de trois* that was staged with the cacophonic sounds of recurring international crises abroad and political disorders or instabilities at home. Long before Iraq, it was first performed in Germany for a full decade after 1945, when Britain acquiesced to Truman's terms of reconciliation with their defeated adversary more readily than did France, even though the British people remained unprepared to forgive for many years after the French had been prepared to forget in the comforting context of a European community from which Britain was absent.

It is after the fall of France, in June 1940, that Britain had to face up to its new security circumstances in the world and, in Winston Churchill's words, to begin to woo America "as a man might woo a maid." In this moment of geopolitical transition, when the United States was assuming a leadership that Britain had claimed as a right of birth, Churchill was the first to understand the new terms of his country's changed vocation. "Never be separated from the Americans," he warned his successors. The assumption was that such faithful followership would permit historically agile governments in London to influence decisively (and to Britain's benefit) their inexperienced counterparts in the United States.[6] Churchill's war was therefore both military and political—not only to defeat Germany's new bid for hegemony in Europe but also to make sure that Britain would be left with enough influence at war's end to keep its relevance as America's partner of choice.[7] Achieving the former demanded that Churchill acquiesce to an American leadership that Britain found to be perpetually indispensable though often contradictory with the latter, especially over matters that had to do with Britain's role in the world and imperial status. As a result, the war ended with a mixture of both triumph and tragedy: the triumph of the only democracy west of Russia that had fought the war in full and now shared center stage with its senior partner, but also the tragedy of a nation that after the war would lose the empire without which it could not maintain its rank as a world power on par with the United States (and Russia) and over its European rivals.

As previously discussed, France too claimed a status in the world that it sought to enforce by relying on those features that had defined its diplomatic style since at least Talleyrand. Unlike most other countries that struggle to forget a defeat, the French prefer to deny it. To that end, governments in Paris readily test their people's gullibility and challenge their allies' tolerance by treating a retreat or even a surrender as a victory, and by elevating some of their defeated military leaders into mythical heroes.[8] Thus defined, France's terms of estrangement from, and Britain's terms of endearment with, the United States also shaped the terms of Anglo-French engagement in Europe, about which their distinct assessment of the U.S. role was often a cause for bilateral discord at the expense of the European institutions that France helped launch and Britain sought to ignore.

This is not to say that Britain and the United States were never at odds within the Atlantic Alliance and about Europe, especially during the earlier postwar years, but rather to say that their disagreements, however frequent, never were cumulative, as was the case between France and the United States.[9] What proved to be cumulative instead were those cooperative moments during which Britain learned to rely on the United States even when it might otherwise disapprove of, or question, its policies. Meanwhile, as France struggled with the United States within the Atlantic Alliance, its well-entrenched differences with Britain about Europe and other substantive policy issues were exacerbated by the intangibles of national practices and political processes, neither of which could be understood, let alone accommodated, on either sides of the English Channel or the Atlantic. In this odd threesome, France, denied special status by the United States within the Atlantic Alliance, often tended to retaliate against Britain in Europe, where the British government was said to be a conduit for America's unwanted influence and overbearing power.

Faithful Britain

In the fall of 1956, the Suez crisis was a defining moment in Anglo-French and U.S.-European relations. The unusual intimacy consummated at the time by both European powers with a joint military intervention in Egypt was influenced by a bitter—and surprisingly open—rift between Secretary of State John Foster Dulles and Prime Minister Anthony Eden, in spite of the latter's ambivalence toward his French socialist counterpart, Prime Minister Guy Mollet. Their failure to achieve vital goals because of an unexpected U.S. decision to "engage [its] authority in the lead against us," as Eden viewed it, should have united Britain and France against what the then-British ambassador to the United States disdainfully dismissed as "an administration of business executives."[10] Instead, the humiliation both countries suffered on an issue each deemed to be of vital interest divided them further at the very moment when the European Community was poised to take off as a benign and unassuming Common Market.

For the first decade of the Cold War, Britain's European credentials had included its exceptional pedigree as a durable and reliable wartime ally and a proven link with the United States, now Europe's most significant but historically least reliable ally. During that period, too, the apparent success of Britain's decolonization policies (especially relative to France and other European imperial powers) had helped refurbish Britain's claim as a consequential power in the world. After Suez, however, these premises could legitimately be questioned in the United States and France, as well as in West Germany and, of course, the Soviet Union.[11] The French hoped to use Britain's military power and political know-how in Egypt and its influence in and over the United States. As a result, Paris had given London the lead in a military operation whose goal was not only to achieve regime change in Egypt, as the Americans had done in Iran three years earlier, but also to reassert Europe's control over a central part of the Middle East. "We entrusted this to the British," reportedly complained de Gaulle at the time. "They commanded on sea, they commanded on land, they commanded on air." Interestingly enough, de Gaulle's complaint was not over the French decision to turn to Britain as a willing ally but on Britain's lack of capabilities to respond to

French expectations: seemingly, he would have favored a U.S. lead that could provide needed capabilities, assuming the United States had the will to do so.[12]

Fifty years later, it is clear that the crisis in Suez defined the postimperial strategic choices of postwar Britain and, as a result, confirmed the terms of Britain's relations with the United States within the Atlantic Alliance, as well as with France in Europe. With the failed Anglo-French intervention in Egypt exposing the tragic realities of Britain's decline, London's dependence on the United States deepened, and so did its resistance to an emerging French vision of Europe, which was correspondingly affected by those events but away from rather than toward the United States. Suez did not make Britain weak, but it exposed the fullness of its weakness and the emptiness of its postwar claims. Nor did Suez alone knot Britain's bilateral ties with the United States, but it exposed the one-sidedness of the relations between Washington and London, with little time left for an unwanted detour via Paris. As a result, Suez also conditioned America's rise to preeminence as a global power that would keep its European allies on a shorter leash to protect the Western alliance from other such embarrassing situations in the future. A post-Suez study prepared for Eden's successor, Harold Macmillan, returned to Churchill's post-Dunkirk warning about Britain's ties with America.[13] Convinced at last of the "certain decline" of their country's "relative power," the authors of the study insisted that Britain's "status in the world will depend largely on [the Americans'] readiness to treat us as their closest ally." Thus positioned, Britain would not need to fear America's power because it could influence and even manage that power. Indeed, if there was power to be feared, it stood across the English Channel where the political consolidation of the newly formed European Economic Community might "dwarf the United Kingdom" to an extent that would gradually reduce London's leverage across the Atlantic. "Whatever happens," the report ominously warned Macmillan and his successors against "finding ourselves in the position of having to make a final choice between the two sides of the Atlantic."

Late in 1962, Macmillan hoped to avoid that predicament when he seemingly followed de Gaulle, the architect of a self-induced regime change in France and now the self-appointed choreographer of an allegedly European Europe. Like de Gaulle, Britain's prime minister, who had been the beneficiary of a change of government in Britain after Eden's humiliation at Suez, was increasingly exasperated with a U.S. tendency to act first and inform next, as evidenced during the Cuban missile crisis in the fall of 1962. Macmillan, who had been especially close to Eisenhower and was initially quite wary of John F. Kennedy, appeared prepared, therefore, to enter into an agreement with de Gaulle on bilateral defense cooperation in the broader context of an emerging European community. As in Suez, however, conflicting perceptions of the United States set strict limits to any such Anglo-French intimacy. According to de Gaulle, cooperation with Britain would make of Europe the equal of the United States "in fifty years."[14] In return, the French president was expected to approve London's agonizing bid for membership in the Common Market—a bid that had been made with full U.S. support. But expectations of a deal floundered a few weeks later, when Kennedy, concerned over de Gaulle's intentions, forced upon Macmillan, to whom the U.S. president had become personally close, the very choice that the prime minister had hoped to avoid—between standing across the Atlantic with the United States or moving along with France across the channel. "There is a perception," noted Blair in Warsaw nearly twenty years later, that "de Gaulle was anti-British. . . . Nothing could be more misguided. . . . [He merely] saw Britain as both a Trojan Horse for the United States and a brake on the necessary strengthening of Europe."[15] Whether de Gaulle was anti-British or even anti-American, his decision—No to Britain in Europe, and No to America in the Atlantic Alliance—not only delayed Britain's entry to the European Community for another decade, until 1973, but it also led to France's departure from NATO, though not from the Atlantic Alliance, in 1966.

After September 11, 2001, relations between Britain, France, and the United States also seemed to take a highly personal turn. Positioned between George W. Bush and Jacques Chirac, Blair was driven by two ambitions—to sustain his country's close partnership with America and also to assert his leadership in Europe. In pursuing these ambitions, Blair relied on the legacies of renewal inherited from his once-removed predecessor, Margaret Thatcher, who had relaunched Britain after a thirty-year winter of postwar decline and discontent and had made *Thatcherism* the code word for resurrecting her nation's heroic image in the United States, though at the expense of her ties with Europe. Blair was eager to duplicate the former and remain America's best ally, but he was equally determined to avoid the latter and become Europe's least favored member. To achieve such a feat, Blair would have to display the same manipulative qualities that had characterized his remarkable ascent to power within a Labor party that he had seized, renewed, and relaunched after its surprising electoral defeat in 1993. In late 1998, eighteen months after Blair's first election, his meeting with Chirac in St. Malo was the first serious Anglo-French dialogue about a common security and defense policy since de Gaulle's meeting with Macmillan in December 1962. In so doing, Blair appeared to restore a pattern of Anglo-French cooperation that, coupled with his demonstrated ability to work not only with Clinton but also with Bush, confirmed his identity as both a steadfast Atlanticist and a convinced European. Coming after Europe's debacle in Bosnia, when the actions taken by the European states and their union had been particularly ineffective, Blair's goal in St. Malo may have been to safeguard Europe's relevance to America, but it was also, and no less significantly, to assert Britain's commitment to Europe.

Across the Atlantic, Bush was not as "complete" and experienced a politician or statesman as Blair or Chirac. His rise to power had been almost fortuitous. Even before Bush's political career had truly started, Blair was the upcoming head of his party, and Chirac was already France's prime minister when Bush was barely coming out of graduate school. The difference between them might have been endearing to Americans who consume their political leaders with the same excesses as all other commodities, but it was puzzling to others in continental Europe where leadership is conceived, leaders born, and reputations earned differently than in the United States. More pointedly, though, it is Bush's singular faith in absolute truths—his impatience with complexities as a man of action rather than a thinking man—that worried Europeans whose caricatures of Bush, drawn with unusual bluntness even before he was elected, symbolized and confirmed everything that Europeans like least and fear most about America (and Americans about Europe).

"He least likes me to say, this is 'complex,'" Condoleezza Rice said of George W. Bush—as had been said, in some fashion, of Ronald Reagan and as had been thought, even earlier, of Truman.[16] Even the temptation to explain Bush's simplicity in terms of his religiosity was neither new nor unique. Whatever the president, and whenever the moment, beliefs—perhaps most of all, religious beliefs—matter.[17] Truman found solace in the Bible and his faith in God, which he placed squarely at the center of America's heritage.[18] Reagan perceived the ungodly "evil forces" at work in the Soviet empire in the context of the godly "good forces" at work in America.[19] But there could be found in Bush a biblical dimension that exceeded any other president before him, including Jimmy Carter, whose reading of the Bible as background for his policies on human rights and his negotiations on the Middle East was notorious.[20]

That dimension, in truth, was the essence of George W. Bush. After September 11, 2001, this trait was reinforced by a permissive domestic consensus on which Bush was able to rest his decisions throughout his first presidential term. For a man who had shown a total lack of curiosity about Europe and the world during his youth, as well as during the maturing years of his personal and political life, September 11 taught Bush everything that needed to be known, and his faith shaped every decision that came after that. "For my thoughts," it is written, "are not your thoughts, neither your ways my ways, saith the Lord. For as the heavens are higher than the earth, so are my ways higher than your ways, and my thoughts than your thoughts."[21] Nothing that might distract Bush's thoughts from the war at hand would possibly compromise its outcome—as would anyone, at home and abroad, who entertained doubts about the war and the cause it served. That characteristic, in a sense, made Bush and Blair converge in ways that were ignored at the time. Whatever their differences, each man saw in the other the piety that distinguished him from most other political leaders, friends or foes, and, conversely, tied them together more spontaneously than any other two political leaders. As it has been observed since, it is the sincerity of their piety that kept them both untouched by the occasional distastefulness or even unscrupulousness of their subsequent decisions or actions—an antinomian faith that "to the pure all things are pure" and even, as a corollary that September 11, 2001, asserted but that subsequent acts of terror in Madrid, London, and elsewhere confirmed, that to the pure all things done to the unpure are pure.[22] In subsequent years, the spectacle of failure did not erode that faith: that Pontius Pilate was Blair's second-favorite figure in the Bible, by his own account, is therefore appropriate.[23]

Compared to both Blair and Bush, Chirac stood as odd man out—a political figure of the Third Republic who presided over a Fifth Republic that had been stalled by François Mitterrand during the decade that preceded Chirac's election in May 1995. For Blair to exist, there had to be Thatcher, and for Bush to prevail, there had to be Reagan; both earlier figures defined a discourse of renewal without which there would have been no place for Blair's ambitions (especially in Europe) or for Bush's convictions (especially about America). But for Chirac to be the "modern" president he wanted to be, there was no benchmark inherited from the 1980s—a period during which Mitterrand became progressively more interested in presiding over Europe than in governing his own country and more concerned over the course of his own history than over that of his nation. Instead, there was, of course, de Gaulle, the founding father of the Fifth Republic: this is who Chirac wanted to be, and for those at home who disapproved of him, an opportunity to sound like de Gaulle was instant redemption.[24] But branding him a Gaullist was enough to make him questionable in America, where de Gaulle was remembered as the tiresome advocate of a French vision that was fundamentally hostile to the United States and actively committed to the emergence of a world in which Europe would stand as an adversarial counter-weight to U.S. power and influence. (To an extent, Gerhard Schroeder suffered from the same handicap: by September 1998, Helmut Kohl's fifteen years of conservative rule, and twenty-five years of party rule, had created an air of political stagnation that Schroeder and the new majority found difficult to clear. Indeed, when Kohl stated his intention to run again, no one within his own party dared stand in his way, and when the aging chancellor began to personalize his attacks against Schroeder during the campaign late that summer, few within the opposition, including the candidate himself, dared respond.)

Still, the hostility that grew between Blair and Bush on the one hand, and Chirac and Schroeder on the other, was not premeditated. In Europe, occasional references to "Schroeblair" or "Blairac" reflected the German chancellor's hopes for a special partnership with Britain and those of the British prime minister for a closer partnership with France. In the United States, Bush too was initially conciliatory, as he hoped "to erase the false lines" still separating the states of Europe, as well as between them and the United States.[25] Neither was entirely right in his approach toward the others, both before and during the debate over Iraq, and neither was entirely wrong either. More important, however, and most specifically, their conflict over Iraq confirmed that political unity in Europe depends on effective cooperation between Britain and France no less, and even more, than it does on France's cooperation with Germany: absent Anglo-French cooperation, Europe's ability to influence the United States—or, to put it more bluntly, to mitigate America's preponderance while asserting Europe's own relevance—is weakened.

What the conflict in Iraq did was not to end America's right to lead, as a matter of fact (namely, its power) and as a matter of principle (which was a post–September 11 need for self-defense) but to alter fundamentally the context in which that right was asserted in Europe and over its principal allies. The decision to go to war was an American decision that Britain accepted, and even shared, in spite of Britain's concerns over its ally's competence in preparing for and managing postwar conditions in Iraq. By making that choice, Blair confirmed a pattern that had been set at Suez nearly half-a-century earlier, and mostly confirmed throughout and since the Cold War—with Macmillan, with Thatcher, and now with Blair. For the latter to do otherwise, and follow Chirac instead, would have been surprisingly off course: there had been no such precedent since the fateful fall of 1956 in Suez. What prompted. a growing public opposition to the war and to Blair's unquestioned commitment to the United States was not Blair's inability to justify his decision to follow Bush and go to war absent the evidence of an imminent threat but rather the lack of a quid pro quo that became especially glaring in Britain as the evidence of failure in Iraq mounted. For Bush, Blair's followership was a choice based on principles and values, and his status as America's partner of choice was an honor that required no reward. There was nothing that needed to be conceded, therefore, on issues that mattered to the British people (such as, say, the treatment of war prisoners) or even on issues where American and British interests converged most visibly (such as, say, various aspects of the Israeli-Palestinian conflict).

The conclusions likely to be drawn by Blair's successors, beginning with Gordon Brown, may well prove to be the reverse of the conclusions that were reached after Suez, thus closing a fifty-year cycle of a bilateral partnership that was made special so long as it met convincingly the related tests of will, efficacy, and reciprocity—a readiness to be there, an ability to do well, and a certainty of shared benefits.

Price of Followership

An Englishman, it is said, works best when others already view his work as coming too late. So it looked for Blair, not only in relation to Europe but also with regard to Britain's relations with the United States, which had deteriorated since Thatcher but to which Blair was no less committed than any of his postwar predecessors. Indeed, what the new prime minister wanted most was the same goal that had eluded Britain since Suez: to remain America's privileged partner *and* to be a leader of Europe—a bridge between the United States and the European Union, as well as between the European Union and NATO.

"I am a passionate pro-European," Blair told the EU Parliament in June 2005. "I always have been." This passion shaped Blair's view of Europe "as a political project . . . never . . . simply an economic market."[26] Eight years earlier, upon his election, Blair's commitment to building "a patriotic alliance in favor of Britain's central place in Europe" had finalized the evolution of his party since the electoral debacle of 1983, when Thatcher's had reigned supreme. With EU membership said to be "overwhelmingly in Britain's interest,"[27] Britain needed at last to assert a leadership that other European states, including France, would have conceded earlier had it not been for Britain's reluctance to join and abide by the discipline of membership after it had joined. "The blunt truth," observed Blair in October 2000, "is that British policy towards the rest of Europe over half a century has been marked by gross misjudgments." At each stage, he continued, "we held back" because, he argued on another occasion, "politicians of both parties" presumed too readily that Europe "wouldn't happen . . . [that] it wouldn't work . . . [and that] we didn't need it."[28]

Renewing Britain's engagement in Europe without compromising his explicit interest in ending its relative estrangement from the United States (where then-president Bill Clinton neither forgot nor forgave John Major's proactive opposition to his candidacy in the fall of 1992) might not be easy, however. To achieve these objectives, Blair sought a third way that bypassed both the anti-European, Atlanticist sealine favored by most of his postwar predecessors, and the anti-American, Gaullist path embraced by many of Britain's postwar interlocutors in Europe. At first, Blair's choices seemed to be eased by his personal affinities—ideologically, politically, and even culturally—with Clinton. Occasional tensions—over Kosovo, for example—were handled by Blair with "a kind of triumphalist subservience which occasionally even shade[d] into an implied superiority" that on the whole did not seem to affect his U.S. interlocutor. This was reminiscent, to an extent, of Churchill's initial approach to Truman, which was quickly aborted, however, with Churchill's unexpected electoral defeat in July 1945.[29] Just as Blair might teach lessons of geography to his constituencies at home about the need for Europe and the significance of closer relations with France, he might also teach a few lessons of history to his senior partner across the Atlantic, whether about the Balkans or about the Middle East. Blair enjoyed the role, and Clinton, the consummate politician but also a quick learner, did not seem to mind it.

Yet, and more important, Clinton's own commitment to a united and stronger Europe erased whatever contradiction there might have been between Blair's related ambitions. On the contrary, strengthening his relations with Washington would reinforce Britain's position in Europe and, conversely, closer relations with Paris would reinforce Blair's position with the United States. In other words, Blair could help America's interests in Europe (and with France), but he would also be in a position to help Europe's interests (and France) in and with the United States. Blair's style of multiple followership was therefore without tears: there was little for him to lose with either side but plenty to gain from all sides. Building on Thatcher's legacy, but less painfully than she did, Blair would reassert Britain's influence "not as a superpower but as a pivotal power" that could comfortably stand at the center of the alliances and the multilateral institutions that shaped the world, including the European Union no less than NATO and even the United Nations.[30] To try out for this part, Blair eagerly accepted a central role in Iraq, where he shared Clinton's interest in containing a regime that, said Blair from the start, was "blind to reason" and "to whom a last chance to do right is just a further opportunity to do wrong."[31] That might separate him from Chirac, who preferred to distance himself from Clinton's air war over Iraq, but the issue still looked marginal relative to other issues over which Blair and Chirac appeared to agree.

At first, the election of George W. Bush complicated Blair's aspirations to pursue two approaches that his domestic, and now his American, critics viewed as contradictory. For one, a more conservative U.S. leadership resented Blair's acrobatic attempt to strike a new deal with France within the European Union while claiming his interest in sustaining the old ways with the United States within NATO. Blair's interest in a European Security and Defense policy especially was said to represent a "historic reversal of decades of British policy"—a quest for membership in a French-led multipolarity brigade that was alleged to be the equivalent of a betrayal of the United States.[32] More broadly, Blair's policy, warned Henry Kissinger, was inconsistent with the entire history of NATO and might cause an inevitable drift toward the political decoupling of the United States from Europe.[33] Worse yet, the personal dimension that had characterized the closest moments in Anglo-American relations since 1945—between Kennedy and Macmillan, Reagan and Thatcher, or even Blair and Clinton—was now missing under ideological conditions that had brought to power Laborites whose youth had been spent bashing America for the messianic rigidities articulated by many of the leading officials who surrounded the new U.S. president from Texas.

Blair's first trip to Bush's America was therefore decisive. Not since Harold Macmillan had there been a British prime minister so intent on making a good impression on his U.S. interlocutor.[34] "I cannot of course ever hope to have anything to replace the sort of relations that we have had," an anxious Macmillan had written his friend, Dwight D. Eisenhower, in late 1960, while awaiting "with great eagerness" his first meeting with Kennedy. Now, Blair's apprehensions were equally pronounced. He had come to appreciate his "intellectual relationship" with Clinton—and to respect Clinton's ability "to discuss a problem" and "proceed more by asking questions than by answering them." These were skills that were said to be lacking in the new U.S. president about whom Blair knew little beyond the caricatures that had flooded the European media during the previous year. Nevertheless anxious to say the right things because of his conviction that close ties with America were fundamental to Britain's well-being, Blair therefore picked on the issues that were known to be central to the new president's thinking—the "rogue states" generally, and Iraq specifically. This emphasis was not merely tactical but also, as noted earlier, responded to convictions about Iraq that Blair had shared earlier with Clinton.[35] But now, Blair's rhetoric about Saddam Hussein, "a serial killer," grew increasingly blunt and quickly endeared him to Bush. "He put on a charm offensive for me and it worked," observed the U.S. president at the close of their first meeting.[36]

Thus the lines were drawn. Without Blair's support on an issue of primary concern to the new administration from the moment it took office, Bush might have looked elsewhere—perhaps to Germany, not only his father's predestined partner in leadership but also his predecessor's favored partner before Blair's rise and Helmut Kohl's fall. But without Blair's assurances on European issues of primary significance to Paris, Chirac too might have turned to Germany, France's partner of choice since the split with Britain and the historic Franco-German Treaty of Friendship in January 1963. To be sure, Chirac gave Blair added power in Europe, as de Gaulle had promised to do for Macmillan, but Bush made of Blair a man of influence in the world, as Kennedy had for Macmillan in response to de Gaulle's entreaties.

"We must steer close to America," Blair told his cabinet in March 2002—"if we don't we will lose our influence to shape what they do."[37] Especially in the context of what was thought to be known in 2002, going to war in Iraq appeared to be a more attractive option than losing a friend across the Atlantic: the pain that was sure to follow separation from the United States was assumed to be much higher than the pain likely to be caused by the war. In coming to his decision, Blair reasoned that his renewed commitment to America and his new commitment to Europe still followed parallel tracks that would ultimately converge. In EU parlance, this was "a two-speed strategy"—America now, within an alliance that was being challenged by the horrific events of September 11, 2001, and Europe next, which the end of the Cold War had moved closer to an institutional finality that Blair wanted to shape.

For Blair, Bush was a reliable interlocutor who understood and even shared his temperament. Conversely for Bush, Blair was an ideal partner. Britain's prime minister did not have to be asked for his friendship, and when the time came he would not even have to be provided with lengthy explanations that the U.S. president, by his own account, does not like to provide.[38] Even their political philosophies could now be made compatible because of the two political giants to whom each was indebted, as Bush's compassionate Reaganism appeared to be converging with Blair's appearance of Thatcherism with a social conscience. Unforeseen by Blair because of his sincere faith in the just cause that Bush was undertaking was that his influence on the U.S. president as the only man who could derail his plans for war would end after the war had demonstrated anew that a righteous and overwhelmingly preponderant America did not need a best ally after all, unless it remained so uncritical and committed as to avoid sustained and public criticism. As a result, the price of followership paid by Blair proved to be superior to the influence that he sought but failed to achieve.

Ironically, Blair's balancing act between America and Europe after his election in May 1997 parallels that of Chirac after his own election two years earlier. However, unlike Blair, whose immediate goal was to restore Britain's good name in Europe, Chirac initially aimed at restoring France's good name in the United States. Chirac's need for the latter was no less self-evident than Britain's interest in the former. Even as the Cold War was ending in Europe, France still stood as America's most predictable critic and was seemingly raising obstacles to the U.S. attempt to achieve a peaceful reunification of Germany and an orderly dismemberment of the Soviet Union. Admittedly, President Bush had felt at ease with Mitterrand, "this sage French leader . . . a dependable ally and friend . . . who told me what he was going to do, then went ahead and did it."[39] But that had not been enough in the Persian Gulf, where Mitterrand's last-minute attempts to delay or prevent war were questioned by his senior ally. After that, France's frustrations with America relied on a vocabulary—"hyperpower," "hegemony," "simplistic"—that lost much of its subtlety in translation and carried an offensive connotation in any language. Yet on the whole, Chirac's surrogate government during the two years of cohabitation with Mitterrand, which preceded his election in May 1995, showed a marked interest in better relations with the United States. To this day, Alain Juppé, who was at the time Chirac's handpicked dauphin, remains one of America's best-liked and most effective foreign ministers of the French Fifth Republic.

As compared to Mitterrand, who had little interest in anything specifically American, or to de Gaulle, whose views about America—its society no less than its history—were unusually simplistic, Chirac is arguably the first French president of either postwar republic who liked both America and Americans.[40] While this penchant for a country where he briefly lived as a young man hardly implied a willingness to agree on all issues, Chirac went to unusual lengths to regain the U.S. trust that would help him proceed with his own vision of Europe—not because this was the phase of *finalité* envisioned by Germany's foreign minister Joshka Fischer but because this was to be a decisive phase of *modalités*, always at the center of France's concerns. In other words, Chirac, like Blair, assumed that in a world transformed by the collapse of the Soviet Union more unity in Europe would help France so long as its government maintained its decisive voice over a united Germany but also resumed a cooperative relationship with Britain. Better yet, to America's satisfaction, more unity in Europe was no longer viewed by Chirac as incompatible with NATO, France's traditional bête noire but now an institutional relic that the French president was prepared to accommodate, as, like any historic monument, it seemed quaint and of little use.

Admittedly, NATO raised the question of U.S. preponderance, to which the French are more sensitive than any other European ally, including Britain but also Germany. But this transatlantic imbalance could only be reduced by a European Union that would grow more powerful even as it became more united and larger. Meantime, such imbalance could at least be managed by transforming the modalities of interstate relations within NATO, within the European Union, and ultimately between the European Union and NATO. Thus Chirac's response to Fischer's call for EU finality had an ambiguity that was pointedly constructive. By asking *"qui fait quoi?"* ("Who does what?"), Chirac was opening a legitimate debate for the European Union but also for NATO, as he implicitly understood that there could be no final resolution of the role of the nation-state relative to the European Union—and of the European Union relative to NATO—without a parallel resolution of the U.S. role in Europe and within NATO.[41]

From 1995 to 1999, Blair and Chirac repeated the choreography staged by de Gaulle and Macmillan after Suez. Just like de Gaulle, whose memorandum of September 1958 had started a strategy that ended badly in January 1963, Chirac's opening gambit was for a renewed Atlantic Alliance that he launched with the announcement that France would rejoin NATO's Defense Planning Committee, as well as its Military Committee. At the time, such a decision was viewed as a major step toward France's return in NATO's integrated military command structure.[42] A few weeks later, Chirac's plea for a new transatlantic charter that would formally renew "the vitality of our alliance" could be heard as France's long-awaited response to Henry Kissinger's call for a Year of Europe thirty years earlier.[43] Although disappointed by the lack of U.S. responsiveness to what Chirac viewed as significant departures from past Gaullist practices, his sudden call for an early election in the spring of 1997 was designed, in part at least, to release the French president from domestic political pressure for the remaining years of his first seven-year term as he prepared to reassert France's leadership of Europe and reappraise his country's role in a reformed NATO. The strategy dramatically misfired, however, when the elections produced instead five years of futile cohabitation with a contentious Socialist majority in the French National Assembly, thereby stalling Chirac's grand designs for Europe and the alliance.

Then as now the issue was over European insufficiencies relative to the primacy of American power. While the war in Kosovo convinced both Blair and Chirac of Europe's military weakness, it also exposed Blair less than Chirac to a post–Cold War, pre–September 11 "unipolar moment" during which the United States, free of any constraints, could succumb to unilateralist temptations that ignored Europe's objections and might ultimately place vital European interests at risk. As a result, Chirac came to support the multilateral frameworks to which de Gaulle's France had objected in the past, including especially the United Nations. At the very least, the United Nations might provide the time needed to await the rise of a multipolar world in which "an engaged, imaginative Europe" would join other "major poles of international equilibrium"—such as "Russia and China, Brazil and Japan, India and Mexico"—to "contribute to building a dense network of organized, harmonious relations" with a (hopefully) "responsible" United States.[44]

Even before September 11, 2001, Islam was an interlocutor of choice for France's renewed interest in the benefits of multilateralism in a unipolar world. For one, countries in the Middle East had never been comfortable with the bipolarity of the Cold War that forced itself in their region after the failed Anglo-French attempt to reassert Europe's regional primacy in the fall of 1956. Yet, it is there more than anywhere else that French interests had a singularity that differentiated them from the United States without separating them from the rest of Europe, including Britain. France's claim was therefore unequivocal: "In the Middle East," boasted then-French foreign minister Hervé de Charette, "we are still able to shape history."[45] And as Islam has emerged as France's (and Europe's) second most populous religion, it is to the 1.2 billion Muslims spread all over the world that France seemed not only to matter globally but also to matter more positively than any other Western power.[46]

Thus the events of September 11, 2001 presented Chirac with an opportunity to test France's theory of primary relevance. No less than Blair and even like Bush, he believed in the centrality of the war on terror that loomed ahead. But more than Blair and unlike Bush, Chirac also believed he had a superior know-how nurtured during his four decades of public involvement in the region, as well as the added legitimacy of a country that had long made of Islam its first priority, initially as a matter of choice but now as a necessity made politically vital by the growing Muslim community in France. Denying America's leadership would carry a price, but such denial would also deliver ample rewards, including a status in the world to which the French felt entitled as a matter of right and which they sought for their own interests. Not surprisingly, the British came to the opposite conclusions.

Endearment and Estrangement

For George Herbert Walker Bush, the 1991 Gulf War loomed like the moment for which he had trained all of his life. Issues of war and peace were the issues with which he was most competent; and these interlocutors—friends and foes alike—were also the sorts of people with whom he was most comfortable. His own diary entry on September 7, 1990, depicts his mood and assessment well: "I have a confident feeling here," he reflected. "Maybe it's the fact that I have been intimately involved . . . with the leaders."[47] Relying on lifelong friendships and personal relationships, and intimately familiar with the subtleties of multilateral diplomacy, the forty-first U.S. president built a universal coalition that helped him to achieve his immediate goal (the territorial status quo anti-bellum in the region) with a reasonable expectation that his ultimate goal (regime change in Iraq) would follow soon and without any more U.S. involvement.

In 2001, his son, now president as well, also thought that September 11 was opening a period for which he too had prepared, spiritually at least, for most of his mature life. "We are at war," George W. Bush immediately told his vice president.[48] In the following months, the president's tone became increasingly confident and his leadership more and more assertive—even, on occasion, feverish (as in "With us or against us") and bellicose (as in "Bring them on") with a touch of juvenile swagger (as in "Dead or alive") that soon because disturbingly provocative to many of those who had initially found such rhetoric enticingly refreshing.

In effect, the leadership unveiled by Bush after September 11 suited well the nation's mood. Nothing had prepared the country for the murderous audacity of these attacks aimed at the symbolic centers of its power. In a shocked, angry, and united America, there was little room for equivocation— arguably less than at any time since the Chinese intervention in the Korean War had shaped a permissive consensus that facilitated Eisenhower's policies for regime change from Iran and Guatemala to the Congo and Chile.[49] From that moment on, even a passing reference to "9/11" could suffice as a credible explanation for every decision and every action—haunting memories out of which Bush found enough clarity and even certainty to shorten policy debates at home and ignore public concerns abroad. Admittedly, as the critics argued, Bush was not prepared for the world, let alone the world that he inherited from the terrorist attacks of September 11. That was his own defining moment, but it had come way too early—more like Kennedy's Bay of Pigs, shortly after his inauguration in 1961, than the Cuban missile crisis eighteen months later—and left him, therefore, a captive of his emotions to the point of restricting any interest he might have had in alternative arguments.[50]

Like Blair when addressing his own constituencies in Britain, but also like Chirac (or Schroeder) relative to America, Bush's aim was not to mislead his interlocutors but to convince them of his own convictions. There was no bad faith in his behavior; but so deep was his confidence in what he believed, and so absolute was his faith in what he was about to do, that he deceived himself by ignoring the facts that might weaken his instinctive sense of the needed action against Saddam Hussein and the dehumanized world of terror the Iraqi dictator embraced. It is as if the horrific events of September 11 were enough to unveil a world gone mad after the end of the Cold War had shown a seductive tendency for the world to get better—a peculiar convergence for the U.S. administration between events in America that few could have imagined and a war in Iraq that many had eagerly awaited. When responding to these conditions as well as to one another, Bush, Blair, and Chirac all misplayed the hands that their countries had become used to holding—the righteous hand of preponderance for America, the principled hand of acquiescence for Britain, and the determined hand of resistance for France.

Although Chirac was the first to rally behind America and its president to share their pain and horror, he did not fully understand the sense of urgency that September 11 created in the United States—unlike Blair, but also unlike Spain's José María Aznar, another star performer in the Euro-Atlantic ballet staged after September 11. Whether that day inaugurated a "new security normalcy," as told by Vice President Cheney, can be debated. But the mere fact that it was so assumed in the United States was enough to make it so: in other words, the world was changed no less by the changed U.S. vision of the world than by the very events that led to the U.S. change.[51] With Americans made aware of a territorial vulnerability from which they had been spared throughout their history, September 11 provided their government with its first obligation in at least seventy years to wage war in the name of America—to protect the nation's territory, to restore its security, and to cater to its own interests in the face of an unprovoked act of aggression aimed at U.S. citizens who must be avenged.

"The importance of the U.S. leadership is brought home to me clearly," the U.S. president's father had written in January 1991 on the eve of the first Gulf War. Now, in 2002, his son agreed that the leadership he was called upon to provide on America's behalf was not only important but also preeminent. Relative to his father's war, however, this war seemed to be easier to justify, wage, and even settle. At home, public and congressional approval was not seriously questioned, and throughout 2002 there remained considerable support abroad as well. What Bush lacked, relative to his father, was a personal interest in the world and an understanding of the need for, and desirability of, consultation with countries toward which he felt, by his own words, "allergic" and whose followership he therefore assumed but did not truly seek.[52] "All countries in the West clearly have to turn to us," the elder Bush had noted, but "the more we get their opinion, the more we reach out no matter what is involved, in terms of time involved, the better it is."[53] In short, relative to the allies no less than to its adversaries, the United States was about to turn imperial even though it had neither the know-how nor the will to be imperialist as well. "Tell the Syrians I am a nasty unilateralist,"

Bush reportedly told a French official in September 2003. Whether the warning was meant for Damascus or Paris is a moot point; most likely, it was meant for both capitals.[54]

Worse yet, unlike Japan's surprise attack on the United States in December 1941, the possibility that the attacks of September 2001 could be repeated—with possibly worse ramifications—haunted America and its citizens. As a result, Bush was hardly the issue, even though that was the way it was construed nearly everywhere in Europe. In a scared and scarred America, Europe's calls for a return of the liberal, compassionate, outward-looking, and even prudent America they knew and liked showed more political partisanship than ever before.[55] Like Blair, Bush could readily agree with de Villepin's description of a world that "is sick, and in considerable disorder."[56] But where such conditions might have been common, and thus tolerable in "Old Europe," they were certainly new, and thus unacceptable, in the United States. Blair instinctively understood that fundamental piece of American history, but Chirac did not. And even if or when he did, the French president did not grasp as well as Blair the sense of urgency that America's new condition conveyed for Americans.

As September 11 changed the psychology of America, it opened a clash of history across the Atlantic and, to an extent, across the English Channel. Where such unprecedented conditions seemed to force the United States to adopt the sort of pagan leadership that had conditioned Europe's collapse during the first half of the previous century, Europe turned to the "transformative" leadership that it had learned from its senior partner during the latter half of the century—one that "like an 'invisible hand,' operated through the shell of traditional political structures."[57] After the initial post–September 11 Euro-Atlantic embrace, and beyond the consensus quickly achieved over the just war in Afghanistan, Chirac's plea for "limitless patience" revived the debate that had divided the three countries since the French ended their participation in surveillance missions in the no-fly zones over Iraq alongside American and British planes, in January 1997.[58] "The choice," argued de Villepin, was "between two visions of the world"—one that did not take the time to distinguish between preventive and preemptive action, and one that took whatever time was needed to achieve the international consensus required to make the use of force legitimate.[59] Chirac still thought there was plenty of time left to make that choice, but Blair knew better precisely because he knew that Bush had already concluded there was no longer any time left.

There is bitter irony in the fact that as early as March 2002 Blair was urged by his most senior advisers to pursue a strategy of delayed showdown— "the least worst option" given their fear of Iraq's postwar disintegration or a popular upheaval in the Muslim world.[60] These private warnings paralleled de Villepin's own public concern about "the tensions and fractures" that would follow a premature use of force in Iraq. "Our choices in Iraq," insisted de Villepin subsequently, "were not made against any particular country (or those among its partners that wanted to follow it) but in the name of a certain idea of collective responsibility and [on behalf] of a vision of the world."[61] The French foreign minister was speaking on his president's behalf, but Chirac's choice was no more understood by Bush than the latter's was in Paris, and Blair had neither enough influence (in Washington) nor motivation (relative to Paris) to convince either side otherwise: not enough influence to convince Bush that Chirac was not wrong in seeking a postponement of the war but not enough motivation in convincing Chirac that Bush was not wrong in wanting a war that would at last topple the "evil" regime in Iraq.

In its broader terms, the Anglo-French rift of 2002–4 was, once again, not only over Iraq or even directly about each other but also and above all over the United States. Blair and Chirac both agreed that Saddam Hussein had to go—the earlier the better. To achieve this ultimate goal, neither man excluded the military option, the worse of the worst. To that end, Chirac might have joined Blair and followed Bush had the U.S. administration or even the prime minister more credibly made the case for an imminent threat—meaning with a body of evidence that could not be provided since, as it was to be confirmed subsequently, there was none: no evidence that Saddam had the dreaded weapons or a credible predisposition to use them imminently, and no evidence that the United States was prepared for the follow-on missions of reconstruction and stabilization that would surely follow regime change.[62] Absent such evidence, Chirac, who had ordered his forces to be ready for any eventuality as late as the first week of January 2003, chose to disengage from the emerging coalition of the willing notwithstanding the private objections made by some of his more senior officials who understood better America's post–September 11 mood.

But containing Iraq was not the sole "principle" invoked in the ensuing debate; also at stake was the extent to which institutional constraints could be placed on the uses of military power, and more specifically American power, not only in Iraq but anywhere else too.[63] Indeed, it is this latter question over which the two European leaders most visibly clashed. Where

Chirac reasoned that a willingness to object would increase his future leverage irrespective of a U.S. decision that he still refused to see as final, Blair assumed that on balance there was little to gain from a refusal to accept a U.S. decision that he applauded even before it had been made public.[64] Unlike Chirac, Blair did not seem to mind being taken for granted by his U.S. counterpart, on personal grounds no less than on grounds of national status. That, Blair felt, was his best option, as his predecessors had invariably concluded in the past. In so doing, Blair would bolster his role as America's best and most faithful partner in Europe, a main prerequisite for the multilateral management of a unilateralist temptation that Blair perceived and wanted Bush to resist. As America's most reliable partner, Blair would also help form a broader and deeper coalition of the willing, which could compensate for the insufficiencies of U.S. postwar planning, which Blair, like Chirac and others, feared all the more deeply as they understood that they could not escape the consequences of failure. And ultimately, having thus demonstrated his influence on the United States, Blair could claim the EU leadership to which he aspired as, following the war, he alone could restore Europe's good name in America.

Ironically, Blair's case proved to be more compelling theoretically—where the French usually excel—than empirically—where the British traditionally do best. As Bush's indispensable ally, Blair could ask, but he could also insist until he was heard—to not take "no" or even "maybe" as an answer because Blair's concerns, if stated publicly, would expose Bush's isolation and America's drift. "Just as America helps define and influence our politics" in Europe, noted Blair's foreign minister, Jack Straw, shortly before the start of the war, "so what we do in Europe helps to define and influence American politics."[65] Not just the politics of America but also, and especially, its policies: In other words, the failure of Blair's leadership is not that he followed Bush in spite of many of his advisors' counsel (which he did), or that Blair was deceived by Bush in spite of much of what Blair knew (which he was not). Rather, Blair's failure is that he allowed the terms of engagement with Bush to become so unequivocal—in together at the first, and out together to the last—that Blair had no credibility left to impact a strategy that his own people questioned in conception, timing, and execution. Thus, after the Pentagon had taken control of the whole planning operation, the Foreign Office warned Blair of its inability to adapt "from high-intensity combat to soft post-conflict peacekeeping."[66] Ignored before the war, the warning was not heeded after the end of major combat operations either. Rather than reasserting his leadership credentials in Europe by assuming coleadership of a coalition that was now facing different and more demanding missions on behalf of an indigenous population that Britain knew especially well, Blair delivered one of the most "American" speeches ever heard from a foreign leader at a joint session of the U.S. Congress—parts of which, reportedly, he insisted on writing himself—that kept him on the sidelines, as the fan he had become rather than the cocaptain he had hoped to be. Even as evidence of postwar failure mounted in 2005, and even as the American war Blair had cosponsored was being turned into a civil war in 2006, Blair's eloquent support of Bush did not waver enough to question publicly his senior ally's most questionable decisions. If Blair felt so strongly about regime change in Iraq, why had he not insisted on such action when Clinton too entertained that thought in late 1998? Having spurned that early opportunity for ridding Iraq and the world of Saddam Hussein, why did Blair not insist on playing as active a role in the planning for postwar Iraq as he had assumed in making the case for war?

With accounts of the U.S. thinking for that period confirming the limits of that thinking in Washington, the question gains additional significance. In late 2003, Blair's seeming lack of influence on Bush did hurt after all, and so did the presence of other allies, including France and Germany, which might have added to the capabilities and relevance of a coalition that was not sufficient for the postwar military missions now about to be addressed. What is known now was known then by many and should have been known to all. When thinking about and planning for postwar Iraq, America's senior officials would have failed any introductory courses in economics or history taught by a British professor in any of the lesser colleges in Britain. Their failure was not even that they knew so very little about the country they were about to invade and occupy. Worse yet was a seeming unwillingness to learn more, unless it confirmed the little they already knew or were able to absorb in two weeks, which is the time that Ambassador Paul Bremer thought he needed "to get read in on the situation in Iraq" prior to his first trip to Baghdad where he was being sent to make Iraq's history conform to either that of America or, worse yet, that of America in postwar Europe.[67] After World War II, Truman's faith in America's power to reform Germany and transform Europe had been rooted in the belief that "only the United States had the power to grab hold of history and make it conform."[68] After the Cold War, that same belief seemed to guide Bush in and beyond Iraq, as he envisioned a new democratic order for the whole region, which would be built with the surplus of American power accumulated for and at the expense of a defunct Soviet Union. After September 11, the "casualness and swagger" with which Bush reportedly made his decisions, and the style with which these decisions were announced and imposed—"contemptuous, dismissive, arrogant and abusive"[69]—confirmed that while America lacked neither power nor resolve, it seemed to fall far short on strategic vision and even outright competence.

"Men of steel," wrote Eliot Cohen, in a book on wartime leaders, including Winston Churchill (but not Franklin D. Roosevelt), which was said to be of supreme interest to President George W. Bush and the most senior members of his administration. In the end, there was perhaps too much of Churchill in Blair—including a command of political rhetoric that enabled him to compensate for his senior partner's shortcomings in shaping a larger vision and a better rationale for the war they were about to wage together.[70] In and of itself, too much Churchill in Blair would hardly have been fatally wrong were it not for the fact that there was not enough of Roosevelt in Bush. "The Roosevelt-Churchill connection, Eleanor Roosevelt said, was 'a fortunate friendship.'"[71] History turned out to be better, much better, because of it. The same may not be true of the Bush-Blair connection, about which less closeness might have been for the better.

As Bush was preparing for war, his senior advisors liked to evoke President John F. Kennedy's textbook management of the missile crisis in October 1962.[72] But there was also too little of Kennedy in George W. Bush to bridge the differences between both crises—including the questionable threat raised by long-standing allegations against Saddam Hussein, as compared to the verifiably imminent threat raised by the deployment of Soviet strategic forces in Cuba. Unlike Kennedy, Bush never reconsidered or even refined his first impulse to use force; instead, his decision was made even before it could be enforced, and it was maintained after there had been enough evidence to question the urgency that had prompted the decision. Unlike Kennedy, Bush ignored different opinions, whether at home or abroad, and there was no attempt by his senior advisors, especially Condoleezza Rice, to make sure that he would be exposed to those opinions. Unlike Kennedy, Bush also depended most heavily on advisers who lacked solid knowledge of Iraq, and he sought or was provided with such knowledge only if it confirmed his (and his advisers') previously held opinions. Unlike Kennedy, Bush dismissed the relevance of world opinion, even as it turned increasingly hostile to the views and interests of the administration. Unlike Kennedy, Bush insisted on humiliating his opponent after its leader had been defeated, thus leaving no room for Saddam Hussein's allies to achieve redemption and thus ease reconciliation. These differences between Kennedy and Bush are, pointedly, the very "lessons" Robert Kennedy drew from the crisis for his brother's successors, and these are all lessons that Bush ignored even as the crisis was used to justify his actions in Iraq.[73]

When Kennedy had turned to de Gaulle midway through the thirteen-day crisis, the French president, who noted the lack of previous consultation, had expressed doubts over the risks raised over a security issue that was not immediately or directly relevant to France and its European partners. In addition, de Gaulle thought Kennedy was overreacting to conditions of territorial vulnerability that, in Europe, were a way of life. "For centuries," the French president noted at the time, Europe has been "living with threats and menaces," unlike America, which "has not had a comparable experience." Still, de Gaulle's support was immediate and unequivocal. "I accept what you tell me," he told Kennedy's emissaries, "as a fact, without any proof of any sort needed."[74] Forty years later, Bush seemed to think there was too much of de Gaulle in Chirac: the problem, really, was the opposite, not only because Chirac hardly showed the same faith in America's credibility as de Gaulle had but also and especially because Chirac thought of Iraq in terms of tactical opportunities rather than in terms of grand strategy à la de Gaulle. Unable to either deny or stall Kennedy's decision, of which he was being informed rather than about which he was being consulted, de Gaulle followed; only after the crisis had been resolved did he draw the consequences of America's nuclear brinkmanship and engage in a strategy that included distance from America and NATO and entanglement with Germany in an emerging European Community. Who is to say what might have happened had there been the same display of Western discord in 1962 as there was over Iraq in 2002? Who is to say what might not have happened had there been the same display of Western unity in 2002 as there had been in 1962? And above all, who is to say what Kennedy might have done if his Soviet counterpart had not blinked? Answers to these questions can only be surmised from the fact that Europe's unblinking endorsement of America's resolve gave sufficient credibility to a decision based on a less than credible threat to avoid its enforcement after all.

As argued here, Blair underplayed his influence. His main asset was the hold he had on Bush, who needed him, as America's best and most credible partner, to start a war to which he was committed and which Bush's senior advisers were seemingly anxious to get started. Nearly fifty years earlier, in April 1954, a comparable situation had been faced when then-secretary of state John Foster Dulles had sought Britain's support to intervene in Indochina to avoid an impending French surrender at Dien Bien Phu.[75] When Anthony Eden, then Churchill's foreign minister, declined to join a fight that the French had already lost and that he knew the West could not win, Eisenhower chose to abstain from action despite Dulles's apparent eagerness for intervention. In February 2003, Blair too had doubts, but he chose to ignore them in return for a second UN resolution that Bush agreed to seek as a prerequisite for Britain's followership. In making such a request, however, Blair forced a counterproductive clash with Chirac—his own within Europe, as well as Bush's within the Atlantic Alliance. Blair's mistake was not that he failed to ask for a second resolution, which had been part of Chirac's initial strategy; but, having made his request privately, Blair should have insisted publicly and thus, like Eden, help avoid or at least delay the war pending approval and enforcement of that resolution. Alternatively, unwilling to insist, Blair should not have asked, especially now that Chirac too was no longer demanding a procedure that he knew to be conducive to a clash that exceeded his own preferences. Absent such a clash, it might have been possible to enlarge a coalition of the willing that was clearly sufficient for the military mission in 2003 but, as could be anticipated, was not sufficiently capable for the postwar missions and the insurgency that followed.

As to Chirac, he overstated his influence, hardly uncharacteristic for him and his country. His trump card was the hold he gained on public opinion in and outside Europe, which reinforced his conviction that he could stall or even reverse the U.S. decision for war. Admittedly, the decision was not communicated to Paris, while Bush and Blair discussed that decision with a growing sense of finality, from their meeting in Crawford, Texas, in April 2002 to the meeting at Camp David in September of that year. Like Blair, Chirac asked, and certainly more than Blair, Chirac insisted, but unlike his counterpart in London, the French president did so too publicly, thereby assuming the role of a spoiler and reinforcing the worst images that have troubled America's and Britain's relations with France over the past several decades. That too proved to be counterproductive. Having been denied, Chirac should have given thought to joining Blair in order to influence Bush and help him prepare for postwar conditions that were equally feared by both Blair and Chirac. In the end, however, the French president had few gains to show for the influence he thought he had and sought to reinforce. Within the alliance, he could neither delay a war that was all but inevitable nor help end the war after it had been allegedly won. In Europe, even before the French rejection of the constitutional treaty in late May 2005, Chirac's stand proved insufficient to regain the leadership he wanted to exert in and for Europe, as the war did not merely weaken the strong governments that followed Bush's leadership but also helped make the weak governments that resisted Bush even weaker.

It may be that asking Blair to speak up and expecting Chirac to hush up would have been asking too much from either man. But the failure of each to do what was asked of him made of Iraq a European failure before it became an American failure. For Blair, who could speak neither in the name of the Atlantic Alliance (which is what Bush claimed on the basis of the majority support he received from other heads of state and government) nor in the name of Europe (Chirac's claim because of the majority support he received from the general public in most European countries), the stakes were too high, and his stack of bargaining chips too small. Asking Chirac to keep quiet might have been against his nature—but so it was for de Gaulle too, and yet he did keep quiet during the Cuban missile crisis, and that alone should have been enough of a reference for Chirac if only he, like de Gaulle, had understood the urgency of the moment.

In short, the Anglo-French clash over Iraq, measured in terms of both countries' distinctive relations with the United States, confirmed that no single European state can effectively either strengthen or challenge America's leadership alone, because none alone can show enough weight to act decisively as an effective counterpart of U.S. leadership, let alone an adversarial counterweight of American power. For both Britain and France, the preponderance of American power, relative to their own weakness, could be neither ignored nor reversed. Yet that fact alone should not have precluded their ability "to make sure," in de Villepin's words, "that the considerable risks of such [U.S.] intervention can actually be kept under control"—meaning, influenced—under conditions, in Blair's words, that might "determine the rest of the world for years to come."[76]

It is that ability—for Europe to influence America for the better—that was squandered by Blair and Chirac, as the terms of their countries' endearment with, and estrangement from, the United States had little impact on the existential crisis whose resolution became the centerpiece of the post–September 11 security agenda of George W. Bush.

Terms of Disparagement

Blair's role between Bush and Chirac must be assessed in the context of Britain's bilateral relations with the United States and with France. For it is there, clearly, that each man did what was expected of him because of France and Britain's estrangement from the United States and Europe, respectively, but also because of France and Britain's differences over the U.S. role in and with Europe. In the end, the verdict is equally harsh on Britain in the European context and on France in the context of the Atlantic Alliance as it is on the United States for both contexts.

As argued previously, France helped launch the awesome and generally successful idea of an increasingly united and progressively stronger Europe. While the United States helped execute the idea, and steadily urged that it be enlarged to an ever-larger number of other countries in Europe, Britain all too often tried to bury, distort, or contain it. To achieve a "special" status relative to the United Sides, Britain spent time positioning itself at the expense of France and to the detriment of Europe but not enough time explaining Europe or even France on behalf of the Europeans. To stay away from Europe, Britain often maneuvered in ways that were generally disruptive of its neighbors' efforts to reorganize their continent *à l'américaine*. Throughout this process, every initiative for Europe, usually inspired in Paris, was met with resistance from London—from the European Coal and Steel Community to the European Defense Community to the Common Market, and after Britain belatedly and reluctantly signed the Rome Treaties, from the Common Market through the single market to a single currency that it permitted but did not adopt. In May 2005, the French opposition to the constitutional treaty helped avoid another rebuttal from Britain, where the very word "constitution" guaranteed a public opposition unlikely to be overcome. How much more ahead would Europe be today had it not been for such objections from a country that was entitled to at least a share of the leadership that others in continental Europe assumed by default?

Such resistance did not serve Europe well, and it was even more damaging to Britain's interests. So long as in Britain's absence Europe stayed small, they also both stayed weak. Nor did Britain's resistance serve the United States well during the Cold War, when the construction of Europe remained a primary goal that never seemed to meet U.S. expectations in full or on time. It may be that the end of the Cold War gave a new voice to American skeptics who, like their counterparts in Britain, questioned the desirability of a project that was exceedingly linked to France and its supposedly anti-American instincts. To make matters worse, with the Soviet threat done and communism gone, the European project no longer seemed safely glued to the United States either. Why, it was asked, should American power be exposed to the countervailing influence of a uniting Europe? Why not, instead, extend the hard-earned unipolar moment with new global arrangements that would favor U.S. interests, goals, and values? The answer was provided in Iraq when it was shown that American power was not sufficient to make that moment last, either because it was not sufficiently efficient or because it was not sufficiently abundant or because it was not sufficiently available given a lack of public taste for it. Echoes of Vietnam when the Nixon administration, having uncovered the limits of American power, announced a Year of Europe, following which it would be possible for the United States to do less on the assumption that its allies of choice were committed to do more. Thus exposed to the limits of U.S. preponderance, Bush returned to Brussels in February 2005, a few weeks after his reelection, to relaunch America's alliance with Europe as a union rather than persist with a string of coalitions that would be organized one national capital at a time.

Call it multipolarity or not, but it is when the limits of American power are most evident that the need to work with the states of Europe also becomes most compelling. To meet that need, and thus do multipolarity right, the states of Europe must do Europe right—and to do Europe right, Britain must amend its relations with Europe, beginning with its relations with France, its most predictable nemesis since General de Gaulle's first "no" to Britain in January 1963. Three consequences emerge from this episode in Anglo-American and Anglo-French relations, each of which, post-Blair, is likely to redirect Britain's attitude toward the United States, but also relative to Europe and in the world.

A first consequence is that the days of faithful Britain are over: beginning with Gordon Brown, no British prime minister will dare support the United States as unequivocally as his predecessors and without the open influence that Blair failed to seek and Bush did not bother to extend.

"If you want me to apologize for the war in Iraq," a defiant Blair insisted in the spring of 2005, "I'm afraid I cannot say that I'm sorry we removed Saddam Hussein."[77] But that is an apology few Britons—or Americans or French or Germans—ever sought. If and when asked, the apology was intended to be over the strategy Blair pursued to achieve this goal, as well as the arguments made to justify that strategy. For even by that early time, in

April 2005, it should have been clear that Saddam's removal did not have the desired effects, and that post-Saddam security conditions in Iraq, slowly pointing to a civil war and the potential disintegration of the country, had taken a turn for the worse. In the end, Iraq became for Blair a political quagmire that built up his reputation in the United States without giving Britain the influence he had hoped to gain, while draining his reputation in Europe to an extent that denied him the leadership he had hoped to assert. That he did not stumble into that quagmire blindly compounds his sin: unlike Bush, it cannot be said of Blair that he should have known better because knowing better is something he did—because of what he knew on his own no less than because of what he learned from his advisers.

Like most other European countries, Britain has had its moments of public anger at the United States—moments when the power of the United States was questioned bitterly over what it sought to achieve no less than what it did or failed to achieve. The sad truth is that at one point or the other, and over any number of issues, every European has been, is, or will be hostile to U.S. policies: anti-Americanism is a recurring phenomenon that knows no boundaries and afflicts allies no less than adversaries. But in a two-party political system like Britain's, such moments tended to be fundamentally partisan, as each of the two main parties ignored its earlier criticism to embrace Britain's sole indispensable ally as soon as it regained control of the government. Now, however, Britain's public anger shows a nonpartisan dimension that regroups conservative and Laborite critics against a "devious" U.S. strategy that Blair proved unable to set straight and from which he could not disengage.[78]

For the decade to come, no prime minister in Britain will respond to a U.S. call to arms without remembering the conditions that surrounded the intervention in Iraq—so wishful in its conception as to border on self-deception, so stubborn in its defense as to suggest deception, and so ineffective in its execution and outcome as to invite separation from the U.S. leaders who ordered it and from the senior ally that bungled it. As Britons are awakened to the difficulties of accommodating a fallen empire that has come home to raise daunting and unprecedented challenges of democratic civility and domestic security, they will be more likely to resist calls from the United States where the post–September 11 "pagan ethos" is part of a European past that Britain does not wish to resuscitate any more than its main European partners do. That legacy from the debate over Iraq is especially significant because it does not extend only to Blair's immediate successor within the Labor party,

Gordon Brown, but also touches the opposition party where a youthful David Cameron's "instinctive" friendship of the United States fails, in his own words, to match his "passionate" commitment to the Atlantic Alliance.

Cameron's distinction between the exclusive framework of Britain's bilateral relations with the United States and the inclusive setting of the multilateral Euro-Atlantic partnership is significant. After Blair and even beyond Bush, it suggests a more evenhanded approach to America and Europe—"a sense of balance, judgment and proportion," Cameron declared in his first comprehensive foreign policy speech delivered, symbolically enough, on September 11, 2006. Like his predecessors, Cameron admittedly understands that "Britain just cannot achieve the things we want to achieve in the world unless we work with the world's superpower." But remaining "America's unconditional associate in every endeavor" would ultimately "combine the maximum of exposure with the minimum of influence" on U.S. decisions.[79] As Britain thus reassesses the limits of its traditional ties with the United States, it follows that a second consequence of the debate over Iraq on Anglo-American relations is that while America remains a central part of Britain's past as a world power, Europe is Britain's best hope for a future as a power in the world.

For the past five decades, Britain has viewed the idea of Europe as a folly she could neither ignore nor control—"not a British, but a France-German, inspired club."[80] At first, there was little wrong in dismissing the idea, or at least in finding it of little relevance to Britain's vocation and interests. Unlike postwar Germany, Britain had made Europe proud during the previous years, and it hardly needed to start anew and reinvent itself, relative to its past and to its people, but unlike postwar France, too, Britain did not have to recast its institutions or even its people. There had been indeed something "splendid" in Britain's postwar isolation from its continental partners, and the terms of the Rome Treaties were such as to cause legitimate concern that entry in the Common Market would more likely accentuate Britain's decline that revive its growth. As Europe grew into an institutional reality, however, Britain's fading splendor was replaced by the ever harsher evidence of a shrinking island whose people could barely remember who they used to be in the knowledge of what they had become. The "folly" now was to continue to disavow what could no longer be stopped, let alone controlled—to be an "extra-European, indeed counter-European" member of a Europe it was joining not because it wanted in but because of the growing evidence that it could no longer afford to stay out.[81]

On occasion the folly seems to persist, expressed with absurd proposals designed to present Britain with alternatives to an ever-closer integration with Europe, such as associate membership with the North American Free Trade Agreement (NAFTA).[82] In practice, however, such proposals grossly underreport, distort, and misrepresent the significance of the European Union to Britain by fragmenting the European single market into its various national dimensions and thus exaggerating the significance of the American market relative to that of Europe as a whole.

The reality is otherwise. Thus, while U.S. companies continue to favor Britain over other EU countries, and even as Britain continues to favor the United States over any other single EU country, the European single market is the primary sources and recipient of Britain's FDI. For the ten-year period 1996–2005, EU countries' FDI in the United Kingdom increased more than fivefold, from £43.9 billion in 1996 to £238.8 billion in 2005, one and a half the total of U.S. FDI (£149.4 billion), which itself nearly tripled during that period (from £56 billion in 1996). The proportions are roughly comparable for Britain's FDI in the European Union and in the United States, with the stock of British FDI in the European Union (£369.2 billion) more than twice that in the United States (£162.9 billion) in 2005. With regard to trade, British exports to the European Union amounted to nearly £150 billion in 2006, as compared to nearly £32 billion to the United States. Again, the proportions are roughly the same for imports—which amounted to £160.2 billion for the European Union and £26 billion from the United States.[83]

Admittedly, it is in Britain more than anywhere else that the case against Europe can still elicit the warmest and most passionate response. But over the years a great deal of that case was based on an ability to make a parallel case for America, which represented, therefore, a trump card that was not similarly available to other EU members. After Iraq, as was suggested earlier, this alternative may no longer be so readily available, and, ironically enough, it is the "case against America" that might best help make the "case for Europe" in the future. Thus, by mid-2006, public opinion polls confirmed that on most issues Britain was as skeptical as Germany or even France. For example, 72 percent of the British respondents found a U.S. strong leadership in world affairs "somewhat" or "very" undesirable. That still compared well with France and Germany (where the rate of disapproval reached 85 percent and 86 percent, respectively—suggesting a skepticism that went beyond the sole person of the U.S. president). But three years earlier, in June 2003, the rate of disapproval in Britain had stood at 57 percent (versus 81 percent and

82 percent in Germany and France, respectively), thereby confirming a disturbing convergence of public perceptions among the three main EU countries as more people in Britain thought that relations between the United States and Europe had worsened during the previous year (48 percent) than in France (47 percent) or Germany (31 percent).[84]

Significantly, as Britain's skepticism about America's leadership has grown, its confidence in Europe's ability to "exert strong leadership" has not improved, even though as many people in Britain as in France or in Germany—roughly 57 percent—agree that the European Union should "take a more independent approach from the United States" (as opposed to 44 percent in 2004, when the corresponding figures for France and Germany stood at 55 percent and 51 percent, respectively).[85] The same trends are confirmed when projected into the future. Thus, while 89 percent of all respondents to a different poll viewed the United States as a preponderant world power in 2006—about the same as in France (also 89 percent) and Germany (90 percent)—the figure dropped to barely over half (53 percent) for the year 2020, surprisingly the same level as the response to the world power status of the European Union.[86] Written into these public perceptions is a fact of failure that targets not only the United States, as a hegemonic power that made ineffective and imprudent use of its power, but also Britain and Europe, as like-minded allies whose willingness to follow, or eagerness to object, was equally ineffective, imprudent, and ultimately self-defeating.

Finally, the debate over Iraq confirms that the end of Anglo-French estrangement is a precondition for a stronger European Union, but it is also a necessity for a cohesive alliance with the United States.

Europe was given birth to by France and with Britain against Germany; it grew with France and Germany but without Britain; for maturity to come, it will need to proceed around both Britain and France but with Germany. Thus, while Blair's passion for Europe was the main casualty of his passion for America, his successors' misgivings about America may well become a catalyst for a renewed interest in Europe. For it is when the former cannot be controlled that the latter can be rekindled.

For the French, the construction of a united and strong Europe was a realist-driven arrangement centrally tied to security issues. It reflected France's primary concern with Germany, but it also acknowledged France's inability to gather the capabilities and the will needed to attend to that concern on its own. Britain was France's ally of choice in Europe, but the French instinctive ambivalence about the two superpowers, strongly reinforced by domestic political pressures, was also resolved on the basis of their respective capabilities—which America enjoyed and which the Soviet Union lacked except in the military dimension. What followed is therefore unfortunate. America should have exerted more pressures on Britain on behalf of the French idea of Europe, and France should have exerted fewer pressures on Britain at the expense of the U.S. idea of the alliance.

For Britain, the realist case for European unity was much less compelling than for its partners on the Continent. For one, there was the United States, with which, as we have seen, each successive government in London was determined to maintain a special relationship that no government in Paris was able to achieve. In addition, unlike France and other European powers, Britain did not suffer from what de Gaulle liked to call "the psychology of the vanquished." For Britain, therefore, a realist case for balance in Europe could still be made with a mixture of British will and American power that could manipulate and assuage the fears that all European states had of each other as well as of Russia. What followed is also unfortunate. Far -sighted across the Atlantic but near-sighted across the English Channel, Britain over-stated America's interest in its identity as a non-European power and ne-glected the U.S. interest in Britain's power because of its European identity.

For its part, the U.S. security interest in a united and strong Europe had four distinctive security goals: to permit a lasting reconciliation among the states of Europe, but also to have these new allies assume a bigger share of the common defense burden with added and usable capabilities, to maintain the centrality of NATO as the security institution of choice and give it a global dimension that compensated for Europe's own descent to parochial-ism, and to provide the United States with a coherent and capable interlocu-tor whose right of first refusal was not a right of veto. For these goals to be met fully during the coming years, there is a need for more cooperation between Britain and France, without which Europe cannot be completed, as well as between France and the United States, without which the completion of Europe could not be achieved to the satisfaction of the United States. But there is also a need for additional contributions from Germany, without which Europe would not be strong enough and therefore might not be rele-vant enough to U.S. interests and expectations.

CHAPTER THREE

Terms of Disparagement

*He was all over me. He was ready to go in the barn and milk my cows,
if he could find the teats. There's only one way to deal with the Germans.
You keep patting them on the head and then every once in a while you
kick them in the balls.*
  —Lyndon Baines Johnson, after a meeting at his Texas ranch
  with then-German chancellor Ludwig Erhard

*The sudden and complete moral collapse of a valiant people, a decadence
the more grandiose in that this people had, until then, known how to
display a will to vanquish, an obstinacy of endurance, a capacity to suffer
that merited . . . the astonishment and admiration of its enemies.*
  —Charles de Gaulle, writing of Germany in 1924[1]

AFTER 1945, France and Britain were the only plausible contenders for leadership in postwar Europe west of Russia. However, for either nation to act accordingly required U.S. support—to tame Germany, to preserve the empires, and to contain Russia. Denied such support, neither Britain nor France could lead, for lack of capabilities and, most likely, a lack of will too. Unlike the situation in 1919, that relative weakness was widely understood in both European capitals where, arguably, a sense of limits prevailed in Paris even more than in London. "It was necessary to warn the Americans," pointedly complained de Gaulle about the Anglo-French debacle in Suez a decade after the war, "and say to them, 'this is what we wish to do.'" De Gaulle might not welcome such dependence on the United States, but he still recognized it at the time, as he added pensively, "If [they] don't approve . . ."[2] He was not wrong, of course, and the lack of U.S. approval transformed the Anglo-French quest for renewal at the expense of Egypt into a retreat that ultimately proved to be costly for the West.

Still, in the new world that had come out of the war, the United States needed a partner of choice, and there were few alternatives to these two aging European powers. In time, Germany might become an option again, but there was no expectation that it could do so quickly. A defeated nation whose collective folly had shamed Europe, it lay as a divided state that was barely entitled to the limited sovereignty its occupiers were willing to grant it—America less grudgingly than Britain, Britain more rapidly than France, and all three less rapaciously and more convincingly than the Soviet Union. The object rather than an active participant of postwar superpower rivalries, Germany now endured as two countries inhabited by one people torn between incompatible ideological allegiances and rigidly kept apart territorially because of the impact that reunification would have on regional and global balances. In short, the geography of East-West confrontation had placed Germany at the center of the newly unveiled bipolar world, but its own history of regional preponderance also kept it at the center of Europe's haunting memories of a seemingly defunct multipolar environment.

While these postwar conditions evolved progressively during the Cold War, neither the United States nor its European partners encouraged Germany to assume the leadership role to which it was otherwise entitled by the capabilities it "miraculously" regained after 1945. The alliance with America and within a strong NATO was its security blanket, and reconciliation with France and with a uniting European Community (EC) was its road to redemption. It is only with the end of the Cold War, therefore, that a newly unified German state found it possible to develop a more active and potentially more assertive foreign policy.[3] For only then did a bigger and better Germany regain at last the legitimacy it needed to seek coleadership of the West with the United States, Germany's most reliable benefactor, and reinforce its leadership of Europe, with or without France, its previously implacable foe and now its most intimate European partner.[4]

An American interest in, and even predilection for, Germany over other states in Europe is not new, although it has often been hidden behind an attitude that Teddy Roosevelt once described as "humorous contempt."[5] In 1871, Germany's unification had been greeted in the United States as an event that was oddly assimilated to the unification of the American colonies almost one hundred years earlier.[6] Nearly fifty years later, after having denied Germany's bid for hegemonic control of Europe during World War I, America was neither willing to help France keep its nemesis in the cage built at Versailles nor amenable to a special relationship with Britain that would have placed the burdens of the European balance, and hence Europe's security, on America's shoulders. For the United States to come home after 1919 was not a wrong choice. This was the wrong peace at the wrong time—a peace bound to remain too vengeful because it came at least three years of murderous killing too late. Attaching the Versailles Treaty to a covenant explicitly designed to build a new European order at the expense of Germany made matters worse, and for the United States to join the League of Nations would have made neither the victorious European powers more compliant nor a defeated Germany charged with the guilt of the war more submissive.[7] Everywhere in Europe, the people's primary allegiance went to a tragic past that had made of "every little garden a graveyard," whose justification would ultimately demand even more graveyards.[8]

America's interest in Germany remained predictably strong after 1945. Dean Acheson, writes historian John Harper, "lacked the deep distrust of Germany that characterized most Europeans . . . while [Chancellor] Adenauer was inclined to trust the Americans more than the British or the French."[9] A decisive U.S. precondition for an entangling alliance with Europe in peacetime was therefore that France and Britain also change their ways and agree to include Germany in the reconstruction that the United States orchestrated soon after the war had been won. To be sure, the 1949 North Atlantic Treaty kept a defeated, divided, and disarmed Germany out of the Western alliance. But that condition was known to be temporary. On grounds of capabilities as well as on political grounds, it is with Bonn more than with London and Paris that Washington best shared its fear of Soviet power and its visceral disdain of the Kremlin, and it is in Germany more than in France or in Britain that defense against a hypothetical Soviet thrust in Europe could best be met. And unlike France, West Germany had no communists, while unlike Britain and France, its Social Democratic Left did not embrace a Marxist ideology.

Admittedly, Germany's rehabilitation did not come easily.[10] Neither France nor Britain welcomed decisions that made Germany a recipient of America's postwar economic largesse and a main beneficiary of its security umbrella, which its Western neighbors felt the newly formed German state had not yet earned. Nor was Germany always content with a partial sovereignty that exposed its leaders to occasional bursts of frustration: toward France (expressed with an initial reluctance to embrace the European Coal and Steel Community or an open resistance to rearm and thus risk paving the way for a revival of the German army) but also toward the United States later in the 1950s (with occasional statements of concern over the reliability of the U.S. commitment or mounting frustrations with the heavy-handedness of U.S. economic policies).[11] Yet, like de Gaulle, the German chancellor understood the limits of U.S. support and leadership no less than the need for it. "Vital necessities for European states," warned Konrad Adenauer in the tense context of the then-approaching Suez crisis, "are not always . . . vital necessities for the United States, and vice versa; there may result differences in political conceptions that may lead to independent actions."[12] Such rebellious moments never lasted, however; they were irrationalities that were quickly corrected by the pressures felt diplomatically from the West, including the United States and France, or exerted forcefully from the East, namely the Soviet Union.

After the war and throughout the Cold War there was no escape from Germany's centrality. Germany's rejuvenation might well be the inevitable consequence of reconstruction, but reconstruction was an indispensable prerequisite for reconciliation. This was a postulate that a compassionate America understood instinctively well. But unlike the situation in 1919, this was also a principle that America was able to communicate to, or impose on, those states in Europe to which it had extended protection and on which it was now bestowing its generosity. That Germany's contribution was indispensable to an effective Western defense was an imperative that Truman's distant and safe America could also accommodate better than any of Germany's neighbors. Ironically, by keeping Germany divided, occupied, and militarily in check, Soviet hostility also provided the insurance policy that convinced the European allies to follow the U.S. lead.[13] A mere decade after war's end, in May 1955, bringing the Federal Republic into NATO, "the bloc within which it was born and to which it belonged by its own choice," while Germany's other half was forced into the Warsaw Pact, sealed the grand bargain for a new security system in Europe that was all the more satisfactory to a tamed Germany as an expansionist Russia was kept at a safe distance by the United States.[14] The paradox is that the more firmly such a bargain asked Germany to deny any interest in using its power unilaterally and on its own behalf, without or at the expense of its neighbors, the more effectively Germany was able to exercise that power multilaterally and for its own self-interests, with and on behalf of its allies.

Recast Germany

During the Cold War, Germany's status in Europe and within the Atlantic Alliance was directly affected by the state of U.S. bilateral relations with Britain and France—the former as America's most faithful partner and the latter as its most quarrelsome ally. After 1958 especially, which is after the Fourth Republic had ended its prolonged institutional agony, mounting exasperation with de Gaulle prompted the United States to hinder France's efforts to cement its own special relationship with a declining Britain. Fearing isolation in Europe between two superpowers that denied France its rank and limited its independence—two of the most cherished words of France's diplomatic language—the Fifth Republic turned to a recast Germany as its new European partner of choice.

The U.S. strategy of isolating the French had worked well in 1956: that is, there is no need for the United States to punish an ally for its challenges to U.S. leadership so long as that ally is denied significant followers of its own. As U.S. pressures forced Britain to abandon its attempt to reassert its status in the Middle East, France predictably gave in too. Six years later, in January 1963, it was President Kennedy's turn to lure a "depressed and desperately tired" British prime minister away from an assertive and domineering French president who wanted to offer Britain a central place in Europe while the United States seemed to be standing in the way of the central role in the world to which London still aspired. Coming days after Macmillan's meeting with de Gaulle, the intent of Kennedy's improvised meeting with Britain's prime minister in the Bahamas was unmistakable.[15] The French and the Americans were openly bidding for Britain's allegiance on vital security issues—including the proliferation of nuclear weapons and the control of the strategic deterrent—and for the first time the French government seemed competitive. But with Kennedy quickly reaffirming the hierarchy of America's bilateral relations with its European allies in Britain's favor, de Gaulle's hopes for a special bilateral partnership with Britain were denied. As George Ball acknowledged subsequently, Britain was "encouraged . . . in the belief that she could, by her own efforts, as long as she maintained a specially favored position with the United States, play an independent great power role."[16] Admittedly, in so doing Kennedy "deflected [Britain] from coming to terms with her European destiny." But no such destiny could satisfy the United States if it was left wholly in French hands and pursued at America's expense. Nor would it prove satisfying to Britain: even after Macmillan had made his bid to join Europe, he remained openly ambivalent about the European Economic Community, which he pointedly viewed as "an economic community, not a defense alliance or a foreign policy community, or a cultural community."[17]

"Macmillan," de Gaulle said later, "has come [to the 1962 Rambouillet Summit] to tell me we were right to build our force de frappe. We also have ours, he said, and we ought to be able to unite the two within a context that would be independent from the United States."[18] De Gaulle's self-serving translation of what he heard may not have matched what he was told, but it reflected well enough the two men's different visions of, and uses for, Europe—one allegedly more autonomous and the other supposedly more Atlanticist.[19] Indeed, the French president was adamant: the subsequent Nassau Summit between Macmillan and Kennedy, he reasoned, confirmed not only America's predilection for Britain over France (and Europe) but also Britain's predilection for America over Europe (and France). "At the Bahamas," de Gaulle concluded, "Great Britain gave the United States whatever poor atomic forces she had. She could have given them to Europe. She has thus made her choice."[20] And the French president added dismissively, in response to Kennedy's offer of Polaris missiles on the same terms as Britain had accepted, "The American proposals . . . will give the United States the possibility of seizing the French atomic forces."[21] The point was made with typical Gaullist exaggeration, but it was not entirely lacking in substance. The Polaris missiles offered by Kennedy to Britain were to be mounted with warheads that were available to the British but which the French had not developed yet, and without which those missiles would have been useless because the French did not have the needed submarines either.[22]

With Britain thus committed to a privileged partnership with the United States to sustain its global role whatever the consequences for its role in Europe, only Germany was left to help France play out its own destiny in Europe, even if at the expense of its role in the world (which the final loss of its empire had sharply devalued anyway, as for Britain). Notwithstanding Adenauer's own expectations, the French goal was not to give Germany co-leadership of Europe, to which only Britain might have been entitled, but to deny the United States the exclusive leadership it wanted, at the expense of

France and other traditional European powers. Like Kennedy and Macmillan, de Gaulle and Adenauer had come to form an odd couple, united by their shared memories of two world wars and their common commitment to a lasting bilateral reconciliation that was to be extended to an ever-larger number of European states. And perhaps better than any other postwar heads of state or government in Europe, both men perfectly understood the historical failures and continued failings of their own nations when left to themselves.

Bilateral intimacy between France and Germany was not merely an effective way to end a contentious past. For de Gaulle, it was also an effective way to build a protective counterweight to the Anglo-American special partnership he had failed to break in the name of Europe and now hoped to resist within NATO. Indeed, the first meeting between these two men, in de Gaulle's home in the quaint village of Colombey-les-deux-Églises, was followed in a matter of days by de Gaulle's call for a NATO triumvirate—a *directoire*—with Britain and the United States, and in a matter of weeks by an opening to Russia, which de Gaulle expected to be especially sensitive to France's new ability to speak for Germany. Presumably, Adenauer was aware of, and potentially concerned about, both initiatives, neither of which was to his liking. But the German chancellor viewed a public reconciliation with France as an end in itself—a step, that is, designed to end at last the harm that each country had inflicted upon the other and, accordingly, to open the door on the peaceful integration of a European community of democratic states. In the summer of 1961, de Gaulle's triumphant tour through West Germany seemed to give two generations of pre- and postwar Germans the historic pardon they needed.[23] But it was only after January 1963, when Britain appeared to confirm the Atlanticist choice it had made in the fall of 1956, also under U.S. pressures, that Germany became the partner of choice for France—a partner that would help build up Europe as a rampart against an Anglo-American partnership whose reliability was questioned by both men, "one old and the other very old."[24]

In this context, Kennedy's intriguing proposal of a Multilateral Force (MLF) served as a quick and effective rebuttal of both Adenauer and de Gaulle. At its simplest, the MLF was designed to remind the German government of its dependence on the United States for security from the Soviet Union, a much more urgent priority at the time than the French offer of partnership in Europe. Of course, the MLF was a bit of a political fake. Kennedy's offer to Adenauer of a limited control of a very small piece of the

U.S. nuclear arsenal was as frankly disingenuous as his offer of Polaris missiles to de Gaulle, without the submarines that could launch them or the warheads that could make them useful after they had been launched.[25] Once again, however, the U.S. goal was not to reward Germany with a coleadership of NATO but to isolate France as Europe's leader within the Atlantic Alliance. Thus understood, that strategy worked: the openly deeper U.S. estrangement from the French not only flowed from the closer U.S. engagement with Britain but also discouraged Germany from any adventure away from Washington.

A side effect of the U.S. manipulation of bilateral differences in Europe could be to stall integration in the absence of a sturdy and dependable bilateral axis around which Europe would continue to be built. At Nassau, Kennedy had been aware of this risk, and he had initially resisted an offer of the Polaris missiles to Britain, which, as Kennedy understood well, could not be made to other allies as well. But Washington's support for a strong and united Europe was not so unconditional as to welcome it in any form and under any condition. "If Europe were ever to be organized so as to leave us outside," warned Secretary of State Dean Rusk, "it would become more difficult for us to sustain our guarantee. . . . We shall not hesitate to make this point to the Germans if they show signs of accepting any idea of a Paris-Bonn axis."[26] Implicit in the U.S. support for European integration, therefore, was the unwritten assumption that even in the absence of Britain, an increasingly united and progressively stronger Europe would remain a credible partner because of the presence of a reliable Germany. Lacking such assurance, the United States could be expected to raise obstacles by collaborating selectively with Atlanticist countries and, on occasion, European political leaders with anti-communist or, now, anti-Gaullist credentials. But nothing the United States did or attempted throughout the Cold War ever stalled European integration for long because Europe's opposition never truly threatened to deny or derail U.S. policies and interests.

For a special partnership between the United States and Germany to emerge as a substitute for, or a credible complement to, the U.S. partnership with Britain, several conditions had to be met, none of which were likely to come anytime soon. First, the Cold War would have to end on terms that were satisfactory to the Germans, meaning reunification, but also to the other European states that, through two world wars, had helped to amputate a country the Cold War had next divided, seemingly irreversibly. In other words, continuing to wage the Cold War to protect a territorial status quo that made room for two small Germanys was preferable to ending the Cold War in a way that resurrected one large and potentially revisionist German state. Accordingly, at the close of the Cold War, it was once again America that stood in the way of an open Anglo-French attempt "to slow up" the German juggernaut of reunification, as Margaret Thatcher put it while attempting to enlist France in that effort.[27] What might have happened had Britain's prime minister convinced the French president to help her stand in the way of Germany's unification will fortunately never be known for sure: for the third time in the twentieth century, America was called upon to save Europe from itself, and Germany from its neighbors, including France and Britain.

In addition, even divided, Germany was to be kept under some control in the EC that was launched after the Federal Republic had found its legitimate place in the U.S.-led Atlantic Alliance. In the United States, reasons for limiting Germany's autonomy had more to do with the threat of Soviet imperialism than with the risks of German militarism. Early in the Cold War, it is only after the enlargement of NATO to the Federal Republic that the Warsaw Pact finalized the division of Europe in May 1955. Given the singularity of Germany's status, any overt U.S. attempt to build it up as the leading West European power risked a conflict with Moscow, which the United States could not have escaped and which it was not willing to wage. In effect, the Soviet Union held the master key of a European security architecture conceived for and around Germany, as it was not only the ultimate guarantor of Germany's division but also the sole plausible provider of Germany's unification, however strong the Americans might make the German half over which they had control.

Thus relying paradoxically on both American power and Soviet hostility, Germany learned to master its history within a European community that was built with much foresight and even imagination. Compelled to be everybody's best ally, the Germans acquiesced to the tangible facts of U.S. leadership in NATO and to the self-fulfilling claims of French leadership in the EC. A consensus emerged, mainly from the top down, as Germans were more anxious to bury their past than to define a future that would require a debate about their condition as a divided country. The main features of this consensus were reconciliation with France in a progressively united Europe and protection from the United States in an increasingly integrated NATO. Accepting French leadership for Europe was the first priority of a recast German state, welcoming Europe was the shared impulse of born-again German citizens, and recognizing the primacy of the United States and NATO over France and the EC was the first imperative of security-conscious German governments. In making these choices, the Germans did not remove the concept of power from their political vocabulary. They did, however, adapt that concept and, in the context of their own national history, civilize it in ways that served their interests increasingly well over the second half of the century.

To be sure, only a close association with the United States in a strong and cohesive NATO could provide postwar Germany with the security to which it aspired. Lacking security, there could not be much political stability either. From 1949 to 1976, the two main political parties of the newly formed Federal Republic increased their share of the votes steadily, from more than 60 percent in 1949 to a peak of more than 91 percent in 1976, with a parallel increase of the total electorate, which grew from 33.1 million in 1949 to 38.2 million in 1976.[28] But the Atlantic Alliance and NATO membership would not have been enough: that was above all a U.S.-led initiative that left Germany without the legitimacy that only its European neighbors could deliver. Joining the European community imagined by the French was therefore a corollary (or even a prerequisite) to being in the transatlantic security community organized by the United States, given the U.S. insistence that there could not be a transatlantic security community without a parallel commitment by the new allies to building a new sort of European community. For the Germans to accept these two complementary ideas, and to move along with both institutions and their respective leaders, was imperative: from Adenauer to Helmut Kohl, there could not be a plausible German claim for unification without a credible German commitment to European integration—but the commitment to European integration could not be made desirable for the Germans without an equally credible security commitment to Germany from NATO.

The Franco-German conflict—which included three wars in seventy-five years—defined Europe after 1871.[29] But in the second half of the twentieth century, each country progressively uncovered the benefits of cooperating with its former enemy as a matter of circumstance as well as a matter of opportunity. At first, these circumstances had to do with the ambivalence of Britain's relations with France and especially with Germany. Relative to France there was the lingering shock of France's unexpectedly quick defeat in June 1940; relative to Germany there were the bitter memories of the air war that soon followed. Relative to both countries, there was Britain's known predilection for negotiation over confrontation. Predictably, that preference was cause for concern in a country partly occupied by a Soviet Army poised to complete during the Cold War what it had started during World War II. As Adenauer saw it, France would guarantee a Western firmness that the German chancellor found to be lacking in Britain and, potentially, in the United States too.[30] While the Fourth Republic appeared to be too weak (and too distracted by its colonial wars) to deliver on such a lofty goal, the Fifth Republic could, especially after it gained a strategic force while losing an empire. De Gaulle especially understood the centrality of the German problem better than any other Western leader, and he could be expected, therefore, to keep the West focused on all of the questions that comprised it, including Berlin, relations with East Germany, reunification, and security from Moscow.

Finally, and reinforcing the case for a special partnership between the Federal Republic and France, there was the fact that unlike Britain, Germany had no traditional zone of influence to defend against its partner's encroachment or to seek at its partner's expense. Quite the opposite: where France viewed Britain (like the United States) as a likely consumer of its influence outside Europe, it embraced Germany as a producer of French influence in its former colonies. That view seemed especially convincing when Macmillan attempted to make of Britain's interests in the commonwealth a precondition for membership in the Common Market—an issue that had not conditioned Germany's receptiveness to the French schemes for a European economic community and subsequent agreements with Third World countries in Africa, the Caribbean, and the Pacific region.

Germany's reconciliation with France was eased further by three developments inherited from the Fourth Republic but reinforced after de Gaulle's return to power in May 1958. First, there was a new sense of security in France, where the development of a small but potentially decisive nuclear force (said to be *de frappe*) gave it a military confidence over Germany that had been lacking since 1871—and to which Germany did not object to the extent that the French force might also add to the Western capacity to deter the Soviet Union. Second, while the Germans were still testing their new democratic institutions, the French constitution adopted in November 1962 gave France an institutional stability that had been missing since the revolutionary overthrow of the *ancien régime* in 1789—and which the Federal Republic welcomed as it set the institutional stage for the centrist evolution it favored for its neighbor. And third, a successful European Common Market,

started in the midst of an impressive economic performance of the underap-
preciated Fourth Republic, pointed to a convincing French bid for economic
parity with a divided Germany—which Bonn did not resent or fear in the
context established by the Rome Treaties. As a result, France could now
substitute Germany for an unreliable Great Britain and welcome its former
enemy as a special partner without which France could not claim a European
leadership that even de Gaulle knew his country could not assert alone. Although the French bid was not always to America's liking, and even though
Germany's response (like Britain's) was occasionally disrupted by the United
States, there was no U.S. strategy of fragmentation whereby American leaders
might have attempted consciously to deepen divisions in Europe for the sake
of U.S. interests.[31] That was made unnecessary by Germany's own appreciation of its dependence on a close relationship with the United States under
the security conditions defined by the Cold War.

Germany's special relationship with France made European integration
possible, and European integration in turn made their special relationship
irreversible. Fundamentally, it is such a virtuous circle that had been the main
objective of postwar U.S. policies: not only to build a new Europe out of the
old European states but also to build new European states out of the ruins
accumulated in the old Europe. Thus understood, the idea of unity in Europe
was an American idea to the extent that unity became possible only after it
had been extended to Germany and accordingly endorsed by the United
States.[32] Not the least U.S. contribution to the idea of Europe was enforcing
it with the conversion of Germany into a state like any other rather than with
an occupation by, or partition among, the three main Western powers. (And
for those who claimed that there was de facto occupation, it could be argued
that the deployment of Western forces was meant to protect Germany from
the East rather than to protect the West from Germany.)

Predictably, the ultimate goals of a French-led Europe that kept Britain
at a distance from both Europe and Germany caused some concern and some
ambivalence about Europe in the United States; by implication, Britain's
status therefore also emerged as an obstacle to closer U.S. bilateral relations
with Germany and, conversely, as a further incentive for more U.S. distance
from France. The issue was not the rise of a strong and united Europe, to
which France and Germany became all the more central as Britain stayed
away from this common European edifice. Rather, the issue of concern for
the United States was a united Europe that would speak with the French
tones of which America had become increasingly resentful during the Gaullist

years, and with a strength that de Gaulle and his successors hoped to make operational outside the NATO context that the United States favored. Yet, such Gaullist tones notwithstanding, Britain's stubborn hostility to the idea of Europe, vigorously confirmed by Margaret Thatcher in the early 1980s, left Washington with few alternatives: either to accommodate French leadership given Britain's marginal influence on its European partners or to continue to encourage German leadership as a counterweight to French influence. Although President Reagan generally worked well with Mitterrand, cooperation with Germany seemed more credible, especially as Chancellor Kohl's stature grew with age, in Europe and across the Atlantic, while Mitterrand merely aged, in his own country and abroad.

Throughout the Cold War, the Germans said little about their own future.[33] Unification was to them what Alsace-Lorraine had been to the French in earlier and less peaceful days—*"N'en parler jamais mais y penser toujours."*[34] Even Germany's new identity, gradually acquired while the Federal Republic grew into an affluent civilian power, did not heal the wounds left by its past. A singularized Germany had goals that were unique, including the well-being of other Germans in the East, pending unification. But instead of a foreign policy based on national interests defined in terms of Germany's resurgent power, the Germans were so historically self-conscious, militarily adverse, and world wary as to depend on proxies that spoke on their behalf: France within the European Union, but surely not in NATO, and the United States within NATO, but obviously not within the European Union. There was no third way for the Germans—only a middle way between France and America within the alliance, between Britain and France over Europe, and between the West and the Soviet Union in the Cold War.[35] At home, each of the two dominant political parties readily endorsed the foreign policy decisions made by the other. Challenges to this externally induced consensus were few: rearmament in the 1950s because America had demanded it and France now tolerated it, Ostpolitik in the early 1970s because both the United States and France had initiated it and could not now oppose it, and the deployment of intermediate nuclear forces (INF) in the early 1980s because America sought it and France was insisting. These challenges were overcome without much damage.

This approach was expected to change when the end of the Cold War left Germany on the side of the victors "for the first time in the twentieth century," as Chancellor Kohl noted.[36] For reasons of size, location, and economic strength, as well as military potential, a reunified Germany was bound to reassert its will to lead. In the United States, this was good news. America and Germany were "co-partners in leadership," announced President George H. W. Bush; their commitment to each other, added President Clinton, guaranteed, "now and forever," that *"alles ist möglich."*[37] Early on, the impending fact of the German leadership that was expected to emerge out of its unification also conditioned a timid Anglo-French rapprochement during the waning days of the Mitterrand presidency, when Thatcher thought she had found an unexpected partner in a French president who seemed as concerned with the pace and ramifications of Germany's unification as she was.[38]

More than any other European country, Britain had remained sensitive to the overbearing image of a German state whose ultimate ambition remained "not to anchor Germany in Europe but Europe in Germany," as Thatcher put it, in imitation of Thomas Mann's contrast between a Germanized Europe and a Europeanized Germany. Indeed, more than anywhere else in Western Europe, the last years of the Cold War resurrected and even hardened Britain's memories of the Third Reich: between 1987 and 1992, public sympathy levels for Germany plummeted from an already low 28 percent to an astonishing 9 percent.[39] Yet, even a de-singularized Germany had few alternatives to the realist normalcy that had taken root during the previous forty years. Distance from the United States and the Atlantic Alliance was not one of these options, on either security or political grounds. Far from seeking the dissolution of NATO, Germany sought its enlargement to other states in Central Europe, as if in acknowledgment of the lingering concerns of states that history had left behind during four decades of Soviet occupation and communist subjugation. Thus more firmly anchored in an enlarged defense community within which it no longer stood as its most exposed member, a unified Germany also had few options in Europe where the ideas and exercise of power politics (*Machtpolitik*) and balancing (*Schaukelpolitik*) were no longer deemed relevant or applicable.[40]

After May 1997, however, Blair's new governing majority in Britain seemed open to more cooperation with the continent and, accordingly, was more receptive to the need to review the terms of its bilateral relations with both Germany and France. As argued earlier, Blair had a passion for Europe: nothing primarily personal but mostly historical, as a sense of Britain's destiny in a renewed Europe. "We can play a role in shaping the future of the EU," announced the new British prime minister on the eve of Schroeder's first official visit to London, six weeks after his first electoral triumph. Schroeder's *Neue Mitte* for Germany paralleled Blair's Third Way in Britain.

But although both Schroeder and Blair—dubbed Schroeblair for short—briefly forged the best bilateral relationship between Berlin and London in nearly three decades, there remained much ambivalence between the two men and their countries, especially with Chirac and France in the middle. Although Franco-German differences had grown after reunification, Anglo-German and Anglo-French differences remained even wider over such vital European questions as the single currency, enlargement, institutional reforms, the role of the European Parliament, and a common foreign and security policy (CFSP) including, most of all, relations with the United States.[41]

At the peak of the Cold War, the United States might have viewed favorably such tensions between Europe's two leading partners—tensions that were said to reinforce America's leadership of the Atlantic Alliance. At first, the Clinton administration proved to be different, however. Arguably, Clinton was the most spontaneous "Europeanist" U.S. president since Truman. Little aware of a Cold War history that Clinton had not lived and did not know, except for the Vietnam War (which he had not fought either, whether as a combatant or even as a dissenter), Clinton was not burdened with the memories of the setbacks that have characterized the construction of Europe and its relations with the United States during the previous four decades. Nor, for that matter, did Clinton understand that construction well, even as his endorsement of the postwar institutional order did not extend to the constraints that institutions place on the United States as much as the constraints they impose on other countries. Still, Clinton was ready to accept the European Union at face value, and as he did so he was also willing to give the new Europe enough time to deliver on its claims and ambitions. The priority Clinton placed on economic issues—"the economy, stupid"—also made him especially sensitive to the benefits for the United States of a full single market in Europe, including the promise of a single currency made by the then-twelve EU member states at their Maastricht summit in December 1991. Finally, Clinton's personal bitterness over Prime Minister John Major's political support for Bush during the 1992 presidential campaign denied Britain the privileged space it had occupied in Washington during the Thatcher years. As a result, even as Clinton showed a close affinity for Chancellor Kohl, he also found much to his liking with Chirac's policies, especially after Chirac's open Atlanticist turn in 1995, when the French president opened the door to France's return to NATO. And even as (or because) the Franco-German engine that had motored the European Union appeared to be sputtering, NATO seemed to rest increasingly on a modern version of the Triple

Entente that might rely on a recast Germany to motivate France and reassure the United States in the combined institutional context of the European Union and NATO.

The Travails of Leadership

In September 1998, Gerhard Schroeder's election was a benchmark in Germany's postwar history—arguably the birth date of yet another Germany.[42] As compared to Kohl, who had been in his early teens in 1945—and thus still too young to fight but old enough to remember—Schroeder had been barely one year old when the war ended. Unlike his predecessors, therefore, he felt no guilt about Germany's past and did not share their complexes about Germany's future relative to France, Britain, or any of Germany's neighbors in Europe, including Russia but also Poland.

War was not even part of Schroeder's vocabulary—a defining conviction that had predated the end of the Cold War and from which Schroeder did not shy when he named Joschka Fischer, a radical from the 1968 days, foreign minister. Unlike any of his predecessors, the new German chancellor did not view Europe as an obligation but as a choice that Germany could now make on its own terms—a choice, that is, to lead or to follow, and if the latter, whom to follow; to abstain or to participate, and if so, where; to influence or to coerce, and if so, when. Nor did the new chancellor share his predecessors' ever-present need to acknowledge what America had done for and in postwar Germany. Rather, he preferred to acknowledge America for what it was and ought to remain—the apostle of a hard liberalism that would know how to use its awesome power with moderation and compassion. In short, Schroeder was a German with a sharp tongue and a short memory, but he had no inclination to wear his forefathers' boots or helmets. Admittedly, the twentieth century had ended on a good note for Germany, but now that the first postwar generations of German leaders had conquered the nation's past, the successor generations could readily address the new issues of the twenty-first century with no complexes and without fearing criticism for their behavior, however firm or even confrontational that behavior might be.

In this context, Germany's dependence on France looked like an imposition that had outlived its usefulness. For one, it kept Britain away from Germany and the United States ambivalent about Europe. Schroeder wanted to escape this condition and actively explore other diplomatic horizons, with

Britain in Europe as well as with the United States within the Atlantic Alliance.[43] That meant a will to engage Blair, whom he personally liked. But that also meant partnering with Clinton, especially as Schroeder (like Blair) associated the U.S. president with his own struggle to move his party to the center of Germany's political spectrum—just as Schroeder had done personally when he had left behind his early dissenting days at the fringe of German politics. This, Schroeder and his followers felt, was a new Germany in a new Europe, and there was nothing left to fear from a new German way that would insist publicly on the need for close consultation "not just about the how and the when, but also," and most ominously, "about the whether."[44]

Unlike Blair, Schroeder did not feel the need to show off the intimacy of his personal relations with Clinton or, unlike Kohl, feel inhibited over his German-ness and, by implication, an obsession with his European-ness. Nor, unlike Chirac, did Schroeder sense a need to convince a new U.S. president of his dependability as a close partner in leadership. If anything, in 2001 Schroeder feared that George W. Bush might not understand the changes that had occurred since the president's father had ended the Cold War —changes that entitled the Germans in particular to their new status as "partners without restrictions."[45] As such, Schroeder argued, Germany's "responsibility" now was to provide Europe with the "full self-assurance" needed to develop its own security concept and to include in this concept the specifically German economic, social, and environmental dimensions that, together, would define a distinctive European approach to global issues. "For heaven's sake," concluded the German chancellor even before his reelection in September 2002, "don't try to make us comparable to the United States."[46] The warning—"not comparable"—referred not only to the new Germans but also to the new Europeans, and a German leadership for Europe was likely to unfold, therefore, in ways that might not fit the U.S. terms of copartnership. No less significantly, the allusion to the United States referred not only to the reality of America's preponderance, which neither Germany nor Europe wished to deny or hoped to overcome, but also to the reality of a changing America that neither wanted to duplicate either.

Even before September 11, there were strict limits to Germany's rethinking of its postwar normality relative to a world in which the rationality of Germany's decisions responded to normative considerations that few of its partners could understand and no other could fully share. Especially with regard to military force, the unease felt by a growing majority of Germans set rigid limits that were not Schroeder's alone but those of the nation he led.[47] Arguably, Germany's first unification, in 1871, produced too much German power for its European neighbors to balance. Conversely, Germany's division in 1945 failed to leave enough German power for its dangerous neighbor in the East to fear—hence the early U.S. calls for rearmament, notwithstanding the apprehensions that were thus raised. In 1989, however, Germany's second unification seemed to produce too much German weakness for its EU partners to compensate, including the economic burdens of reconstructing the eastern territories, which left a unified, safe, and free Germany state obviously larger and more sovereign but paradoxically less powerful and less predictable than divided and at risk.[48] In that regard, Blair and Chirac appeared to move Europe too quickly—as "a superpower" Blair had said after Saint-Malo—and Bush to take the Atlantic Alliance too far—"at war" Bush had pledged after September 11. In other words, torn between the contradictory goals of alliance solidarity, on which Germany still counted for security; European unity, to which the new Germany still aspired for influence; and national values, which the Germans had embraced for redemption, Schroeder could take his people into the world only as quickly and as far as they would allow: by agreeing to some modest military role for the *Bundeswehr*, a role that Kohl had resisted even during the first Gulf War but which the wars in the former Yugoslavia seemed to demand; by endorsing the idea of European defense, but without additional defense spending, which would predictably be required but which he insisted on reducing; and by keeping the Germans as close to America as they might tolerate, which would probably always keep him short of U.S. expectations and even U.S. needs.[49]

This does not mean that nothing changed when Schroeder became chancellor in September 1998. But it does mean that what changed is not the substance of German policies relative to Kohl's years, or the perception of Germany's potential for leadership within and outside Europe, but the internal conditions under which Germany might assume its role amidst internal political divisions and petty personal rivalries that had been absent during the Cold War years. "Who really runs Germany?" is a novel question for and in Europe—a question that has not come up since the Weimar Republic, and one that seems to place politics above policies.[50] As a result, Germany's new normalcy extends beyond its view of, and place in, the world; it also has to do with its internal transformation, away from its remarkable postwar political predictability into an increasingly multiparty system that began to emerge when Helmut Schmidt replaced Willy Brandt in 1976, and which was confirmed by the coalition government forced upon Angela Merkel, notwithstanding her predecessors' durability (which amounted to sixteen years for Kohl and seven years for Schroeder). Indeed, since 1976, the combined percentage of votes received by Germany's two main parties has declined steadily, from 87.4 percent in 1980 (nearly four percentage points below the peak it had reached four years earlier) to a low of 69.5 percent in 2005, while the turnout has declined steadily from a high of 88.6 percent in 1980 to a weak 77.7 percent in 2005.[51]

After September 1998, Schroeder's interest in better relations with Britain and the United States renewed France's concern over the directions and goals of Germany's policies. After a half-century, the French verdict on Germany's history did make room for parole, but its freedom of movement was still expected to remain constrained by France and its European partners. As a result, Schroeder's disquieting presumption of full equality, at least, and his belief in Germany's right to full consultation and even veto on all issues involving Europe were disconcerting. Ironically, Schroeder's populist anti-American campaign in the summer of 2002 also caused concern in Paris because it confirmed a new German willingness to go it alone.[52] At the very least, the campaign seemed to confirm Chirac's worst fears of Schroeder's disruptive heavy-handedness; worse yet, it clashed with Chirac's attempt at the time to build a cohesive EU policy supportive of Bush's policies and goals—as evidenced by the French contributions to ensuring unanimous approval of UN Security Council Resolution 1441 in November 2002.

Different expectations about Germany's willingness to embrace the U.S. strategy in Iraq, whether as an alliance obligation or even as a moral obligation, ignored the widely shared public constraints that had come to define Germany's nonpartisan consciousness on foreign policy and security issues. Had it been otherwise, Schroeder's use of the confrontational card at the expense of the United States would not have been as effective as it proved to be when the outgoing German chancellor unexpectedly won a second term in office in September 2002, in part (or mainly) on the basis of his objections to Bush and his post–September 11 policies. Indeed, three years later, in September 2005, Schroeder nearly won again an election he was sure to lose, thus confirming that his positions on the facts and efficacy of U.S. leadership in the world were deeply anchored into Germany's post–Cold War, post–September 11 consensus. Thus, in June 2006, only 37 percent of the German public held a favorable opinion of the United States, a precipitous decline from where that public had stood in 2000 (78 percent) or even 2002 (68 percent)—with the hard core of such hostility found especially among younger Germans. That the Germans continued nonetheless to hold a favorable opinion of Americans as a people (66 percent, compared to 70 percent in 2000) suggests that such hostility might be attributable directly to President Bush, toward whom only one-fourth of the public showed "a lot" or "some" confidence. But with more Germans (40 percent) finding the United States more dangerous to world peace than North Korea (23 percent) and nearly as dangerous as Iran or the Israeli-Palestinian conflict (51 percent), a tendency to reduce such public ambivalence to Bush alone would be dangerously complacent, as it would neglect an anger over failure that is no less significant than the anger over the decisions that led to those failures.[53] Indeed, by early 2006, 80 percent of all Germans believed that the likelihood of terrorist attacks worldwide had increased since the start of the war in Iraq (as opposed to 76 percent in Britain and "only" 67 percent in France, with a still discreet 55 percent in the United States sharing the same conclusion).[54]

Germany's strains with the United States had been growing for many years prior to Bush and Iraq, and moving away from the former or thinking beyond the latter would hardly be enough to alleviate these tensions. After unification—which also means since the Cold War—the security agenda in and near Europe remained beyond Germany's (or Europe's) ability to address to the satisfaction of America's expectations and absent prior and successful U.S. action: to prevent and end war in the Balkans, to engage and stabilize Russia, to widen and deepen the European Union to the East, and to endorse and enforce policies toward rogue regimes in the Persian Gulf and elsewhere. Admittedly, these tasks were not easy, and the U.S. role was not always benign, beginning with Bosnia, or consistent, as in the Persian Gulf. Still, early claims that with the Cold War over this would now be the "hour of Europe," let alone Germany's moment, hardly materialized—an indictment of Germany's capabilities or will that need not be a condemnation of Germany's goals or intent as well.

After Schroeder's election, however, the rift with the United States deepened further as the bilateral agenda became more contentious, not only on such new security issues as global warming and the environment but also on traditional issues such as the sale of submarines to Taiwan, missile defense and the future of nuclear weapons, relations with Russia, cooperation with France for the development of a European security identity, defense spending, Turkey, and others. Move aside, France—here comes Germany?[55] There could be no better measure of Germany's disparagement than to describe its estrangement from the United States in terms traditionally reserved for

France. A German challenge to U.S. leadership and for Europe's leadership would be cause for concern: unlike the French, who remain quite difficult even when they are not serious, the Germans can be quite serious when they choose to become difficult. With the new German way seemingly taking the new Germany away from the United States, the events of September 11, 2001, exacerbated an unprecedented bilateral gap that Schroeder did not open even though he kept on widening it—and which his successor, Angela Merkel, has been able to contain but is unlikely to close.

At the heart of this bilateral drift is the Germans' understanding of September 11 in the context of their rejection of force as a legitimate tool of action in the world. For Germans of all persuasions, September 11 was a *crime* whose perpetrators had to be punished, but it was not a *war* whose participants had to be eliminated through a preemptive strategy of regime change.[56] As a result, Germans viewed the use of force in Iraq as a violation of the normative code adopted by their country after two suicidal wars had demonstrated the failure of such methods and had imposed an end to the global lawlessness that had characterized Europe and the rest of the world over time. Respect for such a code could not be made a matter of circumstances, as had been the case during the Cold War when Germany was exposed to a serious Soviet threat, and as was now said to be the case for post–September 11 America, now vulnerable to further terrorist attacks.

"Threat magnification" is, of course, something the Germans know well, but it is no longer something of which they can readily be convinced and for which they can be easily recruited. In 2005, only one German in three feared an act of terror for the coming decade, as opposed to more than one out of two in France and two out of three in the United States. Moreover, the debate over Iraq unfolded at a time when the Germans were finally reopening the darkest chapters of their difficult past and when, therefore, an attempt to manipulate their collective memory was likely to meet with strong objections and widespread indignation. That was the case when Defense Secretary Donald Rumsfeld built a curious analogy between their country and Iraq. "Turning our backs on postwar Iraq today," claimed Rumsfeld, "would be the modern equivalent of handling postwar Germany back to the Nazis." Although at about that time a majority of Germans (55 percent) still opposed a withdrawal of the coalition forces until Iraq had been stabilized, the analogy was no more convincing to the Germans than Rumsfeld's further argument that for the United States to leave Iraq "would be as great a disgrace as if we had asked the liberated nations of Eastern Europe to return to Soviet domination because it was too hard or too tough."[57] To Germans in particular, the use of such comparisons to postwar Germany in order to make the case for U.S. policies in Iraq ignored all that Germany's people and governments did to overcome their country's past. Comparing Hitler and Saddam Hussein, the air war with Britain and the war against the Iraqi insurgents, and pre- or postwar Germany and Iraq, was a deconstruction of Germany's (and Europe's) history—an invitation to redefine Germany and its people that was all the more offensive, as few Germans felt any affinity with the conditions and the people in Iraq to which Rumsfeld appeared to refer.[58]

Terms of Entanglement

After 1945, Germany's "quasi natural reflex, engendered by feelings of shame and a wish to defy the victors, was to keep quiet and look the other way."[59] This was not 1919: Whatever anger, resentment, and national urge for revenge there had been after the previous war was gone. The dreadful sights of the destruction to which Germany had been subjected by the Grand Alliance were accepted with unusual resignation and even insensitivity.

Only now does the new post–Cold War generation of Germans dare revisit the country's past not only to bemoan the enormity of what they did to others but also to reflect on the totality of what others did to them. The tour is daunting: "Which victims—which memories—should have priority?"[60] To be sure, the Holocaust overwhelms over everything else our memory of the war. Yet the map of man's past inhumanity to others transcends any country, however aggressive, and any single event, however horrific, and leaves little room for exoneration from the collective guilt that defined Europe during the first half of the twentieth century. Guilty as charged: Coming to terms with their past at last, the Germans but also others in Europe revisit their country's history—sometimes asking to be forgiven for the pain they caused, other times asking to ensure that the pain they too endured is not forgotten, and most of the time seeking both forgiveness for what they did to others and also remembrance of what others did to them.[61]

After 1945, Europe began to close the dark holes of its collective memory with a bit of historical cleansing at the top. But what is left of this history, and how much of what was carefully forgotten can be remembered without causing harm to the present? With the Cold War over, Germany's urge to revisit the past one more time, hopefully the last, provides a final test for a belated confirmation of the nation's rehabilitation, as well as its reconciliation with its former victims and executioners alike. Such detachment from past failings need not suggest indifference: forgive, maybe, but do not quite forget, ever. Even while no justification for what was done is sought, explanations are offered. To no longer feel different from yesteryear's victors might mean for the Germans to feel equal with them, morally as well as politically. Over time, no country in Europe was lastingly better or worse than Germany, however dreadful its actions at specific points in time.[62] To an extent, the debate over, and dissent from, the war in Iraq tested that proposition, although, admittedly, the test proved to be especially demanding for Germany.

"*Ich bin gut*, Hans," echoes Britain's "I'm all right, Jack" of old. After so much time, few are left to tell differently anyway—to tell, that is, of the days in the 1920s when Germany was not doing well and of those days in the 1960s when Britain was not feeling right. For the new European era is not about any single state—whether Germany or Britain or France or any other state or group of states. The new European order is about Europe *über alles*, meaning that it is about the primacy of a resurging Europe that places the discipline of its union over the sovereignty of its fading nation-states, lest it might become about America *über alles*, meaning that it would be about the dominance of the United States over a faded and divided Europe.[63] In the summer of 2002, Schroeder did not so much object to the United States as to what he claimed to be America's "bullying, pure and simple" over policies that he found strategically wrong, morally dubious, and politically self-defeating—especially but not exclusively in Iraq.[64] Years after the fact, Schroeder's regret is not that he attempted to stand in the way of Bush's decision, but that his opposition "did not produce the least effect." And, most telling, the explanation for his relative irrelevance is not that Germany no longer matters but that only a "common European position," which he and Chirac failed to achieve, "could have helped" avoid a U.S. decision "heavy with consequences."[65] This is a conclusion that both Merkel, who never questioned Schroeder's decision to keep Germany out of the war, and Nicolas Sarkozy, who viewed Chirac's opposition as having brought "honor" to France, would readily embrace.

Far from "old," the German chancellor who challenged openly the United States led a "young" country made in America with an assist from France and, to a lesser extent, Britain. Like this new Germany, Schroeder personally showed "a deeply provincial suspicion of anything beyond the psychic borders of his familiar world,"[66] anything, that is, that extended historically before his postwar time and geographically beyond Europe and even across the Atlantic. What characterized his provincialism was a willingness to question the country that, barely known to him, had given Germany another lease on life after a second defeat in fewer than thirty years had nearly brought the nation to its deathbed. In so doing, Schroeder was hardly alone. Standing in the way of the docile Germany Americans and Europeans have learned to know during the Cold War is a German populace that has also learned to live with its past and now knows better what it does and does not want—meaning, a countrywide willingness to assert its preferences and objections no less forcefully than others do.

"*Quel people!*" marveled de Gaulle in the winter of 1944–45, speaking of the Germans amid the ruins of Stalingrad, the farthest point east of Germany's advances during World War II.[67] There is no lasting answer to the German question, because the question itself keeps changing as Germany repeatedly turns into the reverse of what it was supposed to remain.[68] A people that, according to Machiavelli, did not like war and accepted defeat easily was gradually transformed after its unification in 1871 into an awesome military machine that welcomed war and could fight literally to the end.[69] It is this Germany that fought the world to a standstill until it ran out of space in November 1918, when that horrific war threatened to cross the Rhine and spill over into German territory, and until it ran out of bodies in May 1945, when only ruins and corpses stood in the way of advancing allied forces.

The German question, then, was about the need for external obstacles to the accumulation and use of German power, which other European countries were no longer able to balance and contain on their own. With the question thus phrased, the answer called for formal arrangements aimed at defeating Germany's predatory and expansionist instincts and, after 1945, redirect its people's will away from the use of German power for self-interest, let alone out of revenge. During the Cold War it was shown that semi-sovereignty could be the way to a good life—indeed, a good way of life that made of Germany the ultimate institutional state: a state, that is, committed to subjecting the nation's sovereign "I" to the collective discipline of the European, transatlantic, and global institutions to which it belongs. This is less a Cartesian logic adopted from the new privileged partner across the Rhine than a new Nietzschean faith: only to the extent that we, Europe, act, can I, Germany, be a super state; only to the extent that we Germans act, can I, Europe, be a superpower. But unlike what drove Adenauer when he followed de Gaulle, or Kohl when he embraced Mitterrand, Germany's value-sensitive approach is now policy- and facts-driven in addition to being history- and faith-sensitive as it responds to interests no less than to emotions. Within the alliance, this evolution justified Schroeder's challenge of U.S. policies, on grounds of value and efficacy; within Europe, it justified his challenges to France and to the European Union, on similar grounds; and so too will Merkel and her successors justify their own challenges should these policies—whether those of America, France, or Europe—fail to meet the expectations and needs of the new Germans.

The resulting confusion in and about Germany is hardly surprising. Faced with partners that simultaneously ask for and fear too much, but also tired of hearing those calls and sensing such fears, which they no longer understand anyway, the Germans can only strive to prove wrong those with lesser expectations about what they can do anew while upholding the confidence of those who have fewer fears of what they might do again. A balance between the old and the new is difficult to assert, let alone execute. Germany's power has been tamed and the Germans recast, which is to the good for those who remember their past. But that being the case, can such tamed German power be used again, even within its new institutional arrangements, for the good of those who no longer fear that past and thus expect more and even too much?

The lesson from Iraq—not only for Germany but also in the related context of the choices made by France and Britain—is that past Germany's prime, this cannot be Europe's time pending some rethinking of how much more Germany will do in Europe, and how, so that Europe can do more with the United States, and where.[70] In the meantime, two additional conclusions can be drawn from this episode in U.S.-German relations and the related interplay of Germany, France, and the United Kingdom within the European Union.

First, the rhetoric on U.S.-German cooperation is distorted by a U.S. tendency to set too high its expectations about Germany's contributions to the Atlantic Alliance, contrasted with Germany's tendency to keep its contributions to Europe too low.

"It's the economy, stupid." The theme that defined Clinton's leadership for the first presidential election held in the United States after the Cold War has lost much of its significance in the global security environment unveiled since September 11, 2001. Now, emphasis is placed most visibly on culture, history, geography, as well as leadership.[71] Americans and Germans, together with other Europeans, have never been closer culturally, historically, geographically, or otherwise, yet their own leaders have rarely shown less ability to understand and acknowledge what they have become, which is comparable if not similar, and why (out of necessity if not out of choice). This is especially significant in a post–Cold War, post–September 11 security environment in which the absence of a single, readily identifiable threat is conducive to debates over policies that involve judgments rooted in specific local or regional conditions, rather than goals or even values that can be shared even when they are not common.[72]

Early in the twenty-first century, the Germans (and other Europeans) complain of an America that "never had its Verdun." There is some truth to then-foreign minister Joschka Fischer's observation, which suggested an exaggeration in the United States of the nature and significance of the events of September 11.[73] Oddly, the United States is to Germans what Germany used to be to Americans early in the twentieth century, which is not to the better, as it suggests a tendency for the United States to rely on the brutal use of military force to achieve full security, preemptively if needed, and a quasi-messianic urge to expand its Kultur, coercively as needed. Yet, however much the misuse of American power in Iraq may have changed the world, as well as the world's perception of the United States, it is the assaults of September 11 that initially changed America's use of its power after those assaults had seemed to open a new chapter in the country's never-ending quest for 100 percent security.[74] Standing in the way, and even denying an understanding, of what each side has become is therefore a flawed perception of the other's singularity. The more Germans themselves accept their country as a "normal state"—with all due regard for its history but also with a proactive recognition of its potential—the better Germany will be able to play a role commensurate with its power and its interests. The more Germany (and its European partners) accept the United States as a normal state—with all due regard for its failings but also with a respectful acknowledgment of its preponderant power and its legitimate security interests and concerns—the better the United States will be able to assume its leadership role to its allies' satisfaction and to its own.

To be enforced, however, Germany's new antimilitaristic tradition no longer needs a constitution, as was instituted in 1949 to protect the Germans from themselves, or an occupation army, as was the case during the Cold War to protect Europe from Germany and Germany in Europe. For that tradition no longer demands legal or military coercion to be embraced as a matter of belief in, and even as a source of pride for, being a "global peace power."[75] After Kohl took the Germans as far as he could in Europe and within Germany, Schroeder took the Germans as far as he could in the world—much farther, arguably, than was deemed possible, from the first parliamentary authorization of postwar deployment of German troops outside national borders in 1995 to having approximately nine thousand German troops actively involved in worldwide NATO- (Afghanistan and Kosovo), EU- (Bosnia and Congo), and UN- (Lebanon) led missions ten years later. Admittedly, highly restrictive rules of engagement and a deep public skepticism about the relevance and usability of military power are legitimate causes for exasperation in the United States and among some of Germany's allies.[76] Yet realistically in terms of capabilities, and intangibly in terms of political will and public support, Germany will not be able to offer much more for the foreseeable future, and Schroeder therefore deserved more recognition for what he did and for which he finally paid the ultimate political price. After September 11, however, Germany's availability was so much taken for granted in the United States that Schroeder was not merely asked to do more in and about Iraq than he wanted to do: he was asked to do more than his people wanted to do, irrespective of his own preferences. The same error should not be made with his successor over, say, Iran or any other contentious front of the "long war" of September 11.

In short, the U.S. perception that Germany consistently punches below its weight is no more meaningful than Germany's perception that the United States now punches below its heart. Neither country is willing or even able to afford being what it used to be. But while no country in the West wants Germany to return to its old ways either, many would want the United States to do just that and return to the "noble traditions" and "the standards it expects of itself" as the leading world power.[77] Unless there is fuller acceptance of what Germany and America have become, the frustrations of overblown expectations are likely to lead to new rounds of disparagement, from Germany about a senior ally that does too much too poorly, and from the United States about an ally of choice that does too little too late.

A second conclusion of the debate over Iraq is not about Germany and Europe's relations with the United States but about Germany's relations with France, and for both countries with Britain and Europe. In 2003, a common front against the use of American power in Iraq consolidated relations between Chirac and Schroeder, but in 2007, and beyond Iraq, both Germany and France must find new ways to adapt their privileged partnership to a changed Britain and a changing Europe, as well as to their own evolving public attitudes toward Europe and even each other.

As we have seen, postwar France played a leading role in the gradual construction of Europe as a union, but it never was able to move that process alone. The *pas de deux* choreographed in the name of Europe featured France as the ballerina whose pirouettes relied on a strong and reliable partner who could add the reliability of his power to the boldness of her jumps. That is not a role that postwar Britain, France's initial partner of choice, wished to play, and it is not a role that France wished to offer any other state in Europe, with the paradoxical exception of Germany, to which France turned next as its only viable alternative after Britain's repeated rejections of the French solicitations.

In January 1963, reconciliation between Germany and France was a historic achievement—a tribute to the visionary policies of American political leaders who had encouraged it after the war, French and German leaders who were now consummating it, and British and other European leaders who had embraced it. For a while, and in the absence of Britain, Germany and France thus defined and ruled a small European community with limited ambitions and modest expectations. That did not always come easily for either country or for their partners. Adenauer liked de Gaulle, and he might even have envied the latter's intransigence, but he often deplored his policies, especially those of which he failed to be informed, as was often the case. Adenauer's successor, Ludwig Erhard, liked neither de Gaulle nor his policies, let alone his rigidity, and neither did Willy Brandt think well of Georges Pompidou, de Gaulle's most immediate and least remembered successor.[78]

Notwithstanding these recurring moments of German ambivalence about France, its leaders, and its policies, the Franco-German partnership has been the main axis of institutional growth in Europe. Often closer to each other than to the leading members of their own governments, Valéry Giscard d'Estaing and Helmut Schmidt first, and François Mitterrand and Helmut Kohl next, were the coarchitects of a European construction that exceeded the expectations of its initial contractors. Within the framework of the 1963 treaty signed by de Gaulle and Adenauer, Giscard and Schmidt kept Europe going as a shield against the then-prevailing perception of U.S. decline during the latter part of the 1970s. After a difficult resolution of their differences with Thatcher, Mitterrand and Kohl kept Europe moving as an answer to America's renewed power for much of the 1980s and through the 1991 Maastricht Treaty. Later in the 1990s, however, Chirac and Schroeder were not able to match their predecessors' personal intimacy or even share their predecessors' political commitment to Europe. Instead, both briefly thought they could turn to Britain, not as an alternative to each other but for the reinforcement of their respective positions within the European Union—Chirac to compensate for Schroeder's unwillingness to give Europe more power, and Schroeder to compensate for Chirac's interest in assuming too much leadership. Given Blair's own interest in Europe—unprecedented, as we have seen, in Britain—both initially received a warm response in London. But any thought of moving Europe away from the Franco-German axis, let alone extending that axis to Britain, ended when Chirac and Schroeder's divisions with Blair over Bush and the war in Iraq drove the three European leaders apart more sharply than at any time since the first French veto of Britain's bid for membership in the Common Market in January 1963. That, according to Schroeder, Blair never discussed with him the reasons for his position on Iraq is surely telling of the scope of the split that divided Europe in 2003.[79]

After World War II, and for the duration of the Cold War, the construction of an ever-closer Europe was the central idea that motivated the Franco-German reconciliation as a shared rejection of a failed past. After the Cold War, new public challenges to that idea were bound, therefore, to affect the terms of that reconciliation by exposing the two countries' differences over Europe's future—meaning its political finality. Never mind Britain: "Europe" has often been an issue in Europe. The Cold War was barely over when controversial referenda over the 1991 Maastricht Treaty were held in France and elsewhere to confirm a growing public skepticism about institutions deemed to be all the more intrusive, as they seemed increasingly immune to national control. What has been new over the past decade, however, is for "Europe" to become also a political issue in Germany—meaning that German citizens, too, now increasingly disagree over what the European Union is because they question what it does, neglect what it has achieved, and, accordingly, differ over what they want out of it next. After 1945, these were not questions that Germans wished or dared to raise, as the mere idea of Europe served Germany even better than the institutions to which it gave birth subsequently.

For Germany more than for any other European country, the Cold War was a catalyst for European integration—both when it began as a small economic community to welcome the western half of a divided Germany and after it grew into an open-ended union to absorb the eastern part of a reunified Germany. There could be more Germany only to the extent there would be more Europe—meaning, by the same token, more France but hopefully no less America. But with the end of the Cold War and the collapse of the Soviet Union leaving a reunified Germany no longer geographically threatened in the East or even historically embarrassed at home, Germans fail to understand the relevance of the European idea and question the usefulness of the European institutions more directly than most other EU members. As a result, Berlin's cavernous German voice, which used to be muted when translated in Paris in the name of Franco-German unity, adds to the cacophonic sounds of discord heard in Brussels. For the new Germans now, there can be life with less Europe, as well as with less France and even with less America.

In any case, the days when Europe could be ruled as two—two nations, let alone two heads of state or government—are over. The point was made over Iraq especially well. Britain's own coalition of the willing within the European Union included Italy, Spain, and Poland—but lacking either of the other two larger EU powers, that coalition remained insufficient. France and Germany's coalition of the discontent, meanwhile, could count on a number of smaller countries, but lacking any of the other larger states that too was insufficient until Spain's defection following the unexpected defeat of Aznar's hand-picked successor immediately after the horrific acts of terror in Madrid on March 11, 2004. In a European Union with twenty-seven members (including Romania and Bulgaria), even an informal *directoire* between Britain, Germany, and France would not suffice. Such pressing issues as institutional reform, immigration, economic policy, further enlargement, and internal security will require a broader consensus, including at least one more large state—be it Italy, Spain, or Poland—or a larger following of smaller states.

With shifting and overlapping coalitions of interests across the European Union, any leadership core will remain elusive for the balance of the decade. This is especially true, as every new governing majority in the larger EU members introduces new perspectives on the European Union—from Aznar to Zapatero in 2004, from Schroeder to Merkel in 2005, from Berlusconi to Prodi in 2006, from Chirac to Nicolas Sarkozy and from Blair to Gordon Brown in 2007. So much politics in the national capitals stands in the way of too much policy out of Europe and, accordingly, raises additional obstacles to the European Union's ability to perform and deliver for its citizens whose skepticism keeps growing.[80] Indeed, during the coming years a new generation of European leaders may be better remembered for what they refused to do on behalf of Europe than for what they agreed to do in its name—from enlargement, including but not limited to Turkey, to economic reforms, including but not limited to Agenda 2010, and even institutional reforms, including but not limited to some variation of the failed constitutional treaty. Move over Britain, you've got company: this is no longer about the United States and the future of U.S. relations with Europe; it is about the states of Europe and the future of their relations within the European Union.

CHAPTER FOUR

Terms of Entanglement

When you are at the beginning of a big historical transition, it's very tough. . . . I remember what Harry Truman was able to do, which was to take some very difficult circumstances and some fairly unpopular policies and find a few people across the aisle who were ready to support a long-term strategy of containment.

—Condoleezza Rice, in a year-end interview with a small group of reporters in 2006

The spiritual reverse was . . . devastating, for [King] Philip [of Spain] had believed with utter conviction that he was doing God's work, waging a holy war—and God had forsaken him. There was no easy answer to this one. He and his country could turn back upon themselves, search their consciences, and, while heresy triumphed abroad, pledge themselves the more fervently to the defense at home, within the citadel, of the true faith. But the old certainty was gone, and with it the belief in a . . . mission. In their place came the creeping disillusion, the hypocrisy, the divorce between faith and action.[1]

THE WAR IN Iraq stands as a decisive moment in the unipolar world that followed the end of the Cold War—a world that the war certainly defined but also helped to end. Most directly, the war was made possible by the events of September 11, 2001, to which it was linked, even though Saddam Hussein was not directly involved with those events. More than six years later, however, the Bush administration was still in search of a long-term strategy for the war on terror and in need of allies willing to endorse that strategy, but it was also desperately looking for a short-term exit strategy from Iraq and for adversaries that would permit any such exit to be honorable. Notwithstanding Secretary Rice's "memories" of the postwar years, there was little of Truman in President Bush's management of the "very difficult circumstances" he faced. Like Truman, Bush had admittedly inherited a complex conflict, global in its reach and total in its scope—one that he had not sought but from which America could not escape. But unlike Truman, Bush lacked an instinctive sense of the limits of American power, and a common feeling for the need to make a prudent use of that power. Not knowing those limits had made Bush dismissive of allies abroad, and lacking that common touch had kept him oblivious to critics at home—two traits that proved to be especially decisive during and after the debates that surrounded the war in Iraq.

That the events of September 11, 2001, started "a big historical transition" is not in doubt. But that transition too was a legacy of much that had happened earlier. It was a legacy of the post–Cold War years, when America showed an indifference to the world that masked its inability to leave it. During those years, in the 1990s, much that relied on American power to get started remained stalled when that power was unavailable, or unfinished after that power was withdrawn—from the first Gulf War and the conflicts that accompanied the disintegration of Yugoslavia, through the engagement of defeated Russia, through the conflicts in the Middle East, and to South and East Asia. But the "historical transition" started after September 11 is also a legacy of the Cold War, during which the United States became entangled in a region, the Greater Middle East, which Americans barely knew and understood little more than a need to keep the Soviet Union out, Israel in, and Arab nationalism down—from the 1953 coup in Iran, through the 1956 Suez crisis and the 1967 Arab-Israeli war, to the 1975 civil war in Lebanon and the 1979 Iranian Revolution, all the way through the Iran-Iraq war and the Soviet war in Afghanistan, and up to the 1991 Gulf War and even the premature exit from Somalia. Finally, and most broadly, the post–Cold War transition into the "wars of 911" is also a legacy of all the wars that have been fought before, when centuries of national, colonial, and ethnic conflicts left behind territorial corpses that are now resurrected by people who seem to welcome death as the main justification for their lives.[2]

In short, if the three world wars of the twentieth century, including the

Cold War, were for the most part about the geography of Europe, waged in the context of East-West or even North-South adversarial relations, the wars of September 11, including but hardly limited to the wars in Iraq and in Afghanistan, ought to be viewed through the lenses of a history that originates and evolves around the never-resolved relations between Islam and the world, as well as within Islam and, beyond Islam, the struggle between the West and the rest. It is there in the Islamic world that can be found the new "wretched of the earth," as they were known when the Third World was but a geographic generic fraught with Europe's imperial memories. As Jean-Paul Sartre wrote more than four decades ago, "make no mistake about [them]; this mad fury, this bitterness and spleen. . . . Hatred, blind hatred which is as yet an abstraction, is their only wealth. . . . There are those among them who assert themselves barehanded against guns; these are their heroes. Others make men of themselves by murdering . . . and these are shot down; brigands or martyrs, [but] their agony exalts the terrified masses."[3] These were terrifying words then, but they could easily be ignored until they gained unprecedented concreteness, under different circumstances, when terror appeared to be spreading from New York to Madrid to London and elsewhere.

For those who insisted that the war in Iraq was just, history stands as a reminder that a just cause—which it was, for the war did aim at changing a tyrannical, dangerous, and criminal Iraqi regime—does not automatically translate into a just war (which the war in Iraq was not, to the extent that it was a war of choice) and is not symptomatic of justice (which the war in Iraq did not achieve either, to the extent that it failed to bring the national reconciliation that had been announced when the war was started). Indeed, historians will be baffled by a war that was so poorly planned by the United States and subsequently so poorly executed as to lead those who embraced the cause most openly in 2003 to distance themselves from the war three years later.[4] But historians will also be baffled by critics in Europe who became so rigid in their positions as to permit a failure of which they too were bound to be the victims. Thackeray said it best: "The wicked are wicked, but who can tell the mischief the very virtuous do?" Not the least among such mischief is the temptation to use dissent as an avenue to power even if it cannot ultimately produce an effective substitute for lack of workable, desirable, or even necessary alternatives.[5]

For Iraq at least, the verdict came in early. The war had been "pretty much of a disaster," inadvertently acknowledged Blair in late 2006. Bush too turned to the troubling conclusion that "we're not winning, we're not losing," a confirmation of newly appointed secretary of defense Bob Gates's comment that the coalition was "neither winning nor losing."[6] Where it had been argued earlier that failure in Iraq was not an option, the debate now seemed to focus on how and when that failure would be acknowledged—with and after a military "surge" that might permit what Richard M. Nixon had called, late in the Vietnam War, a "peace with honor," or with a diplomatic surge that would merely seek to avoid the humiliating sights of a retreat.[7]

Admittedly, the war in Iraq was too significant an event to permit a final assessment of its legacies: the consequences of the war's failures will take many more years to unravel, depending on the ways in which such failure is consummated in coming years. In the meantime, however, the popular verdict is not merely about Iraq or even Bush, or even about only America and its goals but also about American power and its limits. Claims to be gentle and benevolent do not suffice for legitimacy; equally important is the need to be prudent and effective—two qualities that proved to be grossly lacking in the war in Iraq.[8]

Ending the Beginning

Throughout the Cold War there were recurring expectations that the bipolar structure of power that had defined the world after 1945 would ultimately evolve into a multipolar system that included the rebuilt and ascending great powers of Europe and Asia. Britain's postwar hopes for a "third force"—to not be left "wholly in U.S. hands"; France's subsequent boasts of a force de frappe—to assert the nation's independence in the sovereign area of defense; and even Germany's quest for an Ostpolitik toward Russia—to expand the boundaries of its limited postwar sovereignty—are examples of policies devised by the leading European powers to move without and beyond their senior partner.[9] The military intervention in Suez, which was planned to protect vital Anglo-French interests said to be compromised by U.S. policies; the war in Vietnam, which America fought and lost essentially alone; the first oil crisis during the 1973 Middle East War, as a dramatic instance of Third World challenge to vital U.S. interests; and even the ill-fated Soviet invasion of Afghanistan, which took place in spite of U.S. warnings to abstain from such action, are examples of Cold War events that pointed to a new multipolar assault on the primacy of U.S. power. After the Vietnam debacle especially, the two main strategic architects of U.S. policies anticipated a return to multipolarity that might resemble either Henry Kissinger's "world restored" of a defunct European state system or Zbigniew Brzezinski's new "technetronic age" that would bury that world.[10]

Although neither of these predictions came to be, both were partly justified by subsequent events during and after the Cold War, but also since September 11, 2001. At first, however, the Soviet collapse gave the United States a seemingly insurmountable preponderance. Whatever doubts might still remain about the new unipolar conditions were promptly dispelled when the universal coalition organized by President George Herbert Walker Bush for the first Gulf War also gave America's leadership an international legitimacy that had rarely been achieved before—an unprecedented exercise in collective security that confirmed how much, and how well, the United States had learned about the world since the country joined it.

The first Gulf War was a significant test for the post–Cold War order, but it was also a significant test for the United States as the only power that stood in the way of Iraq's bid for hegemony in a region of crucial significance to all. This was a test that could not be failed. To ignore Saddam's aggression in the fall of 1990 might encourage Americans to come home: to leave war behind at last and finally enjoy the hard-earned peace benefits that had been denied twice before, in 1919 and in 1945. As significant, even the appearance of a U.S. abdication from its role in the Persian Gulf might encourage other rogue regimes, there and elsewhere, to impose their expansionist will on their weaker neighbors. With so much at stake, America enjoyed the right leaders at the right time: the UN-sponsored coalition, brilliantly organized and sustained by George H. W. Bush and his administration, was a tribute to the sort of leadership that had ensured the U.S. triumph in the Cold War, and the overwhelming military capabilities on which the coalition relied had been accumulated during the previous decade for a different sort of war against an altogether different adversary.[11] Criticism of Bush's management of the 1991 Gulf War came only later, when it was argued that more could have been done to destroy the Iraqi army and force Saddam out, thus permitting a quicker withdrawal of U.S. military forces in the region, especially in Saudi Arabia. But, predictably, little of that criticism was heard at the time.[12] On the contrary, the prompt end to the war was greeted with relief, especially abroad where it reinforced America's reputation as a power that remained immune to the imperial temptation that had beset other great powers during their moments of preponderance.

Admittedly, future challenges to U.S. primacy were anticipated, whether by states that would choose to act alone or, more likely, by states that might seek to form countervailing alliances with others. To that extent, the post–Cold War unipolarity could only last "a moment."[13] But America's superiority seemed so compelling that the moment, however finite, was expected to last for some time.[14] If there was, then, an American vision for that moment, it was an extension of the postwar vision that had shaped the U.S. surge in the world after 1945, when the re-creation of the world, wrote Dean Acheson, had been confined to "half the world" only. Now there was an opportunity for the United States to attend to the other half as well and complete the making of the world into America's image. Such a new world order would celebrate the end of history—meaning the final victory of democracy over totalitarianism and the coming of a truly global Age of Enlightenment in a neo-Kantian world of progress.[15]

To be a docile follower of the United States was said to be a reasonable "price to pay for paradise."[16] In Iraq in 1991, even as the United States had demonstrated the completeness of its power—including capabilities, will, and leadership—it had also confirmed its benign intentions: there was no attempt at regime change, no military occupation of Iraq after its hateful regime had been defeated (or of Kuwait after it had been liberated), and no pretense of nation building anywhere in the region. Moreover, given America's perceived ability to replenish and reinforce its power indefinitely and at will, the cost of balancing the United States was deemed too high relative to whatever gains might be expected by a hypothetical challenger. In any case, even under conditions of unipolarity, the United States remained openly committed to acting multilaterally and thus determined to sustain the institutional order that it had developed after World War II.[17] As had been the case when Truman had acted in Korea at the start of the Cold War, there was nothing preordained—indeed, no precedent whatsoever—in Bush's decision to respond to Saddam's aggression in Kuwait with a massive use of U.S. force. Instead, the U.S.-led coalition was formed at the invitation, and with the full support, of U.S. allies, and the war was launched only after it had been "blessed" at the United Nations, with the encouragement of Cold War adversaries, including but not limited to a then-collapsing Soviet Union and even the like of Syria and Iran. Absent such global legitimacy, a U.S. intervention would have been difficult. To put it simply, Americans were not interested.

That a righteous America had reached imperial status was nowhere in question, except in the United States where the idea of empire conveys interests and ambitions that have remained incompatible with its history and vocation. Unlike any past imperial power, Americans did not achieve their dominant status in the world with a sustained and conscious drive for preponderance. If anything, the age of American imperialism, mostly centered on the Western Hemisphere, came early and long before the United States could claim the attributes of an imperial power—at a time, that is, when it showed the required sense of mission but still lacked the capabilities and especially the will to enforce that mission.[18] As it has been noted, "The Anglo-American colonists were in this respect typical Englishmen," and even, more broadly, typical Europeans.[19] In the nineteenth century their expansionist mission was extended with the zeal of a "manifest destiny" that exceeded their strength but confirmed their original imperial instincts. More atypical was America's nearly fortuitous rise to global preponderance in the twentieth century, when its power and its role grew out of the exhaustion and subsequent abdication of other world powers during their own hegemonic drives—Nazi Germany, Imperial Japan, and Stalinist Russia, which the United States helped defeat by joining the other European great powers that proved unable to endure those wars any better. It is to exercise that power during the latter part of the twentieth century that American political leaders were "re-Europeanized"—meaning that they gradually returned to the realist traditions that taught them anew to respect the immediate advantages of stability as a prerequisite for long-term changes in order to avoid the immediate risks of change as a possible precursor of short-term instabilities.

In other words, the maximization of American power never was an end in itself—the inescapable fate of Gulliver-like nation-states trapped in the Hobbesian net of an anarchical world. But irrespective of intent, entering the twenty-first century, the United States stood as a state whose complete capabilities, global interests, and universal saliency readily surpassed those of others. It was the only remaining superpower. With its status thus acquired by default, the American Republic's well-recognized imperial allergies gave its preeminent condition a sort of historic respectability at home—a commitment to doing good even more pressing than an ambition to do well—and global legitimacy abroad, where there was little need for the United States to impose its will, as it continued to be sought out for the benefits it brought. To that extent it was not a "dangerous" nation in the usual imperial way, meaning territorial grabs for traditional goals of self-expansion and self-preservation, but in a cultural sort of way—meaning the imposition of "the" American way under self-serving pretenses of self- abnegation but at the expense of any other ways.

For many in fact, the most pressing danger raised by the rise of American power remained its historic reluctance to make use of that power on behalf of an international order that the world could recognize and welcome. Even during the Cold War, the interventionist élan that followed the Korean War could only last a generation, whether in the United States or among the countries that urged and followed its leadership: it ended in Vietnam when the permissive consensus that had given it legitimacy at home and durability abroad faded dramatically. Notwithstanding the Gulf War, the U.S. reluctance to use force was especially notable during the short decade that followed the collapse of the Soviet Union, when America's abundant deterrent power overwhelmed its usable power.[20] Admittedly, the first President Bush might have liked to show otherwise. His plans for a new post–Cold War world order relied greatly on heavy investments of every dimension of American power.[21] But the public repudiation of the Bush presidency in November 1992 confirmed that in a postwar era Americans still prefer a life of consuming leisure at home to the travails of imperial conquest abroad.

At first, and like many of those who helped elect William Jefferson Clinton, the new U.S. president lacked interest in the world, and whenever interested, he seemed to lack a feel for the world. Absent his predecessor's motivation and experience, Clinton failed to exert the global leadership needed during the moment of geopolitical transition that followed the Cold War—the leadership Truman had shown after World War II. Henry Kissinger, who knew plenty about world leaders, had set the bar high but well when discussing Lyndon Baines Johnson: "One never had the impression that he would think of the topic spontaneously—while shaving, for example."[22] As the unexpected end product of the political machine in a midwestern rural state, Truman gave no reason he might have such thoughts either, of course. But no less, and even more effectively, than any of his successors, Truman had that "spontaneous" feel—an instinctive ability to understand "America's ultimate calling to serve as a fount of freedom and progress for all mankind," but also an uncanny appreciation of the unstated gap between what must be said, as he did in the doctrine that bears his name, and what can be done, as he showed in neglecting the declaratory excesses of that doctrine.[23]

By comparison, Clinton had neither the postwar visionary instincts of Truman nor the stubborn and calculated wartime determination of Johnson. He was, in a sense, Francis Fukuyama's "Last Man"—meaning an "Economic Man, seeking [for his country] prestige through material wealth and related activities, and content to live within a liberal democratic order that perpetuates peace, justice, and equal opportunity."[24] Clinton's own qualities when dealing with domestic issues—a sense of timing, a will for compromises that was facilitated by an understanding that his own convictions might have to be kept flexible, an openness to broad consultation based on a passion for diversity, an explicit predilection for the feasible over the ideal—were compelling; these could have served Clinton well in any kind of world, as would be shown during his post-presidential life when he was transformed into a one-man global institution. But in the 1990s the former governor of Arkansas sadly appeared to discover the world a bit too late and too grudgingly after the midterm elections of November 1994 seemed to deny him the ability to do what he liked best, namely, to govern an unfinished nation rather than to preside over a hard-earned empire.[25]

After September 2001, the debate waged at the UN Security Council over the use of force in Iraq was influenced by countries that hoped to constrain the United States—its capabilities, its intentions, and therefore its policies. While the Clinton administration was able to accommodate such constraints after the Cold War, when the world could still be kept "over there," the Bush administration, which had just been exposed to the first signs of war "over here," felt an urgency that was not shared elsewhere and could not therefore respond to lengthy debates with the allies and permissive arguments at the United Nations. As we have seen, the "principle" that divided Chirac (and Schroeder) from Blair (and Bush) was not over the need to contain or even change the "evil" regime in Iraq. All European leaders generally agreed that a world without Saddam would be better and probably safer, even though all of them, unlike Bush but including Blair, were explicitly concerned over Iraq's postwar condition. Rather, the principle that divided the Europeans had to do with the uses of American military power not only in but also beyond Iraq.

It is over that challenge that these men clashed. Blair and other "willing" coalition members (including Aznar, Berlusconi, and Poland's Aleksander Kwasniewski) assumed that there was little to gain from a refusal to accept a U.S. decision that Blair applauded even before it had been made or, at the very least, before it had been made known to all. Although he did not fully embrace America's worst-case projection of Saddam as an imminent threat, Blair had supreme confidence in the coalition's ability to overcome the postwar difficulties he anticipated more clearly than did Bush.

Ironically, Chirac and Schroeder shared Blair's faith in the efficacy of

American power. To an extent, therefore, their objections were over the consequences of success, not failures, especially in the Middle East, where the U.S. intervention might create a burst of violence aimed at Western interests and exacerbated by a U.S. neglect of regional priorities (including the Israeli-Palestinian conflict). But like Blair and others who chose to join Bush, Chirac and Schroeder could not readily imagine the failure that followed. As a result, their challenge was expected to cause little harm. After all, this would not be the first time that Europe's support for the United States, especially in the Middle East, would only be extended after its policy had worked. Moreover, Chirac, but also Schroeder, though to a lesser extent, reasoned that a readiness to follow, even on an issue of vital relevance to them, might dangerously weaken their ability to stand apart from the United States when they might differ over goals no less than over policies. In short, irrespective of the U.S. response, a willingness to object now might reinforce the allies' ability to influence later.

In the meantime, intra-European alignments relative to the United States within NATO served to define new alignments in the European Union. In a union about to be made significantly larger, European countries that accompanied Britain into the U.S.-led coalition (including most new members in the East, in addition to Spain and Italy) hoped to rely on their ties with the United States to balance the inordinate weight exerted by France and Germany in the European Union. Some of Chirac's rhetoric—including an ill-advised verbal slap to Poland for having "missed a good opportunity to remain silent"—defined the clash for balance within the European Union with unusual (and self-defeating) bluntness.[26] But rhetoric aside, Blair was equally blunt when, together with Aznar and with Bush's blessing, he engineered letters that sounded like "manifestos" designed to isolate his EU adversaries within NATO even at the expense of a split within the European Union between the reported "old" and the allegedly "new" in Europe.

The year 2002 was "a missed opportunity," later complained Schroeder: "A common European position could have helped the United States avoid making a mistake heavy with consequences."[27] While Europe's divisions made it look much weaker than the sum of its capabilities, America's unity at home made it look even stronger than the facts of its power: to that extent, Bush's interest in consultation never aimed at achieving a consensus, even, or especially, within the coalition of the willing. Rather, consultation presupposed a consensus, which neither Chirac nor Schroeder were prepared to endorse without further evidence of Saddam's involvement with the attacks of September 11. It is only in the absence of such evidence that Chirac and Schroeder's opposition became irreversible, and so did, therefore, Bush and Blair's hostility. Balancing each other's weaknesses and power on behalf of overlapping interests and in the name of common goals is what alliances do. Unlike "coalitions," alliances are thus occasionally expected to desist—when some of the allies would otherwise wish to insist over what to do or not do. That, for sure, is a principle about which none of the architects of the war in Iraq were ready to agree, or even to acknowledge and respect. For this debate was waged during a unipolar moment, when accommodation was viewed by the United States as an unnecessary sign of weakness and by many of the states in Europe as an undesirable sign of subservience.

Whether a more cooperative strategy would have served the French (or German) interests better can be argued. Admittedly, the events that followed vindicate Chirac and Schroeder's objections to the war—including the absence of an imminent threat; the need to prepare better for postwar conditions in Iraq; the consequences of the war on neighboring states, including Iran; and the urgency of other issues, such as Afghanistan and the peace process in the Middle East. A few years later, these were mainly the terms of reference for the severe indictment of U.S. policies presented by the "study group" that had been formed the previous spring to report on the conduct of the war and to point to a new "way forward" in Iraq.[28] But had the French president followed the U.S. lead, France would have bolstered her role as America's best partner on the continent, which had been Chirac's initial goal in 1995, and thus enjoyed a carte blanche for leadership in Europe, which had been France's earliest goal in 1945. By supporting the U.S. attempt to act within a UN framework, Chirac would also have reinforced the legitimacy of the United Nations, which Bush continued to solicit. After the war, Chirac and other European dissenters might have helped compensate for the insufficiencies of U.S. postwar planning and could have contributed actively to the reconstruction of post-Saddam, postwar Iraq. And in each case, by openly speaking justice to power, Chirac's voice would still have been heard at home and abroad, especially in the Islamic world, with a specificity that boosted France's advantages as a principled and influential Western leader.

That is a powerful case to be made against a French strategy that had otherwise no reasonable chance to stop Bush, whose appreciation of the U.S. stakes in Iraq at the time was too urgent to suffer further delays. Arguably, Schroeder could have helped make that case to the extent that without him Chirac would have stood alone in Europe and possibly fearful of alternative alignments. But like Blair relative to Bush, Schroeder chose to do otherwise, as his own personal convictions, combined with the ambitions he had for Germany, converged with Chirac's more than they did with those of either Blair or Bush.

Coming under the new security conditions opened by the attacks of September 2001, divisions among the main European countries and with the United States are cause for regret and even dismay. These divisions exceeded what any of their main proponents anticipated or wanted. As a result, the Atlantic crisis that ensued was a collective failure in diplomacy for all concerned, and so was the subsequent European crisis, which also proved to be a political loss for all. Chirac and Schroeder, as well as Blair and his main EU partners, may have been able to delude themselves for a while in thinking that they could reinforce their respective influences on the United States while moving on separately with the construction of their own union in Europe. But the architecture they hoped to leave behind was never clearly explained. Did Blair think he could recast Europe around Britain, but without, let alone against, France and Germany? Did Chirac think he could build a powerful Europe with Germany, but without Britain and possibly against the United States? Did Schroeder think he could redirect Germany by following France, dismissing Britain, and ignoring the United States?

In May 2005, France's rejection of the constitutional treaty drafted at its insistence to outline the modalities of Europe's institutional finality confirmed the depth of Europe's divisions, not only in the European Union but also within each of its members. The very idea of "Europe" has become a political issue in Europe—meaning unprecedented public ambivalence from the bottom up, because citizens now disagree over what it is, question what it does, neglect that which it has achieved, and differ over what they want out of it next. Who speaks for Europe? As heads of state and government come and go, the question, which defined many a debate over Europe in the past, seems to have lost its intensity. Instead, the question of what is Europe is emerging as a more credible focus of today's passions. In other words, the question is no longer about what Europe does but about what Europe is—less a matter of facts than a matter of feelings extended not only to the ways in which Europeans view and like each other but also to the ways in which they view and like others, including Americans. To that extent, Iraq helped define the end of the beginning for Europe, which may also lead to a new beginning for America and its relations with Europe.

New Beginning and False Start

"Here we are, condemned to live in the world as it is," concludes François Furet about "the passing of an illusion"—the "idea" of communism—that changed the world for the greater part of the twentieth century.[29] After 2003, the war in Iraq too meant the passing of an illusion—a democratic illusion that, relying on a post–Cold War surplus of American power and beginning in Iraq, was expected to spread throughout the Middle East after a quick start in Iraq. Admittedly, a new beginning in that region was overdue, but Iraq was hardly the right place to get started.

Part of the illusion that ended during the war in Iraq was linked to the unipolar moment that had been sighted after the Cold War and appeared to peak immediately upon the completion of the military phase of regime change in Baghdad in the summer of 2003. For the war exposed anew three limits of American power: first, the difficulties the United States faces to compel an adversary that refuses to be defeated—meaning the lack of a credible and lasting public will to kill and be killed after deterrence has failed and war has been won with an awesome display of military power; second, an American ability to identify, sanction, and coerce new enemies with greater ease than making, courting, and keeping new friends—meaning a capacity to reward no less convincingly than a capacity to punish, to entice no less than to threaten, and to reason and convince no less than to assert and impose; and third, a U.S. predilection for the desirable over, and even at the expense of, the doable—meaning a tendency to rely on a reality that seems more based on faith (including convictions and emotions, as well as religion and traditions) than on facts (including those rooted in historic traditions, as well as those shaped by geographic imperatives and cultural values).

Early in the Cold War Truman and his successors learned to overcome these weaknesses during a highly regulated clash with the Soviet Union. They learned how to deter the adversaries with threats that remained credible even when the execution of those threats challenged the nation's own definition of credibility, as well as the limits of allies' reliability. The 1962 missile crisis is a case in point. To this day, who knows what John F. Kennedy would have done had the Soviet regime failed to blink and cancel its planned strategic deployment in Cuba? The saving grace for Kennedy was not only that his counterpart in Moscow could never be sure of what Kennedy might do but also that he did not know what Moscow knew all too well—namely, the scope of usable Soviet forces already in place, which reduced even further the possibility that a conflict between the two superpowers could be kept limited. But how to explain, then, the allies' willingness to endure silently the risks of annihilation while kept in the dark over Kennedy's intentions until it might have been too late to change his decisions?

Still, on occasions when deterrence failed during the Cold War, America also learned quickly how to defend itself—its citizens and its territory—by limiting the use of its power to faraway places where U.S. casualties might be high, as they were in Korea and in Vietnam, but would remain nonetheless lower than would have been the case had the U.S. president succumbed to America's historic passion for instant gratification—total victory and unconditional surrender. To this day, thinking of what might have happened had Truman listened to General Douglas McArthur in December 1950, or had Johnson listened to General Westmoreland in January 1968, is a challenge to imagination: a planned assault on China, a last-minute 230,000-troop surge in Vietnam?[30] In a sense, every bit of history and geography America learned during the Cold War was exhibited by and during the Bush presidency at the close of that conflict—in the fall of 1989, as the Berlin wall was crumbling and the Soviet Union retreating until its collapse two years later, but also in the Persian Gulf one year later, as preparations were made for the United States to force Iraq's humiliating withdrawal. These were lessons of patient resolve and elementary prudence that America had learned well, as the first President Bush confirmed, but these were also lessons in geopolitical thinking and multilateral diplomacy that America could now teach other parts of the world that had seemingly forgotten them. For the United States, the way the Cold War ended and the first Gulf War waged seemed to end the past disparity between ends and means, power and interests, realism and ethics: not only to go to war and when, but also why and with whom; not only to win a war but also, and possibly above all, when to end it and how.

America's on-the-job "great power" training during the decades that followed World War II left it with the reputation of a benevolent hegemon that acted mainly with forbearance and used force mostly (but not always) with restraint—a hegemon that, by that time, was not "dangerous" if only relative to any alternative hegemonic pretender.[31] In Western Europe especially, where the United States put in place and managed an effective institutional order, the rewards of both America's leadership and the allies' followership were compelling. They took the form of security, to be sure, but also that of unprecedented stability and affluence in an increasingly orderly world. Even for Britain, where serious postwar misgivings about the quality of U.S. leadership had been quickly overcome, the price of followership proved to be small: Europe always remained within reach, as confirmed by Macmillan in 1962, when France was still pursuing a new bilateral intimacy with its rival across the English Channel; by Harold Wilson in 1973, when Britain finally joined the European Community after two short-lived French vetoes; by Margaret Thatcher in 1987, when she signed a Single European Act that made the process of Britain's integration in Europe irreversible; and ultimately by Tony Blair in 1998, when the new British prime minister attempted to revive earlier efforts for close cooperation with France.

While there were a lot of false starts in Britain's descent into Europe, there was no ambiguity about its ascent as a renewed economic power in Europe: ranked seventh out of seven in the G-7 when Blair was first elected in 1997, Britain stood second only to the United States in national income per capita by 2006.[32] Among other allies, the Anglo-French disparagement of Germany did not affect America's interest in Germany's return to preeminence, while the U.S.-French estrangement lacked substantive and lasting consequences for either country and for either of the two institutions to which they were most committed, NATO and the European Union, respectively. Elsewhere in the world, anticommunism was enough to define the identity of individual proconsuls and viceroys—a U.S.-favored alternative to Europe's defunct imperialism and Russia's unprecedented imperial bid outside Europe. The temptation for the United States to overdo it was always there, and so was its capacity to act unilaterally, in spite, and potentially at the expense, of its allies. But that temptation was usually resisted: with the primary exception of Vietnam, which still stands as an aberration for the ways the war was fought as well as for the way it ended, the United States often did less than it could and even, on some occasions, less than it should.

It is such capacity for moderation in the face of Soviet excesses and even allies' impatience that in the end made of the Cold War a "long peace" during which the United States was gradually normalized into a country like any other, willing to talk when possible and to fight when necessary, but also willing to accept a military or diplomatic tie that remained short of a success otherwise deemed too costly.[33] For America's allies in Europe and elsewhere, including Japan, the paradox was that their own transformation into the peaceful countries they became—when they seemingly moved from the planet Mars to the planet Venus—depended on the United States' making the opposite passage, moving, that is, from the Kantian world Americans had inhabited in isolation during their nation's formative imperial years in the nineteenth century into the harsher world they acknowledged and joined during the latter half of the twentieth century. The European passage had occurred through two wars that left the states of Europe first void of will and then void of power. Similarly, the American passage, too, came in two legs: after 1945, when America led but did not seek to dominate, and after 1991, when America seemed ready to dominate but did not appear eager to lead.

In each case, the most conclusive tests were faced by the United States in Europe, first because of the unfinished security business inherited from the two world wars, and next because of the new security business caused by the abrupt collapse of the Soviet empire. Either way, these tests were not easy, and the American passage was often stormy. From the 1948 Berlin blockade to the 1989 fall of the Berlin wall, two generations of Americans embraced a permissive bipartisan commitment of U.S. power and leadership in and beyond Europe. From the first Gulf War at the start of the 1990s to the war in Kosovo at the close of that decade, another generation of Americans seemed prepared, however reluctantly, to walk away from the peace benefits and assume additional responsibilities for the post–Cold War order. How well America did is not a matter for debate: if nothing else, we at least know now that on the whole America made better use of its power than did any of its predecessors.[34] Neither Britain nor France or Germany could convincingly pretend more success during their years of preeminence up to the mid-twentieth century, at which time their recovery could not have been managed without a controlling assist from the United States and could not have been completed without some rethinking of their earlier Westphalian ways.

Beyond the Cold War, the events of September 11, 2001, started a third leg in America's passage. It is one that may last as long as the previous two—a time measured in generations rather than in years or even decades. During that time, Europe will no longer stand at the center of America's security concerns because it no longer stands as the central challenge to the sort of world order that would best serve America's interests and values. However, this need not mean that Europe will no longer be at the center of America's interest in like-minded allies. Indeed, more than ever before, it is in and with Europe that America is most likely to find its most indispensable allies, because the issues of greatest U.S. concern are in the Middle East, a region that America does not know well, and certainly knows far less well than its counterparts in Europe, for whom the Middle East is an old historical acquaintance.

Challenges in the Greater Middle East are daunting and make the postwar challenges faced in Europe small by comparison. Never mind the inability to define the boundaries of the new regional center of global disorders,[35] after 1945, these boundaries were not self-evident relative to the Soviet Union either. Sixty years later, in May 2005, the inability of all NATO and European Union members to celebrate jointly the end of World War II was a reminder that peace in Europe was achieved only on different timetables and only one piece of Europe at a time. As the newly liberated states of Eastern Europe and the newly independent former Soviet Republics insisted, peace had hardly come to them when Germany's surrender gave way to Russian military occupation and Soviet communist subjugation—and few of the anniversaries used as benchmarks for the enforcement of Truman's vision, including the 1947 Marshall Plan, the 1948 Berlin blockade, and the 1949 Washington Treaty, were relevant to former Warsaw Pact countries and Soviet republics that had been abandoned to their fate to make half of Europe rich and free.

Never mind, too, the absence of a historic relationship between the United States and Islam, the prevailing identity of the Middle East region, however defined geographically or ideologically. Throughout the Cold War, the two superpowers had little in common, except for their gluttonous appetite for nuclear weapons. But at least, they both learned, relatively quickly, to accept rules of strategic engagement that neither dared to break because of the consequences each knew it could expect from the other. To compare Truman and George W. Bush, Germany and Iraq, and postwar Europe and post–September 11 Middle East is so wrong as to be irrelevant and so misleading as to be dangerous. It would be much better, assuming any need for analogies, to turn to the Hobbesian turmoil of eighteenth-century Europe rather than to the regulated environment of the Cold War, the Kantian conversion of Germany, or the grand rehabilitation of Westphalian Europe.

For one, unlike post-Vienna Europe in 1815 or postwar Europe in 1945, most states in the Middle East are not war-wary. Indeed, the opposite is true: for many Arab countries in the region, and for most people in all of these countries, there is nothing to restore and little to rebuild. Left helpless and destitute by corrupt governments and aggressive neighbors for far too long, citizens have grown collectively angry and individually hopeless. Their desperation is not over war, which they have endured long enough to accept it as a way of life, but over peace, which has proven elusive for so long as to no longer have credible meaning. War might not feed them and it is likely to kill them, but it can also provide them with a dignity that has not been found in the peace to which they are used, which also fails to provide adequate measures of life and food. These are Dostoyevsky's new Possessed, recognizable for their "ungovernable wildness" and their "unusual gift for crime" caused by their "great revulsion at life."[36] For those who insist on making of history the flashlight that will bring clarity in an obscure moment, the precedent is therefore more that of post-Versailles Europe in 1919 than that of post-1945 Europe—a moment, that is, when defeated and embittered states were bent on revenge and the victorious states on punishment, as opposed to redemption for the former and reconciliation for the latter.

That distinction is all the more significant as neither the United States nor the states of Europe can seemingly rely on a special partner in the area. America's decision to stay in Europe after World War II grew out of the availability of privileged partners, including, as we have seen, Britain especially but not excluding France, at least for a while. Absent such partners, America might have gone home again, as had been done in 1919, when Americans were not ready for Britain and the French were not ready for America. Even the democratic process that Americans favored for postwar Europe was distorted to preserve the credible partners the United States needed, as the communist parties were denied a voice commensurate with their large political constituencies—especially, but not only, in France. By comparison, privileged partners in the Middle East are hard to find, and the quasi-democratic elections held since 2004, including in the like of Lebanon, Palestine, and Iraq, not to mention Iran, have made it even harder. To be sure, Israel is one such privileged partner—arguably "the" U.S. partner of choice but also, for Europe, a case of conscience that cannot be totally ignored or forgotten. But Israel lacks both regional and even, to an extent, global legitimacy, especially under conditions that would demand that force be used, and it will not be able to play a central peacemaking role in the Middle East for many years after the negotiated emergence of a sovereign Palestinian state. For local partners to emerge elsewhere in the Middle East would require centrist forces that can replace autarchic governments that no longer have the aura of anticommunist respectability they had during the Cold War. That too is not a likely outcome for many years to come, if ever, and in the meantime would probably facilitate the rise of theocratic regimes that have become the legitimate focus of Western apprehensions since September 11.

"The levels of brutality we've seen [in Iraq] are truly horrifying," noted Richard Perle in late 2006, as he reflected on the "disastrous" condition of a war that he had sponsored to the best of his considerable influence. And, he adds, "I underestimated the depravity."[37] Even to the uninitiated, however, it should have been clear that to think of Iraq as a model for democratizing the Muslim world, just as Germany had emerged as a model for transforming Europe after 1949, was a creative fantasy—a reassuring manipulation of history for a Bush administration whose faith in its policies was designed to neutralize the facts used by its critics. These are not only echoes of Truman's years but also echoes of the Reagan years, when U.S. pressures on behalf of regime change in the Philippines served allegedly as a model for the democratic revolutions that followed in the name of the Reagan Doctrine—past South Korea and all the way to Eastern Europe and ultimately the Soviet Union.[38] After Truman, however, came Eisenhower, whose attempts at regime changes in Iran, Guatemala, Lebanon, Cuba, and, of course, Vietnam, exceeded Truman's vision and carried unintended consequences for the next three decades, from the 1961 failed Bay of Pigs invasion to the 1979 Islamic revolution in Iran and the 1983 debacle in Lebanon—not to mention Southeast Asia.

Even to the most indulgent and sympathetic observer, the comparison that was initially made between post-Saddam Iraq and postwar Germany remains historically preposterous and intellectually embarrassing. The very least that should have been known about the central dimensions of Germany's recovery after 1945 was enough to end any such comparison: a national will to reinvent itself after the war, a homogenous people anxious to redeem themselves, a homegrown political leadership of unusual vision and impeccable wartime credentials, and, not least, the country's willingness to accept an open-ended military occupation that limited its national sovereignty in a region that had, on the whole, lost its taste for war and hence its interest in revenge. The sort of people and the sort of leadership found in post-1945 Germany might have been able to rebuild and rehabilitate Iraq as quickly as the Bush administration assumed in the summer of 2003, but those, clearly, were not available among post-Saddam Iraqis, and the minimal U.S. forces deployed for regime change were neither sufficient nor prepared for the military occupation that followed, pending decades of reconstruction, rehabilitation, and reconciliation for the country, the state, and its various sectarian communities. Ambassador Bremer, we have noted, was looking for an Iraqi equivalent of Ludwig Erhard: but why try so hard by aiming so high? In 2003, there was not even an Iraqi Shah, an Iraqi Chamoun, or even an Iraqi Pinochet—someone, in short, who could fill the vacuum left by Saddam's removal, as there had been in Iran, Lebanon, and even Chile. All there was

was a deviously manipulative Ahmed Chalabi, who, like so many others who contracted American power on their behalf in the past, "had nothing to do with Communist or liberal or royalist and everything to do with blood feuds" of no distinct and lasting relevance to U.S. interests.[39]

At least, the centrality of the Greater Middle East region early in the twenty-first century is more widely acknowledged in the United States than that of Europe was early in the twentieth century. Before 1914, the United States remained indifferent to the "gathering storm" across the Atlantic: to this day it is truly remarkable that at no point that spring, on the eve of the defining cataclysm of the twentieth century, was there any discussion in Europe of U.S. preferences and any discussion in the United States of unfolding events in Europe.[40] After 1919, the United States passively watched the forces of totalitarianism sweep over most of Europe until its forced intervention in 1941: to this day, too, it is shameful that the Roosevelt administration entered the war against Germany only after Hitler had declared war on the United States. And after 1945 America abandoned a large chunk of the short-lived Nazi empire to an "evil" regime and a hostile ideology bent on acquiring more of the continent if granted the opportunity: to this day the predilections for power over justice, and stability over equity, are cause for embarrassment in many parts of the so-called new Europe.

By contrast, the case against disengagement from Iraq starts with the known difficulty of letting go of even a small part of the Middle East to radical forces that are intrinsically hostile to the most fundamental U.S. interest, which relates to the safety of American citizens wherever they might be, not to mention economic and strategic interests to which the Middle East is of unquestioned and vital relevance. Given a demonic potential in radical goals that aim not only at denying the United States and its allies but at killing their people, it would not be enough for America to go home, because even at home America might be threatened and hurt, as it was in September 2001—and as some of America's closest allies were after that, including Britain and Spain. It may well be that even in this context the war in Iraq was the wrong war for the wrong reasons, waged against the wrong enemy and at the wrong time—a strategic mistake comparable to the French intervention in the Ruhr nearly eighty years earlier, when the small coalition of the willing put in place by a vengeful French government caused so much resentment in Germany as to end the postwar years and, for all purposes, launch a long and agonizing wait for what would be World War II. But however the war in Iraq continues to be fought, whether overtly with U.S. forces or more or less covertly by proxy and with forces imported from the region, this war will last for a while.

Unlike Vietnam, which began as a civil war before Johnson turned it into an American war that bore little relevance to U.S. interests, the conflict in Iraq is an American war that has turned into a civil war in which the United States has vital interests that cannot be abandoned. And unlike Vietnam, which had the unity and the power needed to keep neighboring countries at bay after the war, Iraq will be the target of territorial ambitions from its neighbors lest somehow U.S. power can effectively keep them at a distance while they resolve the sectarian issues that define their civil war. In short, even the withdrawal of U.S. forces from Iraq will not end the war in and for Iraq, just as the end of the Vietnam War hardly put an end to the Cold War for and beyond Europe. For viewed as the beginning of a longer conflict, Iraq is more like the Korean War: in June 1953, the departure of U.S.-led UN forces began America's prolonged rise to global interventionism during the Cold War.

Comparing Iraq to the war in Vietnam and assimilating the consequences of a defeat in Iraq to those of the defeat in Vietnam is misleading, and it can even be reassuring. Whereas the war in Iraq has been fought in a country and a region of undisputable relevance to the United States and to world order, the war in Vietnam was fought as a mindset that bore little resemblance to reality—the "inordinate fear of communism," as President Carter called it in the spring of 1977.[41] Admittedly, the U.S. retreat from Vietnam caused political chaos in the United States, a crisis of authority within the Atlantic Alliance, a global Soviet challenge that seemed to peak as America was said to be declining, and the emergence of "new influentials" around the world. But none of this lasted, and a few years proved to be sufficient to still the political chaos at home, restore U.S. leadership in the alliance, bury the Soviet challenge abroad, and even stall the rise of the emerging new powers in Asia or elsewhere. By comparison, the growing evidence of a public humiliation of U.S. power in Iraq has already been a catalyst for increasingly chaotic conditions in the Middle East, compromised efforts to contain the spread of weapons of mass destruction, and, most broadly, the end of the unipolar moment during which a new world order had been expected to emerge after the Cold War.

On this score at least, the war in Iraq produces an inescapable verdict that history has rendered many times in the past: whatever is thought of a strategy of preponderance, it is not nearly as bad as a strategy of preponderance that fails. To that extent, Iraq is the true quagmire that Vietnam did not have to be—not only for the United States but also for others, irrespective of where they stood when military combat began in March 2003.

Peering into the Multipolar Moment

When first elected, George W. Bush did not seem to have thought much about the world, about which he cared little and which he knew even less. The "vision" came later, and it was just that—not so much an intellectual construct that might even define a "doctrine" but the horrific sights of September 11, 2001, which he was determined to not see ever again. The vision of the events of that day has not left him since, and, accordingly, the commitment he made then has remained equally firm ever since. That too is not the least of the differences between the situations in Iraq and Vietnam. At the least, Johnson came to understand and believe that the United States should not have gone to, and should not remain in, Vietnam. He just did not know how he could get out. Bush shows no such understanding.[42] "We'll succeed unless we quit," he continued to insist even as a growing majority of Americans had become convinced that success was no longer an option.[43]

"People want you to change," complained Bush in September 2006. "It's tactics that shift, but the strategic vision has not, and will not, change."[44] Admittedly, the U.S. president shifted tactics on occasion: when he went to the United Nations in September 2002 to gain the same universal support as his father had more than a decade earlier; when he traveled to Brussels, Belgium, in late February 2005 to restore a semblance of institutional normalcy in his relations with the allies in Europe; or even when he spoke to the nation in January 2007 to respond to the findings of a study group on Iraq with a recognition of past mistakes and an allegedly "new way forward" of his own. But in none of these cases did Bush depart from his most fundamental belief: that the dangers of inaction are much superior to whatever dangers action might actually cause, which in turn suggests to Bush that it is better to act too early than to act too late and that an excess of force is more forgivable than a display of weakness even if and/or when it comes late (which is therefore better than never). To that extent, the war debate, at home and with the allies, was too narrow. Rather than insisting on operational decisions, critics should have discussed the strategic choices that motivated and guided those policies. In other words, Iraq was an important issue, but it was hardly "the" issue: September 11 was. To Bush, that day's events conveyed the sight of a world run amok and America on the edge of the precipice. Unless it could be shown that the perils raised by September 11 had been such a historic aberration that they could never be repeated, the hypothetical costs of not doing away with Saddam Hussein were deemed to be so significant that they justified a decision to go to war, irrespective of its consequences.[45]

Still, the war went terribly wrong—worse than even the harshest critics imagined when they began to make the case against the war. "We gave the Iraqis a republic," wrote a noted neocon columnist, "and they do not appear able to keep it."[46] The assessment is a convenient alibi for failure—a prelude to a blame-and-run approach that this same columnist adopted when he warned, a few weeks later, that the spectacle of Saddam Hussein's hanging— "beyond travesty"—was enough to let the Iraqis "have [their] sectarian war . . . without us."[47] The Iraqis, however, could not be expected to keep something they never had—whether a Republic or sectarian peace. More convincingly, the war went wrong because there were too many ill-founded judgments that shaped the decision to go to war and were made by an administration that was determined to stifle debate: "I know we've made tactical errors—thousands of them," acknowledged Secretary Rice, notwithstanding her earlier tendency to deny access to critics who questioned the judgments that produced those errors when she served earlier as the president's national security adviser.[48] With the very foundations of its decision-making process gravely—indeed, fatally—flawed, the Bush administration did not question but grossly exaggerated the reach of American power and thus simply assumed the irrelevance of its allegedly weak allies in Europe. But even the conclusion that Bush chose global domination over leadership is incomplete, however convenient such a conclusion might also be. Equally relevant is the fact that, irrespective of the way the war was argued by Bush, planned by his administration, and waged by his generals, it went wrong because the allies too exaggerated the reach of their own influence while neglecting the risks of a U.S. failure and its consequences to their own interests in the region. Move over, though not aside, Mr. President: Chirac and Schroeder, as well as Blair, also need their day in court.

Failure in Iraq did not obscure the objective dimensions of U.S. primacy—which neither the French president nor the German chancellor (and their own followers) ever questioned. What became questionable, however, and what was therefore questioned, was the legitimacy and even relevance of American power (meaning its usability) and American leadership (meaning its efficacy). Unlike the situation in 1945, after World War II, and even unlike that of 1991, after the Cold War, the United States was no longer "invited" to lead. After 2003, U.S. global leadership, explicitly welcomed after September 11, was found to be lacking as the war in Iraq left Bush and his administration seemingly in denial—rigid in what they sought, unfocused in what they did, righteous in what they said, and, most of all, ineffective for what they accomplished. An excessively military outlook on security issues, a near-obsessive concern with global terrorism, and contradictory demands on allies and adversaries alike deflated not only the world's expectations as to what the United States could do, both how and how well, but also, and even more significantly, America's own expectation of what its government could do, both where and how.

This broad assessment of ongoing U.S. policies, which some might find harsh, was admittedly not unusual. It was often heard, at home and abroad, during the Cold War, when periodic warnings of U.S. failure were proven wrong, and when perceptions of decline proved to be easily reversible. But in the post–September 11 world, the combined impact of the many wrong decisions made early in the war may not be easily managed, let alone reversed. Late in 2006 there was no harsher indictment of U.S. policies than that provided by a bipartisan study group on Iraq, which was cochaired by former secretary of state James Baker and former congressman Lee Hamilton and included the participation of leading personalities from both political parties in all three branches of the U.S. government. Ironically, the Baker-Hamilton analysis paralleled a great deal of the Chirac-Schroeder earlier warnings and endorsed much of their agenda. "If current trends continue," Baker and his group unanimously agreed, "the consequences could be severe" for Iraq, the region, and the "global standing" of the United States. House arrest for the Bush administration was the apparent sentence, as the commission attempted to force the president into a rigid menu of recommendations and a fixed timetable that could not "guarantee success" but might at least help avoid further damage and eventually "improve" the prospects for a "grave and deteriorating" situation not only in Iraq but also in Afghanistan and relative to Iran and Syria, as well as to the Israeli-Palestinian peace process.[49]

Abroad, an even harsher condemnation of U.S. policies pointed to the risk of an America that would be isolated in an increasingly hostile and dangerous world. "I can be a little allergic for people overseas," Bush had curiously said while praising Blair in early 2006.[50] By then, however, the allergy had become contagious, and other great powers now appeared to worry less about each other and more about the United States—not only for what had become of the wars in Iraq and Afghanistan but also for what might next happen (in Iran) and how (in the Middle East). A tattering Afghanistan, a civil war in Iraq, a challenging Iran, an unsettled Lebanon, a collapsing Somalia, a stalled Arab-Israeli peace process, and, farther away from but linked to the region, a defiant North Korea conveyed a sense of U.S. weakness and disarray. In 2007, all these were examples of the dangerous spectacle of American power increasingly at the mercy of events that it could no longer control, except for a presumed ability to make matters worse with military "surges" (in Iraq and even in Afghanistan) and punitive sanctions prior to preemptive air strikes (in Iran and in North Korea).

This is hardly the picture that had been envisioned after the downfall of the regime in Baghdad in May 2003, when Bush's triumphant tone celebrated the new unilateralism that he had embraced since September 11: a subdued Afghanistan that seemed to be on its way after a quick and effective military campaign, a mission in Iraq that was said to be "accomplished" and near finality after Saddam's capture in December 2003, an intimidated Iranian government that was seeking accommodation on U.S. terms that summer, and even a tamed North Korean regime that looked for some protection from China to balance Washington's pressures.[51] Three years later, with NATO urged to take over in Afghanistan (and a related French call for an assist from Iran); with the European Union, led by its main three powers, assuming prime responsibility for negotiating with Iran (with an assist from Russia) until it turned to the United Nations for sanctions (where China's support will be crucial); and with China gaining a controlling interest in North Korea (with a related involvement of Japan), America was moved to the sidelines—more than an interested bystander, to be sure, but no longer the decisive terminator of global instabilities and executioner of failed regimes, lest other like-minded countries that had bitterly complained earlier of Bush's unilateralism provide the support that had been sorely lacking in Iraq.[52]

Changes in the number and identity of the principal powers that compose the international system have significant consequences. After 2003, failure in Iraq did not suffice to cause any such changes, but it made them more visible more quickly. Everywhere the principal parties that will compose the recast international system can now make their voices heard with growing assertiveness, including China, India, and Russia, to be sure, but also, and most ominously, Iran and a related group of regional influentials that hope to exploit such new international volatility to their advantage.

By itself, a global devolution of power is not necessarily harmful to U.S. interests. Bipolarity, which we lived through the Cold War, is dangerous, and unipolarity, which we experienced after the Cold War, is exhausting. Any breakdown of bipolarity is possible cause for a global war that might be difficult to control, as was shown in 1914, under conditions of distorted bipolarity, and as was nearly shown during the Cuban missile crisis in 1962 and was still possible as the Soviet Union was nearing collapse nearly forty years later. Under conditions of unipolarity, a crisis anywhere in the world is a possible challenge to primacy—raising tests of durability as well as of efficacy that no world power has been able to endure since the Roman Empire and that, as we have just seen, America could not endure for long either. By comparison, multipolarity is demanding, but it is also potentially less dangerous and certainly less exhausting for the power that must protect its primacy against those many states that sooner or later come to resent or fear it for its capacity to impose or deny changes they fear or seek. To that extent, unipolarity can only be a short-lived moment of geopolitical transition during which the preponderant power moves from one unpredicted or unprecedented situation to another, making desperate uses of history to justify each decision while its interlocutors gather strength and regroup.[53]

To be sure, how desirable the new multipolarity might be depends on where power goes and to what ends. As argued by Stanley Hoffmann three decades ago, "An abstract theorist could argue that any system of autonomous units follows the same basic rules, whatever the nature of these units. But in practice, that is, in history, their substance matters as much as their form."[54] For both, substance and form can best define the alignments that are most likely to emerge as forces for stability or instability in the system as a whole. Whatever the theorist may claim, history offers no iron laws. The acquisition of power by a state does not mandate aggressive behavior until the overriding and ultimate aim of that power has been achieved: "to be a hegemon—that is the only great power in the system."[55]

The other major powers that will influence the emerging multipolar moment are known, assuming there is no significant discontinuity along the way. Russia still qualifies, if only in the short term, and so do China and India, now and for the *longue durée* that defines the antieventism of French historian Fernand Braudel.[56] While none of these powers show a substance that match or might ever match Europe and even Japan's like-mindedness with the United States, they need not point to a conflictual relationship with the United States, at least for the short- to mid-term (*courte* and *moyenne durée*). Instead, they might form a cooperative environment somewhat akin to the five-power concert that kept order in nineteenth-century Europe between 1818 and 1848—an implicit agreement to find common ground on issues of shared concern while respecting each other's sovereignty even on foreign issues over which the concern of one or two of those powers might not be shared by the others.

Take Russia, whose history during the first fifteen post-Soviet years has been especially unpredictable, moving from near collapse and bitter compliance to apparent renewal and proud defiance.[57] Nostalgically, Russia longs for its past imperial days, and relations with its former dependencies appear reckless at times, occasionally reminiscent of frightening Soviet practices. History neither ends nor fades away; it just seems to linger. In the 1990s, it was not prudent for either the United States or its European allies "to deny or forget a thousand years of Russian history, replete with wars of imperial aggrandizement, the Russification of ethnic minorities, and absolutist, authoritarian, and totalitarian rule."[58] Within a few years it was hard to remember who lost the Cold War, as Vladimir Putin derided the United States' failed attempt to impose "one center of authority, one center of force, one center of decision-making" on the world.[59] But that, too, will pass. As Russia's economy eventually runs out of gas, so to speak, it may find itself short of power after a protracted period of military neglect, and even out of people after a protracted sequence of self-induced genocide characterized by falling birth rates and reduced longevity made worse than elsewhere because of inadequate state policies on health and the environment. Such an underdeveloped, defanged, and depopulated Russia will hardly turn to China for comfort—a China that would seem by then enticingly affluent, increasingly powerful, and dangerously overpopulated along three thousand miles of the common border it shares with Russia. While Russia will thus welcome closer economic and political relations with Europe, this would not be enough unless a much closer relationship with Europe also entails closer security and economic relations with the United States.

In the meantime, China will likely continue to depend on a benign security environment within which it can focus its attention on economic growth while attending to the massive societal problems that loom ahead for that immense and immensely populated country: growing inequalities, an aging population, an archaic political system, and ambitious neighbors and rivals. Like Russia, but also like India, China cannot easily sustain its rise to and taste for primacy in isolation from world markets and the financial institutions that shape them—or even in open conflict with the main powers that rule them. The last thing China can afford is an adversarial relationship with its economic partners of choice, the United States and the European Union, even as it competes with them over old-fashioned issues of imperial intrusiveness into those parts of the world that provide the raw commodities without which China cannot continue to grow. The same is true of an over-populated India, whose people lack the sort of homogeneity found in China and whose genuine democratic system has thus far not been exposed to the perils of inclusiveness. India never had much of a lasting interest in Russia, including in Cold War days when the Soviet Union attempted to exacerbate India's occasional bursts of anti-American sentiments.[60] Nor is any Indian government likely to find much interest in an exclusive strategic partnership with China, at the presumed expense of the United States, or with the United States, at the explicit expense of China: if the former, why; if the latter, how?

Under such conditions, neither China nor India (as well as some of their most influential neighbors in Asia) nor even Russia would gain from so much transatlantic friction as to induce America and Europe to seek new privileged partnerships exclusive or at the expense of each other. Rather than thinking of the European Union as a weight to be used to help counter U.S. power, the emerging poles of the new multipolar order would rather hope to see the European middle powers emerge as a strong and cohesive union that can restore "the better America—the liberal, outward-looking and generous US that found itself momentarily out of place and out of friends in Iraq."[61] Paradoxically, therefore, no change in the international system would be more consequential than the collapse of an Atlantic alliance that stands as the only available axis of stability for the new multipolar order. That, in the end, is what the clash within Europe and between Europe and the United States over Iraq threatened to cause when it compromised and nearly derailed fifty years of transatlantic solidariy and European unity.

Implicit in all of this is a final thought. For all of the ambivalence that surrounds America's relations with the leading powers of Europe, as well as Europe's leading powers with each other, two things stand as certainties: when divided, Europe is too weak relative to the United States to be or try to be a significant partner, but if united, Europe is too entangled with the United States to be or wish to become a genuine adversary. Blair, Chirac, and Schroeder overlooked the need for European unity and as a result were left powerless in their efforts to influence Bush. Whatever they did in following or opposing U.S. policies did not protect their countries, or each of them personally, from the consequences of U.S. failures, which their unity, however expressed, could have helped avoid or at least mitigate. Similarly, however, by ignoring Blair's concerns and dismissing Chirac and Schroeder's relevance, Bush overlooked the need for transatlantic solidarity and confirmed that in the security environment of the twenty-first century, no nation, however peerless its power, can remain for long without like-minded allies, however difficult some of them may be at times. As a result, there was little that those four men built—Bush and Blair, Chirac and Schroeder. Rather than the visionary architects they claimed or wanted to be, they were acrobats whose capacity to perform on the Euro-Atlantic stage that they inherited from their predecessors—Truman and Churchill, de Gaulle and Adenauer—was fatally affected by the delusions that conditioned their act and shaped their discourse.

NOTES

INTRODUCTION

1. These images are borrowed from Robert Kagan, "Power and Weakness," *Policy Review* 113 (June–July 2002): 3–28, and Richard Haass, *The Reluctant Sheriff: The United States after the Cold War* (New York: Council on Foreign Relations, 1997).

2. Marc Danner, "Iraq: The War of the Imagination," *New York Review of Books* 53, no. 20 (December 21, 2006): 81–96.

3. Asked what "one thing" he would "change about [his] Presidency," President Bush responded, "my rhetoric early on in the war on terror. . . . I said, 'dead or alive.' And the truth of the matter is, probably, a little too much cowboy talk that might have sent bad signals." Ron Claiborne and George Stephanopoulos, "A Chat with the President," *ABC News*, October 20, 2006.

4. Jon Meacham, *Franklin and Winston: An Intimate Portrait of an Epic Friendship* (New York: Random House, 2003).

5. Tony Blair, "Prime Minister's Policy Speech—Third in a Series of Three," Georgetown University, May 26, 2006. See also Dick Cheney, "Remarks by the Vice President to the Veterans of Foreign Wars 103rd National Convention," Nashville, Tennessee, August 26, 2002.

6. Robert Kagan, "Embraceable EU," *Washington Post*, December 5, 2004; Robert Kagan, *Of Paradise and Power: America and Europe in the New World Order* (New York: Vintage Books, 2004), p. 158.

7. The reference is to Walter Jones (R-NC).

8. Gregor Dallas, *1945: The War That Never Ended* (New Haven, Conn.: Yale University Press, 2005), pp. 297–98.

9. Tony Blair, "Prime Minister's Speech to the U.S. Congress," Washington, D.C., July 18, 2003.

10. Quoted in John Newhouse, *De Gaulle and the Anglo-Saxons* (New York: Viking Press, 1970), p. 31.

11. Adrian Hyde Price and Charley Jeffery, "Germany and the European Union: Constructing Normality," *Journal of Common Market Studies* 39, no. 4 (November 2001): 689–717.

12. Peter J. Katzenstein, "Same War—Different Views: Germany, Japan, and Counterterrorism," *International Organization* 57 (Fall 2003): 734.

13. Quoted in Roger Cohen, "Schroeder Visits Bush," *New York Times*, March 29, 2001.

14. For a while at least, Eliot A. Cohen's *Supreme Command* (New York: Free Press, 2002) was said to be a must read at the White House and the Pentagon. For comments by Cohen, Kenneth Adelman, and other neocon intellectual figures, see David Rose, "Neo Culpa," *Vanity Fair* (January 2007): 82–90ff.

15. Harvey Sicherman, "The Rest of Reagan," *Orbis* 44, no. 3 (Summer 2000): 498.

16. Peter Rodman, *More Precious Than Peace: The Cold War and the Struggle for the Third World* (New York: Charles Scribner's Sons, 1994), p. 548.

CHAPTER ONE

A shorter version of this chapter appeared as "Terms of Estrangement: French-American Relations in Perspective," *Survival* 47, no. 3 (September 2005): 73–92.

1. James A. Baker III, with Thomas M. DeFrank, *The Politics of Diplomacy: Revolution, War and Peace, 1989–1992* (New York: G. P. Putnam's Sons, 1995), p. 370. De Gaulle is quoted by C. L. Sulzberger, *The Last of the Giants* (New York: Macmillan, 1970), p. 55. Echoes of André Gide: "Though I may agree to serve . . . I want the terms upon which I lease out my life to be both freely consented to and renewable at any given moment." *Journal, 1889–1939* (Paris: Gallimard, 1948), p. 670.

2. Quoted in John Harper, *American Visions of Europe: Franklin D. Roosevelt, George F. Kennan and Dean G. Acheson* (New York: Cambridge University Press, 1994), p. 219.

3. Michael Brenner and Guillaume Parmentier, *Reconcilable Differences: U.S.-French Relations in the New Era* (Washington, D.C.: Brookings Institution, 2002).

4. Transcript of interview, French Foreign Ministry, December 14, 1999.

5. "En définitive," de Gaulle told his cabinet on May 10, 1967, with specific reference to the then-unfolding debate over Britain's membership in the Common Market, "on passera par où la France le voudra. Ce n'est pas une situation désagréable." Quoted in Roger Peyrefitte, *C'était de Gaulle* (Paris: Fayard, 2000), 3:272.

6. See also Simon Serfaty, "France-Etats-Unis: La querelle permanente," *Relations Internationales et Stratégiques*, no. 25 (Spring 1997): 52–59; "Anti-Europeanism in America and Anti-Americanism in Europe," in *Visions of America and Europe: September 11, Iraq, and Transatlantic Relations*, ed. Christina V. Balis and Simon Serfaty (Washington, D.C.: CSIS Press, 2004), pp. 3–22. See also the wonderful portraits of the "quarrelsome French" and the "baffling Americans" presented by Luigi Barzini in *The Europeans* (New York: Simon & Schuster, 1983), pp. 115–54 and 217–54.

7. Eugen Weber, "Of Stereotypes and of the French," *Journal of Contemporary History* 25, no. 2 (1990): 199.

8. Stanley Hoffmann, "To Be or Not to Be French," in *Ideas and Ideals: Essays on Politics in Honor of Stanley Hoffmann*, ed. Linda B. Miller and Michael Joseph Smith

(Boulder, Colo.: Westview Press, 1993), p. 32. As a corollary, Hoffmann also played a significant and constructive role in teaching America, and American power, to the French, as he was over the years a pole of reference for a French elite that needed such "education" arguably more than any other group in Europe.

9. As noted already by Alexis de Tocqueville, and as repeated often since—by André Siegfried, for example, when he referred to "*la place à part*" held by France in the United States (and, he could have added, the United States in France). Cited in Pierre Guerlain, *Miroirs transatlantiques* (Paris: L'Harmattan, 1996), p. 9.

10. In the 1990 American census, 10.3 million Americans reported a French ancestry, as compared to 13.6 million in the 1980 consensus. Jacqueline Lindenfeld, *The French in the United States: An Ethnographic Study* (Westport, Conn.: Bergin & Garvey, 2000), p. 8; Damien-Claude Bélanger and Claude Bélanger, "French Canadian Emigration to the United States, 1840–1930," *Quebec History*, Web site of Marianapolis College, August 23, 2000. The rich cultural tradition embodied by these early French emigrants, mostly from Canada and Arcadia, began to fade at the turn of the century. Eager to blend into American society, "many stopped speaking French, changed their names, and tried to blend into the melting pot." Peter Woolfson, "The Aging French-American and the Impact of Acculturation," *Ethnic Groups* 8 (1990): 181. In 1990, fewer than 120,000 people living in the United States claimed to have been born in France, and a majority of them had not sought U.S. citizenship. Laurie Collier Hilstrom, "French Americans: Overview," *Gale Encyclopedia of Multicultural America*, 2nd ed. (New York: Gale Research, 1995), 1:660. These are the few who, rather than "immigrate, settle, and die in their adopted countries," merely "move on to other places" where they settle as permanent misfits. François Lagarde, *The French in Texas: History, Migration, Culture* (Austin: University of Texas, 2003), pp. 310–11.

11. Note, in this context, France's interest in the U.S. Constitution, which was to become a bestseller of sorts. Bernard Bailyn, *To Begin the World Anew: The Genius and Ambiguities of the American Founders* (New York: Alfred A. Knopf, 2003).

12. Walter Isaacson, *Benjamin Franklin: An American Life* (New York: Simon & Schuster, 2003), p. 329.

13. David McCullough, *John Adams* (New York: Simon & Schuster, 2001), p. 192.

14. Quoted in Charles G. Cogan, *Oldest Allies, Guarded Friends: The United States and France since 1940* (Westport, Conn.: Praeger, 1994), p. 200. On this issue, as on nearly everything else, Hamilton disagreed, as he rejoiced over his belief that "there is no resemblance between what was the cause of America and what is the cause of France"—a difference, he insisted, that "is no less great than that between liberty and licentiousness."

15. France "is the great country it is probably because it was molded down the centuries by antagonisms and tensions between tribes, clans, cliques, coteries, guilds, camarillas, sects, parties, factions within the parties," and much, much more. Barzini, *The Europeans*, p. 138. France, observes Michel Wieviorka, "a trouvé sa justification dans une certaine capacité ou une certaine prétention . . . à délivrer à toute la planète, et à chacun de ses propres citoyens, le message des droits de l'homme et de la raison" ("found its

justification in a certain capacity or pretension . . . to deliver the message of human rights and reason for the entire planet and to each of its own citizens"). Michel Wieviorka, "Qu'est-ce qu'être français aujourd'hui? La désacralisation de l'identité française," *Le Figaro*, June 11, 2004.

16. "Allocution du Général de Gaulle," December 31, 1962, in André Passeron, *De Gaulle parle* (Paris: Plon, 1966), 2:263. Some French characteristics that are found most irritating abroad are usefully discussed in Joseph K., *Stratégie du déclin: Essai sur l'arrogance française* (Paris: Desclée de Brower, 2000). That the two French authors of this essay would have chosen to remain anonymous by relying on a pseudonym borrowed from Franz Kafka is not without interest.

17. De Gaulle's predilection for France over the French is well known but hardly exclusive. So it was, for example, with François Mitterrand, his most persistent and unforgiving adversary. Like de Gaulle, Mitterrand liked to speak of France, about which he was passionate, rather than of the French, about whom he felt more ambivalent. See Jacques Attali, *C'était François Mitterrand* (Paris: Fayard, 2005), p. 96. In Germany, Konrad Adenauer had comparable instincts. "My God," he worried, "I don't know what my successors will do if they are left to themselves without a clearly delineated path to follow." Such a path, he firmly believed, was Europe: "When I am no longer on hand," he had noted earlier, "I don't know what will become of Germany, unless we still manage to create Europe in time." Quoted in Gordon A. Craig, *The Germans* (New York: Putnam, 1982), p. 47.

18. Hubert Védrine with Dominique Moïsi, *Les cartes de la France à l'heure de la mondialisation* (Paris: Fayard, 2000), p. 10.

19. Jean-Philippe Mathy, *French Resistance: The French-American Culture Wars* (Minneapolis: University of Minnesota Press, 2000), p. 57.

20. George F. Kennan, *Realities of American Foreign Policy* (Princeton, N.J.: Princeton University Press, 1954), p. 15.

21. George Scott, *The Rise and Fall of the League of Nations* (New York: Macmillan, 1974), pp. 96, 255. An ailing President Wilson went so far as to wish "he could tell the French ambassador to his face that he would like to see Germany clean up" his country. Quoted in Selig Adler, *The Isolationist Impulse: Its Twentieth Century Reaction* (New York: Free University Press, 1957), p. 144.

22. Andrew Shennan, *The Fall of France, 1940* (New York: Longman, 2000), p. ix.

23. Douglas Porch, "Military Culture and the Fall of France in 1940," *International Security* 24, no. 4 (Spring 2000): 157–58.

24. Thierry de Montbrial, "Franco-American Relations: A Historical-Structural Analysis," *Cambridge Review of International Affairs* 17, no. 3 (October 2004): 459–60.

25. See Stacy Schiff, *A Great Improvisation: Franklin, France, and the Birth of America* (New York: Henry Holt and Company, 2005).

26. John Ikenberry, "Rethinking the Origins of American Hegemony," *Political Science Quarterly* 104, no. 3 (Fall 1989): 390–91.

27. Goethe said something comparable about the Germans, as quoted in Craig, *The Germans*, p. 15.

28. Quoted in Robert Dallek, *An Unfinished Life: John F. Kennedy, 1917–1963* (Boston: Little, Brown and Company, 2003), p. 396.

29. See, Simon Serfaty, *La France vue par les Etats-Unis: Réflexions sur la francophobie à Washington* (Paris: Institut Français des Relations Internationales, 2003).

30. George Bush and Brent Scowcroft, *A World Transformed* (New York: Alfred A. Knopf, 1998), pp. 76, 475. Condoleezza Rice does not show the same indulgence: Mitterrand's position, she noted, was nearly always confrontational. Condoleezza Rice and Philip Zelikow, *Germany Unified and Europe Transformed: A Study in Statecraft* (Cambridge, Mass.: Harvard University Press, 1995), p. 237 and passim.

31. Justin Vaisse, "America Francophobia Takes a New Turn"; Edward C. Knox, "Déjà Views: How Americans Look at France"; and Jean-Philippe Mathy, "The System of Francophobia," all in *French Politics, Culture and Society* 21, no. 2 (Summer 2003).

32. Baker, with DeFrank, *Politics of Diplomacy*, pp. 259, 314 (emphasis added), 324, 370.

33. As noted by the Israeli historian Elias Sanbar, who came to that conclusion while observing Secretary Baker and his associates in the early 1990s. "La France, Israël et les Palestiniens," *Le Nouvel Observateur*, February 10–17, 2005.

34. Reportedly asked by Secretary of State James Baker in a conversation with French ambassador to the United States Jean-David Levitte. Quoted in Peter Slevin, "U.S. and France Find Making Up Is Hard to Do," *Washington Post*, September 23, 2003. According to other accounts, Baker had raised a similar question with then-foreign minister Roland Dumas. Michael Gonzalez, "Can America Trust the French?" *Wall Street Journal*, November 23, 1999.

35. Quoted in Jim Mannion, "NATO Should Reconsider Including France in Decision Making," *Agence France Presse*, February 12, 2003; Martin Walker, "Top Pentagon Adviser Says France No Longer U.S. Ally," *Washington Times*, February 5, 2003. Thomas Friedman, "Our War with France" and "Vote France Off the Island," *New York Times*, September 18, 2003, and February 9, 2003, respectively.

36. David Gelernter, "Replacing the United Nations," *Weekly Standard*, March 17, 2003, p. 25.

37. In all fairness, the point takes the form of a leading question: "Is it not possible that . . ." Richard Z. Chesnoff, *The Arrogance of the French: Why They Can't Stand Us—and Why the Feeling Is Mutual* (New York: Sentinel, 2005), p. 23.

38. Michael Ledeen is quoted by Stuart Reid, "The Anti-Europeans," *The American Conservative*, January 27, 2002. Niall Ferguson, "Europe's Highs and Lows Depend on Where You Stand," *New York Times*, February 23, 2003.

39. Charles Krauthammer, "Europe and 'Those People,'" *Washington Post*, April 26, 2002; George Will, "'Final Solution,' Phase 2," *Washington Post*, May 2, 2002.

40. Wolfowitz is quoted in Glenn Kessler and Karen de Young, "After Iraq, U.S. Debates the Next Steps," *Washington Post*, April 13, 2003. Also, Tony Blankley, "France Blackmails Poland," *Washington Times*, February 19, 2003.

41. Adrian Basora, then a senior staffer with the National Security Council and

previously posted at the U.S. Embassy in Paris. Quoted in Rice and Zelikow, *Germany Unified*, p. 206.

42. Gordon Smith, "A Message to Britain and Europe," *European Journal* 7, no. 6 (April 2000): 5–6.

43. Timothy Garton Ash, *Free World: America, Europe, and the Surprising Future of the West* (New York: Random House, 2004), p. 88.

44. Quoted in Henry Steele Commager, *The Defeat of America: Presidential Power and the National Character* (New York: Simon & Schuster, 1974), p. 30.

45. Hubert Védrine with Dominique Moïsi, *France in an Age of Globalization*, trans. Philip H. Gordon (Washington, D.C.: Brookings Institution Press, 2001), p. 2.

46. Geir Lundestad, *Empire by Integration: The United States and European Integration, 1945–1997* (New York: Oxford University Press, 1998).

47. Richard F. Kuisel, "What Do the French Think of Us? The Deteriorating Image of the United States, 2000–2004," *French Politics, Culture & Society* 22, no. 3 (Fall 2004): 93–94. Moises Naim, "Anti-Americanism's Nasty Taste," *Financial Times*, February 24, 2003.

48. Barzini, *The Europeans*, pp. 219ff.

49. Invoking the "very high risks" resulting from "the kind of action" that was being considered by Kennedy, Secretary of State Dean Rusk warned, "It's one thing for Britain and France to be isolated within the alliance over Suez. But it's quite another thing for the alliance if the United States should get itself in the same position." Ernest R. May and Philip D. Zelikow, eds., *The Kennedy Tapes: Inside the White House during the Cuban Missile Crisis* (Cambridge, Mass.: Harvard University Press, 1997), pp. 127–28.

50. "The French," emphasized Margaret Thatcher, "were the only European country, apart from ourselves, with the stomach for a fight." Margaret Thatcher, *The Downing Street Years* (New York: Harper Collins, 1993), p. 819.

51. Christopher Meyer, *DC Confidential* (London: Weidenfeld & Nicolson, 2005), p. 258.

52. Interview, "Kay: No WMDs in Iraq," *CNN Wolf Blitzer Reports*, January 28, 2004.

53. In an interview with CBS and CNN just as the war was about to begin, Chirac, actually concerned over both the impending war and his own "war" with his U.S. counterpart, pleaded: "France is not pacifist. We are not anti-American either. We are not just going to use our veto to nag and annoy the U.S. But we just feel there is another option . . . than war." Quoted in Mark Danner, "The Secret Way to War," *New York Review of Books*, June 9, 2005, p. 73.

54. Baker with DeFrank, *Politics of Diplomacy*, pp. 283–85. Glenn Kessler and Mike Allen, "U.S. Missteps Led to Failed Diplomacy," *Washington Post*, March 16, 2003.

55. "Global Opinion: The Spread of Anti Americanism," in *Trends 2005* (Washington, D.C.: Pew Research Center, 2005).

56. Among the French, favorable opinion of Americans fell from 63 percent in 2002 to 39 percent in 2006, with a low of 37 percent in 2004. The figures for Germany are

broadly comparable. Favorable opinions of Americans rose from 58 percent in 2003 to 65 percent in 2006. Compare these to foreign opinions of President Bush, which stood at 15 percent in 2006. Pew Global Attitudes Project, "America's Image Slips," June 13, 2006, pp. 1 and 10–11. See also German Marshall Fund of the United States and Compagnia di San Paolo, *Transatlantic Trends, 2006*.

57. Mathy, "System of Francophobia," p. 24.

58. Jacques Andréani, "*Les Européens auront les Américains qu'ils méritent*" ("The Europeans will have the Americans they deserve"), *Commentaire* 24, no. 94 (Été 2001): 295–302. Nancy L. Green, "*Le Melting Pot*: Made in America, Produced in France," *Journal of American History* 86, no. 3 (December 1999): 1189.

59. Kuisel, "What Do the French Think of Us?," pp. 91–119.

60. Aragon's verse comes from his delightful poem "Plus belle que les larmes," quoted in Alain Peyrefitte, *Le mal français* (Paris: Plon, 1976), p. 376. Jules Renard is quoted in Nathan Leites, *The Rules of the Game in Paris* (Chicago: University of Chicago Press, 1969), p. 62.

61. Michel Crozier, *The Stalled Society* (New York: Viking Press, 1973). Also David Thomson, *Democracy in France since 1870* (New York: Oxford University Press, 1964).

62. As Chirac had put it at the time of the legislative elections of 1978. See, Simon Serfaty, "French Intellectuals and the Political Debate," *Washington Review of Strategic & International Studies* 1, no. 2 (April 1978): 92–98.

63. Philip H. Gordon, "The Crisis in the Alliance," Iraq Memo #11 (Washington, D.C., Brookings Institution, February 24, 2003).

64. See Paul Pillar, "Intelligence, Policy, and the War in Iraq," *Foreign Affairs* 85, no. 2 (March–April 2006): 15–27.

65. Christiane Amanpour, Interview with Jacques Chirac for CNN and CBS, March 16, 2003; Elaine Sciolino, "Focus on Chirac," *New York Times*, March 19, 2003.

66. Quoted in Bob Woodward, *Bush at War* (New York: Simon & Shuster, 2002), p. 38.

67. Quoted in Jonathan Alter, *The Defining Moment: FDR's Hundred Days and the Triumph of Hope* (New York: Simon & Schuster, 2006), p. xvi.

68. Gaddis Smith, *Dean Acheson* (New York: Cooper Square, 1972), p. 416.

69. An improvement in bilateral relations in 2005 helped improve the U.S. perception of France (from 46 percent in 2005 to 52 percent in 2006) but caused a sharp rise of negative views of France elsewhere, especially in Muslim countries. Earlier, among twenty-three major countries chosen from all parts of the world, France was the country most widely viewed as having a positive influence, while the United States was viewed as the country with the most negative influence. That condition changed for France in 2006 but was strangely reinforced for the United States, whose presence in Iraq was considered by the French as more of a danger to world peace (36 percent) than Iran (31 percent). Pew Global Attitudes Project, "America's Image Slips," p. 3.

70. More on this theme in Simon Serfaty, *The Vital Partnership: Power and Order* (Lanham, Md.: Rowman & Littlefield, 2005), pp. 17–28.

71. Jim Hoagland, "Chirac's Multipolar World," *Washington Post*, February 4, 2004. U.S. Ambassador to NATO, Victoria Nuland, spoke of a "re-understanding" to Daniel Dombey, "Washington Chooses an Awkward Time to Seek Transformation of NATO," *Financial Times*, January 24, 2006.

72. Daniel S. Hamilton and Joseph P. Quinlan, *Transatlantic Economy, 2006* (Washington, D.C.: Center for Transatlantic Relations, 2007), p. 92. See also Raymond J. Ahearn, "U.S.-French Commercial Ties," Congressional Research Service, May 19, 2006.

73. Theodore White, *Fire in the Ashes: Europe in Mid-century* (New York: Sloane, 1953), pp. 6–7.

74. Alain Minc, *Ce monde qui vient* (Paris: Grasset, 2004), pp. 1–43.

75. Antony J. Blinken, "The False Crisis over the Atlantic," *Foreign Affairs* 80, no. 3 (May–June 2001): 35–48.

76. See Benoît d'Aboville, "Où va l'OTAN aujourd'hui?" *Commentaire*, no. 115 (Autumn 2006): 579.

77. "Bush's News Conference on Iraq and the Likelihood of War," *New York Times*, March 7, 2003; interview given by Jacques Chirac to TF1 and France 2 television stations, March 10, 2003. See also the account provided by Pierre Péan, *L'inconnu de l'Élysée* (Paris: Fayard, 2007), pp. 422ff.

78. Quoted in Brian Crozier, *De Gaulle* (New York: Scribner, 1973), p. 292.

79. See Stanley Hoffmann, "Perceptions and Policies: France and the United States," in *Decline or Renewal? France since the 1930s* (New York: Viking Press, 1974), pp. 334–40ff.

80. Dwight D. Eisenhower, *Waging Peace, 1956–1961: The White House Years* (Garden City, N.Y.: Doubleday, 1965), p. 413.

81. James A. Bill, *George Ball: Behind the Scenes in U.S. Foreign Policy* (New Haven, Conn.: Yale University Press, 1997), pp. 129–30.

82. See Jacques Delors, *Mémoires* (Paris: Plon, 2004), pp. 156–57.

CHAPTER TWO

1. Meacham, *Franklin and Winston*, p. xvii. The Thatcher-Blair meeting is reported in Con Coughlin, *American Ally: Tony Blair and the War on Terror* (New York: Ecco, 2006), p. 14. President Bush is quoted in Caroline Daniel, "Blair Not a Yes Man for White House Policies, Bush Insists," *Financial Times*, January 24, 2006.

2. Thatcher, *Downing Street Years*, pp. 733, 730.

3. De Gaulle, wrote Churchill, "had to be rude to the British to prove to French eyes that he was not a British puppet. He certainly carried out his policy with perseverance." Winston S. Churchill, *The Second World War*, vol. 2, *Their Finest Hour* (Boston: Houghton Mifflin, 1949), p. 509. According to Foreign Secretary Lord Curzon, Poincaré was "a clever, hard, rigid, metallic lawyer" whose "explosive temper" added to "the inherent perfidy and insincerity of French policy." Quoted in Scott, *Rise and Fall of the League of Nations*, p. 94.

4. Newhouse, *De Gaulle and the Anglo-Saxons*, pp. 10–11.

5. These formulas are adapted from Salvador de Madariaga: "one Englishman, a fool; two Englishmen, a football match; three Englishmen, the British Empire." *Englishmen, Frenchmen, Spaniards* (New York: Hill and Wang, 1969), p. 18. Indeed, de Madariaga added, "to make up the British Empire, it is not necessary to bring together three Englishmen; one is enough."

6. David Reynolds, "Friend and Ally," *Washington Post*, January 31, 2006.

7. Robert Skidelsky, "Imbalance of Power," *Foreign Policy*, no. 129 (March–April 2002): 48. See also Skidelsky, *John Maynard Keynes: Fighting for Freedom, 1937–1946* (New York: Viking Press, 2000), p. xiii; and Basil Collier, *Barren Victories: Versailles to Suez, The failure of the Western Alliance, 1918–1956* (Garden City, N.Y.: Doubleday & Company, 1964), p. 281.

8. Barzini, *The Europeans*, p. 136. No French diplomat turned defeat into victory more convincingly than Talleyrand, who lectured the victorious coalition that France was the only country that "is asking for nothing . . . [except] respect." Turning to an overmatched Czar Alexander, the legendary French diplomat asked, "pounding the paneling . . . 'Europe! Europe! Poor Europe! . . . Shall it be said that you destroyed her?" Jean Orieux, *Talleyrand: The Art of Survival*, trans. Patricia Wolf (New York: Alfred A. Knopf, 1974), pp. 459–61. Much later, de Gaulle proved to be equally masterful at the "art of survival," although his style, quite different, certainly failed to amuse Roosevelt and often irritated Churchill. "It was a question of power," writes one of de Gaulle's biographers about his relationship with Churchill. "Churchill had it, and de Gaulle, lacking it, made up for it with a rigid pride," which, in Churchill's eyes, "often seemed unrealistic to the point of absurdity." Crozier, *De Gaulle*, p. 110.

9. Suez is a case in point. After the crisis, Washington's reconciliation with London in NATO came quickly—which was clearly not the case between American and British representatives and their French counterparts, not all of it attributable to de Gaulle's return to power in May 1958. Edgar S. Furniss Jr., *France, Troubled Ally: De Gaulle's Heritage and Prospects* (New York: Harper & Brothers, 1960), pp. 464–65.

10. Anthony Eden, *Full Circle* (London: Cassell, 1960), p. 559. Britain's ambassador, Lord Caccia, is quoted in Thomas Risse-Kappen, *Cooperation among Democracies: The European Influence on U.S. Foreign Policy* (Princeton, N.J.: Princeton University Press, 1995), p. 83.

11. Richard N. Rosecrance, *Defense of the Realm: British Strategy in the Nuclear Epoch* (New York: Columbia University Press, 1968), pp. 233–34. Also William I. Hitchcock, *The Struggle for Europe: The Turbulent History of a Divided Continent, 1945 to the Present* (New York: Anchor Books, 2004), p. 177.

12. De Gaulle is quoted in Newhouse, *De Gaulle and the Anglo-Saxons*, p. 9.

13. I am indebted to Philip Stephens for leading me to the government document cited here and the argument that follows. "Future Policy Study, 1960–70," marked "Top Secret" and dated February 24, 1960.

14. Geoffrey Warner, "Why the General Said No," *International Affairs* 78, no. 4 (October 2002): 876.

15. Tony Blair, "Prime Minister's Speech to the Polish Stock Exchange," Warsaw, Poland, October 6, 2000.

16. Quoted in Nicholas Lemann, "Without a Doubt," *New Yorker* 78, no. 31 (October 14–21, 2002): pp. 164–80. On Reagan's "slabby, alabaster-like quality," see Edmund Morris, *Dutch: A Memoir of Ronald Reagan* (New York: Random House, 1999), pp. xv and 4. About Truman's reliance for right and wrong "coming directly from the Bible," see David McCullough, *Truman* (New York: Simon & Schuster, 1992), p. 54.

17. Robert Dahl, *On Democracy* (New Haven, Conn.: Yale University Press, 1998), p. 32. See Richard McElroy, *Morality and American Foreign Policy: The Role of Ethics in International Affairs* (Princeton, N.J.: Princeton University Press, 1992), p. 13.

18. Michael T. Benson, *Harry S. Truman and the Founding of Israel* (Westport, Conn.: Praeger, 1997), pp. 29–37 and 187.

19. Raymond Garthoff, *The Great Transition: American-Soviet Relations and the End of the Cold War* (Washington, D.C.: Brookings Institution, 1994), pp. 9–11.

20. Zbigniew Brzezinski, *Power and Principle: Memoirs of the National Security Adviser, 1977–1981* (New York: Farrar, Straus & Giroux, 1983), pp. 9, 32, 49, 69, and 89–90.

21. Isaiah 55:8–9 (New International Version). Also applicable to Bush's biblical personality is his faith that "for all that is in the world, the lust of the flesh and the lust of the eyes and the vain glory of life, is not of the Father but of the world" (1 John 2:16).

22. Geoffrey Wheatcroft, "The Tragedy of Tony Blair," *Atlantic Monthly* (June 2004): 60.

23. Andrew Gimson, "Commons Sketch Blair Switches to Auto-Pilate and Washes His Hands of Iraq," *Daily Telegraph*, February 22, 2007.

24. Chirac's feistiness over Iraq in 2003, and his assertiveness over Lebanon in 2006, gained him points at home irrespective of the impact of his actions in the United States and around the world. "As in the era of the General," it was approvingly noted at the time, "France, despite its small army and big deficits, offers a counter-model." Charles Lambroschini, "Le verbe et le muscle," *Le Figaro*, September 25, 2003.

25. George W. Bush, "Remarks by the President in Address to Faculty and Students of Warsaw University," Warsaw, Poland, June 15, 2001.

26. "PM Speech to EU Parliament," Brussels, Belgium, June 23, 2005. See also, for the sake of consistency, Tony Blair, "Speech by the Prime Minister on the British Presidency—Europe Working for People," London, December 6, 1997.

27. "Speech by the Prime Minister—Change: A Modern Britain in a Modern Europe," The Hague, January 20, 1998.

28. "Prime Minister's Speech to the European Research Institute—Britain's Role in Europe," Birmingham, UK, November 23, 2001.

29. Mark Lawson, "Bill and Tony Swap Roles—Briefly," *Guardian*, June 12, 1999.

30. In a speech in London, November 22, 1999. Quoted in James K. Wither, "British Bulldog or Bush's Poodle? Anglo-American Relations and the Iraq War," *Parameters* 33, no. 4 (Winter 2003–4): 71.

31. "Prime Minister's Statement to Parliament Concerning Iraq," London, December 17, 1998.

32. Peter W. Rodman, *Drifting Apart? Trends in U.S.-European Relations* (Washington, D.C.: Nixon Center, 1999), p. 14.

33. Henry Kissinger and George P. Shultz, "The End of NATO as We Know It?," *Washington Post*, August 5, 1999.

34. Harold Macmillan, *Pointing the Way, 1959–1961* (New York: Harper, 1972), pp. 312, 359. Macmillan's friendship with Kennedy was an added irritation for de Gaulle, who, in September 1966, still saw the Americans as "Englishmen who wanted to live their lives when they became older. But," he liked to add, "they remained brothers." Quoted in Peyrefitte, *C'était de Gaulle*, p. 145. To make matters even more personal, de Gaulle had viewed Macmillan with "friendship" (a term he rarely used) since the war years, when Macmillan had often mollified Churchill over de Gaulle. See Dallas, *1945*, p. 108. A first-hand account of Blair's initial meeting with President Bush is found in Christopher Meyer, *DC Confidential*, pp. 176ff.

35. "You can agree or disagree with Blair on Iraq," writes Ambassador Christopher Meyer, who "introduced" Blair to both Clinton and Bush. "But you cannot fault him on consistency. He was a true believer in the menace of Saddam." Meyer, *DC Confidential*, p. 228.

36. James Hardy, "I Luvya, Tony: Blair's a Charmer, Says Bush as They Meet to Cement Special Relationship," *The Mirror*, February 24, 2001. Also Bob Woodward, *Plan of Attack* (New York: Simon & Schuster, 2004), p. 177.

37. Quoted in Robin Cook, *The Point of Departure: Why One of Britain's Leading Politicians Resigned over Blair's Decision to Go to War in Iraq* (New York: Simon & Schuster, 2003), p. 116.

38. "I do not need to explain why I say things," reportedly confided Bush. "That's the interesting thing about being the president. . . . I don't feel like I owe somebody an explanation." Quoted by Judy Keen, "Bush Exhibits Political Skills on Global Stage," *USA Today*, November 25, 2002.

39. Bush and Scowcroft, *A World Transformed*, p. 74.

40. "Nothing about America touched him," observes Jacques Attali, Mitterrand's closest advisor for more than two decades. *C'était François Mitterrand*, p. 97.

41. See Simon Serfaty, "American Reflections on Europe's Finality," in *The European Finality Debate and Its National Dimensions*, ed. Simon Serfaty (Washington, D.C.: CSIS Press, 2003), pp. 1–20.

42. "The Atlantic Alliance: A New NATO," *Economist*, December 9, 1995, p. 51. Craig R. Whitney, "France Says It Is Willing to Discuss Its Nuclear Role in NATO," *New York Times*, January 18, 1996.

43. As urged by Chirac when addressing the U.S. Congress on February 1, 1996: "the adoption, in due time, of a transatlantic charter that would formally acknowledge, for the next century, the vitality of our alliance."

44. Jacques Chirac, "Speech on the 25th Anniversary of the Institut Français des Relations Internationales," Elysée Palace, Paris, November 4, 1999.

45. Hervé de Charette, Interview with *Paris Match*, May 2, 1996; see Simon Serfaty,

"Bridging the Gulf across the Atlantic: Europe and the United States in the Persian Gulf," *Middle East Journal* 52, no. 3 (Summer 1998): 337–50.

46. "Arab Attitudes Towards Political and Social Issues, Foreign Policy, and the Media," polls conducted jointly by Professor Shibley Telhami, Anwar Sadat Chair for Peace and Development, University of Maryland, and Zogby International, October 2005.

47. George Bush, *All the Best, George Bush: My Life in Letters and Other Writings* (New York: Scribner, 1999), p. 478. The same inner confidence in his preparedness for leadership appears in what Winston Churchill thought when he "acquired the chief power in the State . . . [and] went to bed . . . as if I were walking with destiny, . . . that all my past life had been but a preparation for this hour and for this trial." Winston S. Churchill, *The Second World War*, vol. 1, *The Gathering Storm* (New York: Houghton Mifflin, 1948), pp. 666–67. Reportedly, this was also a "feeling" shared by Vice President Richard Cheney in the immediate aftermath of the terrorist attacks of September 11, 2001. As reportedly told by Chief of Staff I. Lewis Libby to James Mann, and quoted in Mark Leibovich, "In the Spotlight and on the Spot," *Washington Post*, October 23, 2005.

48. Woodward, *Plan of Attack*, p. 17. Prior to September 11, Bush acknowledged, he "didn't feel that sense of urgency, and my blood was not nearly as boiling." Woodward, *Bush at War*, p. 39.

49. For the duration of the Cold War, only the Eisenhower administration received bipartisan support across the House and the Senate on more than half of the foreign policy votes. James M. McCormick, *American Foreign Policy and Process* (Belmont, Calif.: Thomson Wadsworth, 2005), p. 452.

50. William Appleman Williams, *Some Presidents: From Wilson to Nixon* (New York: Vintage Books, 1972), p. 93.

51. As argued by this author in the weeks that followed those horrific events. Simon Serfaty, "The Wars of 9/11," *International Spectator* 36, no. 4 (Fall 2001): 5–11.

52. Quoted in Daniel, "Blair Not a Yes Man for U.S. Policies."

53. Bush, *All The Best*, p. 478.

54. Quoted in "France—Etats-Unis: Histoire d'un retournement," *Le Monde*, April 6, 2006.

55. Bush is quoted in Woodward, *Bush at War*, p. 38. As an example of Europe's calls on behalf of America's benign hegemony, see Christopher Patten, Cyril Foster lecture, Balliol College, Oxford University, January 30, 2003.

56. Press Conference by M. de Villepin, Minister of Foreign Affairs, January 20, 2003. These themes are discussed at greater length in Serfaty, *Vital Partnership*.

57. Mark Leonard, "Europe's Transformative Power," Centre for European Reform, *CER Bulletin*, Issue 40, February/March 2005. Also, Robert D. Kaplan, *Warrior Politics: Why Leadership Demands a Pagan Ethos* (New York: Random House, 2002).

58. Quoted in Claire Tréan, "'Il faut tout faire pour éviter de tuer des femmes et des enfants,' declare Jacques Chirac," *Le Monde*, February 14, 1998.

59. Address by French Minister of Foreign Affairs Dominique de Villepin before the U.N. Security Council, March 19, 2003.

NOTES TO PAGES 67–70   153

60. House of Commons, "Review of Intelligence on Weapons of Mass Destruction," Butler Report, July 14, 2004, para. 268. Available at http://www.butlerreview.org.uk/report. Dominique de Villepin, Address before the UN Security Council, March 19, 2003.

61. Entretien avec Dominique de Villepin, "Diplomatie et action," *Politique Internationale*, no. 102 (Hiver 2004): 5–62.

62. Philip H. Gordon and Jeremy Shapiro. *Allies at War: America, Europe, and the Crisis over Iraq* (New York: McGraw-Hill, 2004), p. 142.

63. Judith Kelley, "Strategic Non-cooperation as Soft Balancing: Why Iraq Was Not Just about Iraq," *International Politics* 42 (2005): 153–73.

64. In a report commissioned by the French Ministry of Defense prior to September 11, I noted that Iraq would present the best opportunity for France to mend its relations with the United States "since the Revolutionary Wars." Simon Serfaty, "France and US," Center for Strategic & International Studies, November 2001, p. x.

65. Jack Straw, House of Common Foreign Affairs Select Committee, March 4, 2003. At the White House, "all" agreed that losing Blair "would be a real disaster." Woodward, *Plan of Attack*, p. 341.

66. Coughlin, *American Ally*, p. 318.

67. Ambassador Bremer's references to postwar conditions in Germany as an implicit model for Iraq's reconstruction were apparently not questioned by the senior staff that he quickly assembled and who also lacked, with one exception, any experience with Iraq. Bremer's "lament" early on that "there's no Ludwig Erhard in Iraq—or at least we haven't found him yet" is truly puzzling. L. Paul Bremer III, with Malcolm McConnell, *My Year in Iraq: The Struggle to Build a Future of Hope* (New York: Simon & Schuster, 2005), p. 201.

68. Gaddis Smith, *Dean Acheson*, p. 416.

69. John Batiste, "A Case for Accountability," *Washington Post*, April 19, 2006. Lieutenant General Greg Newbold (Ret.), "Why Iraq Was a Mistake," *Time*, April 17, 2006.

70. Admittedly, Blair lacked Churchill's ability to probe, however—an ability that might have helped his advisers talk him out of the errors they thought he was about to commit. Cohen, *Supreme Command*, pp. 114 and 132–33.

71. Meacham, *Franklin and Winston*, p. xviii.

72. "President Kennedy did not wait," observed Secretary Rumsfeld, "until the Soviet missiles were in Cuba or until one was fired at the United States . . . [but] determined that the risk to our country . . . was simply so great that he had to stop it before the United States was attacked." "Department of Defense News Briefing, Secretary Rumsfeld and Gen Myers" (News Transcript), October 22, 2002. "In terms of precedents," it was urged at White House press briefing, "look at the Cuban missile crisis . . . where there was a decision made without the United States being attacked." "Press Briefing by Ari Fleischer," White House, Washington, D.C., March 19, 2003. For other references to the Cuban missile crisis, see, for example, "Dr. Condoleezza Rice Discusses President's National Security Strategy," Waldorf Astoria Hotel, New York, October 1, 2002, and "Re-

marks by Deputy Secretary of Defense Paul Wolfowitz at the IISS," Arundel House, London, England, December 2, 2002.

73. Robert F. Kennedy, *Thirteen Days: A Memoir of the Cuban Missile Crisis* (New York: W.W. Norton, 1969), pp. 89–106. Also James G. Blight, Joseph S. Nye Jr., and David A. Welch, "The Cuban Missile Crisis Revisited," *Foreign Affairs* 66, no. 1 (Fall 1987): 172.

74. Risse-Kappen, *Cooperation among Democracies*, p. 157. Also Michael Beschloss, *The Crisis Years: Kennedy and Khrushchev, 1960–1963* (New York: HarperCollins, 1991), pp. 306–7.

75. An air raid aimed at the perimeter of the fortress was to be carried out with two hundred U.S. planes from the Philippines and the Seventh fleet. Atomic weapons were reportedly available for the contingency of a large-scale Chinese retaliation. Targets in China were even selected, later acknowledged Dulles, although "no great population centers like Shanghai, Peking or Canton." See James Shepley, "How Dulles Averted War," *Life,* January 16, 1956, pp. 70ff. Also Mel Gurtov, *The First Vietnam Crisis* (New York: Columbia University Press, 1967), pp. 95ff.

76. Dominique de Villepin, "Speech at the United Nations Security Council," New York, February 14, 2003; Blair is quoted in Woodward, *Plan of Attack*, p. 399.

77. Quoted in Coughlin, *American Ally*, p. 356. Two years later, when announcing an exit strategy that appeared to parallel the recommendations made by the Baker-Hamilton Study Group for a U.S. strategy that Bush had ignored, Blair was equally determined: "I am proud of the interventions we made in removing dictatorships," he insisted while announcing an initial withdrawal of British forces from Basra and a redeployment of the remaining forces for use only if the local security forces lost control. Alan Cowell, "Britain to Trim Iraq Force by 1,600 in Coming Months," *New York Times*, February 22, 2007, and Andrew Pierce, "Unspoken Truth behind Blair Interview," *Daily Telegraph*, February 23, 2007.

78. Blistering attacks by Michael Howard before he relinquished his party's leadership to David Cameron so angered the Bush administration that Howard was told he would no longer be welcome at the White House. See Ben Hall, "Tory Criticism of Iraq War Risks Upsetting Charm Offensive in US," *Financial Times*, February 16, 2006.

79. David Cameron, JP Morgan Lecture at the British America Project, "A New Approach to Foreign Affairs—Liberal Conservatism," London, September 11, 2006.

80. Robert Skidelsky, "Britain: Mrs. Thatcher's Revolution," in *Recasting National Economies,* ed. David Calleo and Claudia Morgenstern (Lanham, Md.: University Press of America, 1990), p. 128.

81. David P. Calleo, *Britain's Future* (London: Hodder and Stoughton, 1968), p. 67.

82. John C. Hulsman, "The World Turned Rightside Up: A New Trading Agenda for the Age of Globalization," Heritage Lectures (Washington, D.C.: Heritage Foundation, January 24, 2000).

83. UK National Statistics, Business Monitor MA4, Foreign Direct Investment 2005, www.statistics.gov.uk, pp. 31–34, 89–92. For trade figures, consult www.uktradein-

fo.com. See Clyde Prestowitz, "Europe, America, and the New Globalization," in *Visions of the Atlantic Alliance*, ed. Serfaty (Washington, D.C.: CSIS Press, 2005), p. 117.

84. "British and Canadians Criticize Leaders for Following U.S. Lead," Program on International Policy Attitudes, August 9, 2006. For additional figures that confirm these downward trends, consult BBC World Service Poll, "World Views of U.S. Role Goes from Bad to Worse," conducted across twenty-five countries between November and December 2006 by GlobeScan and the Program on International Policy Attitudes, January 22, 2007.

85. German Marshall Fund of the United States et al., *Transatlantic Trends, 2006*, p. 6.

86. *Who Rules the World? World Powers and International Order: Conclusions from an International Representative Survey* (Berlin: Bertelsman Stiftung, June 2, 2006), pp. 13–16.

CHAPTER THREE

1. Robert Dallek, *Flawed Giant: Lyndon Johnson and His Times, 1961–1973* (New York: Oxford University Press, 1998), p. 87. "I know my Germans," Johnson used to insist, having been raised with a German grandmother near German settlements in Texas. Frank Costigliola, "Lyndon B. Johnson, Germany, and 'the End of the Cold War,'" in *Ost-West-Beziehungen: Konfrontation und Détente, 1945–1989*, ed. Gustav Schmidt, Band 2 (Bochum: Brockmeyer, 1993), p. 201. Charles de Gaulle, *La discorde chez l'ennemi* (Paris: Berger-Levrault, 1944), quoted in Crozier, *De Gaulle*, p. 40.

2. Jean-Raymond Tournoux, *Secrets d'État* (Paris: Plon, 1950), p. 154. In this context, de Gaulle's fist visit to Washington, in July 1944, remains telling. Although de Gaulle showed his usual intransigence, he was anxious to impress upon Roosevelt that he understood France's needs for material and political aid from the United States—"to regain her vigour, her self-confidence and therefore her role." Charles de Gaulle, *Mémoires de guerre*, vol. 2, *L'Unité* (Paris: Plon, 1956), pp. 237ff.

3. Richard Holbrooke, *To End a War* (New York: Random House, 1998), p. 32. Elizabeth Pond, "Germany in the New Europe," *Foreign Affairs* 71, no. 2 (Spring 1992): 112.

4. R. G. Livingston, "United Germany: Bigger and Better," *Foreign Policy*, no. 87 (Summer 1992): 157.

5. President Johnson's remark, which opens this chapter, is illustrative of this attitude, although his attempt at humor is not convincing. Roosevelt is quoted in Harper, *American Visions of Europe*, p. 15.

6. The welcome extended by President Ulysses S. Grant in February 1871 reflected America's interpretation of the other national and democratic movements that had spread throughout Europe during these years—in Greece, Hungary, Italy, and a republican France—either as reflective of "the American system of union" or as indicative of "the peaceful influence of American ideas." See Detlef Junker, *The Manichean Trap: American*

Perceptions of the German Empire, 1871–1945, Occasional Paper No. 12 (Washington, D.C.: German Historical Institute, 1995), p. 12.

7. For a persuasive argument that the League of Nations, as construed at Versailles, was structurally bound to fail, see F. H. Hinsley, *Power and the Pursuit of Peace* (London: Cambridge University Press, 1963), p. 309.

8. In Willy Brandt's daunting words, quoted by Craig, *The Germans,* p. 35.

9. Harper, *American Visions of Europe,* p. 290.

10. "Selling the American vision . . . was no mean chore. . . . The European core . . . had compelling reasons to resist American plans." Thomas J. McCormick, "America's Half Century: United States Foreign Policy in the Cold War," in *The Cold War in Europe: End of a Divided Continent,* ed. Charles S. Maier (New York: Markus Wiener, 1991), p. 32.

11. On Chancellor Adenauer's early misgivings, see Wolfram Hanrieder, *West German Foreign Policy, 1949–1963; International Pressure and Domestic Response* (Stanford, Calif.: Stanford University Press, 1967), pp. 94–112; and Desmond Dinan, *Europe Recast: A History of European Union* (Boulder, Colo.: Lynne Rienner, 2004), pp. 50–55 and 58–61.

12. Quoted in Gerald Freund, *Germany Between Two Worlds* (New York: Harcourt Brace, 1961), p. 115.

13. Simon Serfaty, "Odd Couple," in *Ost-West-Beziehungen: Konfrontation und Détente, 1945–1989,* ed. Gustav Schmidt, Band I (Bochum: Brockmeyer, 1993), pp. 73–83.

14. Anton DePorte, *Europe between the Superpowers* (New Haven, Conn.: Yale University Press, 1979), p. 155.

15. According to then-undersecretary of state George Ball, who accompanied Kennedy to Nassau, these were "the worst prepared summit meetings in modern times." Quoted in Bill, *George Ball,* p. 127. The immediate issue between the two governments had arisen from the U.S. decision to not proceed with the development and procurement of the Skybolt air-to-ground missile, which Britain had planned to acquire for its own fleet of strategic bombers. See William W. Kaufmann, *The McNamara Strategy* (New York: Harper & Row, 1964), pp. 124–25. Kennedy and British ambassador David Ormsby Gore worked out an initial arrangement in half an hour on the plane that was taking them to Nassau. After Macmillan declined this initial offer, a new proposal made Polaris missiles (minus the warheads) available to Britain. Arthur M. Schlesinger Jr., *A Thousand Days: John F. Kennedy in the White House* (Boston: Houghton Mifflin, 1965), pp. 863–65. Also David Nunnerley, *President Kennedy and Britain* (New York: St. Martin's Press, 1972), pp. 151–61.

16. Quoted in Douglas Stuart and William Tow, *The Limits of Alliance: NATO Out-of-Area Problems since 1949* (Baltimore: Johns Hopkins University Press, 1990), p. 118.

17. Macmillan, *At the End of the Day, 1961–1963* (London: Macmillan, 1973), p. 111; Bill, *George Ball,* p. 126; George Ball, *The Discipline of Power* (Boston: Atlantic Monthly Press, 1968), p.215.

18. Statement of February 6, 1963. Passeron, *De Gaulle parle,* 2:199. See Simon Serfaty, *France, de Gaulle, and Europe: The Policy of the Fourth and Fifth Republics toward the Continent* (Baltimore: Johns Hopkins University Press, 1968), pp. 126–27.

19. For Macmillan's own account, see *At the End of the Day*, pp. 347–48.

20. Statement of January 24, 1963. Passeron, *De Gaulle parle*, p. 207.

21. Statement of January 5, 1963. Ibid., p. 200.

22. Michael M. Harrison, *The Reluctant Ally: France and Atlantic Security* (Baltimore: Johns Hopkins University Press, 1981), pp. 79–80.

23. Fritz Stern, *Five Germanys I Have Known* (New York: Farrar, Straus and Giroux, 2006), p. 332. For de Gaulle's account of his relationship with Adenauer, see his *Mémoires d'Espoir: Le Renouveau, 1958–1962* (Paris: Plon, 1970), pp. 184ff.

24. As the then-seventy-two-year-old de Gaulle described himself—an "old Frenchman"—and his eighty-two-year-old counterpart—"a very old German." Quoted in Paul Legoll, *Charles de Gaulle et Konrad Adenauer: La cordiale entente* (Paris: L'Harmattan, 2004). See also Peyrefitte, *C'était de Gaulle*, 2:223.

25. Schlesinger, *A Thousand Days*, p. 872.

26. Quoted in Christopher Layne, "Iraq and Beyond: Old Europe and the End of the U.S. Hegemony," in *Visions of America and Europe,* ed. Christina Balis and Simon Serfaty, p. 58.

27. "If there was any hope of stopping or slowing down reunification," writes Margaret Thatcher, "it would only come from an Anglo-French initiative." *Downing Street Years*, p. 796.

28. Alfred Grosser, *Germany in Our Time: A Political History of the Postwar Years* (New York: Praeger Publishers, 1973). See also Simon Serfaty with Derek Mix, "Germany Stalled?" *CSIS Euro-Focus* 11, no. 3 (September 21, 2005): 2.

29. Raymond Aron, *The Dawn of Universal History: Selected Essays from a Witness to the Twentieth Century,* trans. Barbara Bray (New York: Basic Books, 2002), p. 10.

30. Edward A. Kolodziej, *French International Policy under de Gaulle and Pompidou: The Politics of Grandeur* (Ithaca, N.Y.: Cornell University Press, 1974), pp. 262–63.

31. John Van Oudenaren, "Containing Europe," *National Interest,* no. 80 (Summer 2005): 58.

32. This theme is developed at greater length in Simon Serfaty, *Stay the Course: European Unity and Transatlantic Solidarity* (Westport, Conn.: Praeger, 1997).

33. Alvin Z. Rubinstein, "Germans on Their Future," *Orbis* 43, no. 1 (Winter 1999): 128–29.

34. The admonition had come from Léon Gambetta—"Let us always think of what we have to do, but let us never talk about it." Herbert Tint, *The Decline of French Patriotism, 1870–1940* (London: Weidenfeld and Nicolson, 1964), p. 20.

35. Gerhard Schröder, "Politique étrangère: Y a-t-il une troisième voie?" *Le Monde,* September 7, 1999.

36. Quoted in *New York Times,* September 26, 1992.

37. George H. W. Bush, speech in Mainz, Germany, May 31, 1989; William Clinton, speech in Berlin, Germany, July 12, 1994.

38. Reports that Mitterrand repeatedly attempted to block, or at least delay, Germany's reunification have been exaggerated. See Frederic Bozo, *Mitterrand, la fin de la Guerre Froide et l'unification allemande* (Paris: Odile Jacob, 2005).

39. Derrik Ferney, "Xenophobia: A Barrier to Educating the Euro Generation," *Independent (London)*, October 30, 1997.

40. Peter J. Katzenstein, "United Germany in an Integrating Europe," in *Tamed Power*, ed. Peter J. Katzenstein (Ithaca, N.Y.: Cornell University Press, 1997), p. 9.

41. Hans Stark, "France and Germany: A New Start?" *International Spectator* 34, no. 2 (April–June 1999): 21.

42. The fifth of the many known by Fritz Stern during his remarkable career as the foremost American historian of Germany—a man influenced by his German past, of which he always remains aware, and sensitive to the fullness of his American life, to which he became fully committed. See Stern, *Five Germanys I Have Known*, pp. 4–6.

43. See, for example, "Oil That Motor: The French Fear That Gerhard Schröder May Pay Them Too Little Attention," *Economist*, October 3, 1998. Even Schroeder describes his relations with Chirac as initially "distant" and "cold." Gerhard Schröder, *Ma vie et la politique*, traduit de l'allemand par Geneviève Bégou, Laurence Caillarec, Marie Gravey, Violette Gubler, and Pierre Richard (Paris: Odile Jacob, 2006), p. 181.

44. Quoted by Steven Erlanger, "Traces of Terror: Perspectives," *New York Times*, September 5, 2002.

45. Quoted in Cohen, "Schröder Visits Bush Today," *New York Times*, March 29, 2001.

46. See Schroeder's interview with *Die Zeit*, "Wir schicken Soldaten, um sie einzusetzen," February 28, 2002.

47. Adrian Hyde-Price and Charlie Jeffery, "Germany in the European Union: Constructing Normality," *Journal of Common Market Studies* 39, no. 4 (November 2001): 690.

48. Timothy Garton Ash, "Germany's Choice," *Foreign Affairs* 73, no. 4 (July–August 1994): 66–67.

49. Hans Maull, "Germany and the Use of Force: Still a 'Civilian Power?'" *Survival* 42, no. 2 (Summer 2000): 56–80.

50. "Who Really Runs Germany," *Economist*, November 21, 1998; "Who's Running Germany?" *Economist*, December 5, 1998. Schroeder, it was argued for nearly one year after his election, is caught between Oskar Lafontaine's "commanding presence" and the "steady but safe" Hans Eichel, or between Rudolf Scharping, "the measured warrior," and Joschka Fischer, "Germany's reluctant statesman." *Economist*, October 3, 1998, and March 20, April 3, October 24, 1998, respectively. Ash, "Germany's Choice," pp. 66–67.

51. Serfaty with Mix, "Germany Stalled?" p. 2.

52. Joachen Hehn, "Paris ist erstaunt [astounded] uber die kompromisslosen Deutschen," *Die Welt*, September 6, 2002. Also John Vinocur, "German Position on Iraq Could Be Destabilizing for Allies," *International Herald Tribune*, September 7, 2002.

53. See the Pew Global Project Attitudes Project, "America's Image Slips." On the immediate reaction to President Bush's reelection, see "After the U.S. Election: A Survey of Public Opinion in France, Germany, and the United States," German Marshall Fund of the United States, February 7, 2005.

54. BBC World Service Poll, "World Public Says Iraq War Has Increased Global

Terrorist Threat," conducted in thirty-five different nations between October 2005 and January 2006 by Global Scan and the Program on International Attitudes (University of Maryland), February 25, 2006.

55. Jeffrey Gedmin, "Wer schmutzt, fliegt raus," *Sueddeutsche Zeitung,* July 26, 2001. Also "The New Europe and Its Implications for the United States," *AEI on the Issues,* March 29, 1999.

56. Katzenstein, "Same War—Different Views," p. 734.

57. Donald H. Rumsfeld, "What We've Gained in 3 Years in Iraq," *Washington Post,* March 19, 2006.

58. Richard Herzinger, "German Self-Definition against the US: America's One-Time Protégé Turns against Its Patron," *Internationale Politik,* Transatlantic ed., special issue (February 2006): 51–57.

59. See W. G. Sebald, *On the Natural History of Destruction* (New York: Random House, 2003), especially pp. 3–13.

60. Tony Judt, "From the House of the Dead: On Modern European Memory," *New York Review of Books,* October 6, 2005, pp. 12ff.

61. History does not offer any statute of limitation: during the thirty-year war that erupted in 1618, Germany as a whole suffered a loss of about one-third of the prewar population of 21 million, and in 1648 the "peacemakers" recognized more than three hundred German states as sovereign entities. Craig, *The Germans,* pp. 20–21.

62. Herzinger, "German Self-Definition," p. 56.

63. Josef Joffe, *Überpower: The Imperial Temptation of America* (New York: W. W. Norton & Co., 2006).

64. Peter Rudolf, "The Myth of the 'German Way': German Foreign Policy and Transatlantic Relations," *Survival* 47, no. 1 (Spring 2005): 133–52.

65. Schröder, *Ma vie,* pp. 165–71.

66. Jane Kramer, "A Once and Future Chancellor," *New Yorker,* September 14, 1998.

67. Quoted in Stern, *Five Germanys I Have Known,* p. 3.

68. Andrei S. Markovits and Simon Reich, *The German Predicament: Memory and Power in the New Europe* (Ithaca, N.Y.: Cornell University Press, 1997), pp. 3–5.

69. Samuel J. Newland, *Victories Are Not Enough: Limitations of the German Way of War,* Letort Papers, U.S. Army War College, December 2005.

70. Simon Serfaty, "Half before Europe, Half Past NATO," *Washington Quarterly* 18, no. 2 (March 1995): 49–58.

71. As argued by Zbigniew Brzezinski, "My invocation is, it's leadership, stupid." "America in the World Today," in *Complexity, Global Politics, and National Security,* ed. David S. Alberts and Thomas Czerwinski (Washington, D.C.: National Defense University Press, 1997), p. 29. Also Simon Serfaty, *Memories of Europe's Future: Farewell to Yesteryear* (Washington, D.C.: CSIS Press, 1999), pp. 124–40.

72. Cathleen S. Fisher, *Reconciling Realities: Reshaping the German-American Relationship for the Twenty-First Century,* American Institute for Contemporary German Studies, Policy Report No. 16 (2004), p. 51.

73. Interview with Joschka Fischer, "Amerika hatte kein Verdun," *Der Spiegel,* March 24, 2003.

74. As the first secretary of defense, James Forrestal, is quoted in D. F. Fleming, *The Cold War and Its Origins* (Garden City, N.Y.: Doubleday, 1961), p. 487.

75. See Stephen Fidler, "Taking Charge: Germany and Japan Strive to Regain Their Military Might," *Financial Times*, November 16, 2006.

76. Witness the debate over national caveats pursued within Germany as well as with the United States and other leading NATO countries with regard to engaging Taliban forces in Afghanistan.

77. For instance, Will Hutton, *The World We're In* (London: Little, Brown & Co., 2002), p. 3.

78. See William Friend, *The Linchpin: French-German Relations, 1950–1990* (New York: Praeger, 1991).

79. Schröder, *Ma vie*, p. 154.

80. See Vivien Schmidt, *Democracy in Europe: The EU and National Policies* (Oxford: Oxford University Press, 2006).

CHAPTER FOUR

1. Glenn Kessler, "Rice Stresses the Positive amid Mideast Setbacks," *Washington Post*, December 20, 2006. William C. Atkinson, *A History of Spain and Portugal* (London: Penguin Books, 1960), p. 165, quoted in Edmund Stillman and William Pfaff, *Power and Impotence: The Failure of America's Foreign Policy* (New York: Random House, 1966), p. 225.

2. Serfaty, "Wars of 911," pp. 5–11.

3. Frantz Fanon, *The Wretched of the Earth*, preface by Jean-Paul Sartre, trans. Constance Farrington (New York: Grove Press, 1963), pp. 17–18.

4. See Rose, "Neo Culpa," pp. 82–90.

5. See Simon Serfaty, "No More Dissent," *Foreign Policy* (Summer 1972): 144–58.

6. James Blitz, "Iraq War a Disaster, Signals PM on Al-Jazeera" *Financial Times*, November 18, 2006, and Peter Baker, Michael A. Fletcher, and Michael Abramowitz, "President Bush on Iraq, Elections and Immigration," *Washington Post*, December 20, 2006. Secretary Gates's observation, drawing from an off-the-record statement attributed to General Pace, was made during his confirmation hearings.

7. Frederick W. Kagan, *Choosing Victory: A Plan for Success in Iraq*, A Report of the Iraq Planning Group at the American Enterprise Institute (January 5, 2007); and Wesley Clark, "A Diplomatic Surge," *Washington Post*, January 8, 2007.

8. Francis Fukuyama, *America at the Crossroads: Democracy, Power, and the Neoconservative Legacy* (New Haven, Conn.: Yale University Press, 2006), p. 193.

9. See Christopher Layne, "The Unipolar Illusion Revisited: The Coming End of the United States' Unipolar Moment," *International Security* 31, no. 2 (Fall 2006): 17.

10. Henry Kissinger, *A World Restored* (Boston: Houghton Mifflin, 1973). Also Zbig-

niew Brzezinski, *Between Two Ages: America's Role in the Technetronic Era* (New York: Viking Press, 1970).

11. Michael Mandelbaum, "The Bush Foreign Policy," *Foreign Affairs* 70, no. 1, "America and the World," supp. (1990–91): 12ff. See also Simon Serfaty, "Defining Moments," *SAIS Review* 12, no. 2 (Summer–Fall 1992): 51–64.

12. This is not to say that there were no divisions within the administration— especially as the views of Defense Secretary Richard Cheney came to converge, after the war, with those of Paul Wolfowitz, one of his most trusted advisers. Ten years later, the legacy of these divisions "still hung in the air, unacknowledged but undeniable." See James Mann, *Rise of the Vulcans: The History of Bush's War Cabinet* (New York: Viking, 2004), pp. 184ff.

13. Charles Krauthammer, "The Unipolar Moment," *Foreign Affairs* 70, no. 1, "America and the World," supp. (1990–91): 23–33.

14. For an early and notable exception see Christopher Layne, "The Unipolar Illusion: Why New Great Powers Will Rise," *International Security* 17, No. 4 (Spring 1993): 5–51.

15. Francis Fukuyama, *The End of History and the Last Man* (New York: Free Press, 1992), pp. 57–60.

16. See Kagan, *Of Paradise and Power*, p. 101.

17. Van Oudenaren, "Containing Europe," pp. 57–64.

18. See George Liska, *Imperial America* (Baltimore: Johns Hopkins University Press, 1968), and Robert W. Tucker and David C. Hendrickson, *The Imperial Temptation: The New World Order and America's Purpose* (New York: Council on Foreign Relations, 1992), as well as Simon Serfaty, *La tentation impériale* (Paris: Odile Jacob, 2005).

19. Robert Kagan, *Dangerous Nation: America's Place in the World from Its Earliest Days to the Dawn of the Twentieth Century* (New York: Alfred A. Knopf, 2006), p. 13.

20. Joffe, *Uberpower.*

21. See Mann, *Rise of the Vulcans*, pp. 198–215.

22. Henry Kissinger, *White House Years* (Boston: Little, Brown, 1979), p. 18.

23. Henry Kissinger, *Diplomacy* (New York: Simon & Shuster, 1994), pp. 424–25.

24. See Hans Binnendijk and Richard L. Kugler, *Seeing the Elephant: The U.S. Role in Global Security* (Washington, D.C.: Potomac Books, 2006), p. 19. "Clinton," observes Zbigniew Brzezinski, "viewed foreign affairs as a continuation of domestic politics by other means." *Second Chance: Three Presidents and the Crisis of American Superpower* (New York: Basic Books, 2007), p. 85.

25. This theme is developed at greater length in Simon Serfaty, "Memories of Leadership," *The Brown Journal of World Affairs* 5, no. 2 (Summer–Fall 1998): 3–16.

26. Press conference by President Jacques Chirac, Brussels, Belgium, February 17, 2003. Subsequently, Chirac deplored his outburst. Péan, *L'inconnu de l'Élysée*, pp. 434–45.

27. Schroder, *Ma vie*, p. 171.

28. James A. Baker III and Lee H. Hamilton, Co-Chairs, *The Iraq Study Group Report* (New York: Vintage Books, 2006).

29. François Furet, *The Passing of an Illusion: The Idea of Communism in the Twentieth Century*, trans. Deborah Furet (Chicago: University of Chicago Press, 1999), p. 502.

30. See, for example, Truman's own account of MacArthur's dismissal, *Memoirs*, vol. 2, *1946–52, Years of Trial and Hope* (New York: Time, 1955), pp. 440–50; and Brian VanDeMark, *Into the Quagmire: Lyndon Johnson and the Escalation of the Vietnam War* (New York: Oxford University Press, 1999).

31. Stephen M. Walt, *Taming American Power: The Global Response to U.S. Primacy* (New York: W.W. Norton & Company, 2005), pp. 223ff.

32. Martin Wolf, "This Stable Isle: How Labour Has Steered an Economy Going Global," *Financial Times*, September 18, 2006.

33. For example, Christopher Gelpi, Peter D. Feaver, and Jason Reifler, "Success Matters: Casualty Sensitivity and the War in Iraq," *International Security* 30, no. 3 (Winter 2005–6): 7–46.

34. Walter Russell Mead, *Special Providence: American Foreign Policy and How It Changed the World* (New York: Alfred A. Knopf, 2001), p. 10; John Lewis Gaddis, *We Know Now: Rethinking Cold War History* (Oxford: Clarendon Press, 1997).

35. The region needs some definition: "the huge area from North Africa through Egypt, Israel and the Tiger-Euphrates valley, through the Persian Gulf region into Turkey and on to the Caspian basis." Robert Blackwill and Michael Stürmer, eds., *Allies Divided: Transatlantic Policies for the Greater Middle East* (Cambridge, Mass.: MIT Press, 1997), p. 1.

36. Geir Kjetsaa, *Fyodor Dostoyevky: A Writer's Life*, trans. Siri Hustvedt and David McDuff (New York: Viking, 1987), pp. 255–57.

37. Rose, "Neo Culpa," p. 85

38. Mann, *Rise of the Vulcans*, pp. 134–36.

39. Zachary Karabell, *Architects of Intervention: The United States, the Third World, and the Cold War* (Baton Rouge: Louisiana State University Press, 1999), p. 175.

40. According to White, *Fire in the Ashes*, p. 384.

41. President Carter's speech at Notre Dame University, May 22, 1977.

42. "I know we oughtn't to be there [in Vietnam] but I can't get out," reflected Johnson in 1966. Quoted by David A. Fahrenthold, "Vietnam and Iraq: Looking Back and Looking Ahead," *Washington Post*, March 12, 2006.

43. Caroline Daniel, "Bush in Vietnam Admits Parallel with Iraq," *Financial Times*, November 20, 2006.

44. Peter Baker, "Stubborn or Stalwart, Bush Is Loath to Budge," *Washington Post*, December 17, 2006.

45. David C. Henrickson and Robert W. Tucker, "A Test of Power," *National Interest*, no. 25 (September–October 2006): 51.

46. Charles Krauthammer, "Why Iraq Is Crumbling," *Washington Post*, November 17, 2006.

47. Charles Krauthammer, "The Hanging: Beyond Travesty," *Washington Post*, January 5, 2007.

48. Secretary Condoleezza Rice, "Remarks at BBC Today—Chatham House Lecture," Ewood Park, Blackburn, United Kingdom, March 31, 2006. As argued in these pages, the war in Iraq had little in common with the war in Vietnam. But the pattern of failure, as explained here, repeats previously seen patterns during the long escalation of the Vietnam War. See Robert S. McNamara, *In Retrospect: The Tragedy and Lessons of Vietnam* (New York: Time Books, 1995), p. 33.

49. Baker and Hamilton, *Iraq Study Group Report*, pp. ix–xiv. Thus the report presented a total of seventy-nine recommendations that were "comprehensive . . . [and] not [to] be separated or carried out in isolation." The first of these recommendations spelled out "a major diplomatic initiative" that would "have to be launched before December 31, 2006"—meaning barely more than a month after the report had been made public—with a withdrawal of "all combat brigades not necessary for force protection" completed "by the first quarter of 2008." Malcolm Rifkind, "In Some Areas, Sovereignty Should Be Shared in Europe," *Financial Times*, December 13, 2006.

50. Quoted in Daniel, "Blair Not a Yes Man."

51. Glenn Kessler, "In 2003, U.S. Spurned Iran's Offer of Dialogue," *Washington Post*, June 18, 2006.

52. Ivo Daalder and James Goldgeier, "America and Europe Must Learn about Alliances," *Financial Times*, December 15, 2006.

53. Peter J. Taylor, "Tribulations of Transition," *Professional Geographer* 44, no. 1 (February 1992): 10–12.

54. Stanley Hoffmann, "Obstinate or Obsolete? The Fate of the Nation-State and the Case of Western Europe," *Daedalus* 95, no. 3 (Summer 1966): 862–916.

55. John J. Mearsheimer, *The Tragedy of Great Power Politics* (New York: W. W. Norton & Company, 2001), p. 3.

56. Fernand Braudel, *On History* (London: Weidenfeld and Nicolson, 1980).

57. See Andrei P. Tsygankov, *Russia's Foreign Policy: Change and Continuity in National Identity* (Lanham, Md.: Rowman & Littlefield, 2006).

58. Ariel Cohen, "A New Paradigm for U.S.-Russian Relations: Facing the Post–Cold War Reality," The Heritage Foundation *Backgrounder*, no. 1105 (March 6, 1997), p. 11.

59. Vladimir Putin, speech at the 43rd Munich Conference on Security Policy, Munich, Germany, February 10, 2007.

60. Richard Haass, *The Opportunity: America's Moment to Alter History's Course* (New York: Public Affairs, 2005), pp. 439ff. Also Zbigniew Brzezinski, *The Choice: Global Domination or Global Leadership* (New York: Basic Books, 2004), pp. 100–103.

61. Hutton, *The World We're In*, pp. 368–69.

INDEX

Acheson, Dean: on France's post–World War II role, 14; on German trustworthiness, 83; on U.S. influence, 117

Adams, John Quincy, 17

Adenauer, Konrad: de Gaulle and, 87; on de Gaulle, 108; reliance on France by, 91; trust for U.S. of, 83; on U.S. support, 84

Afghanistan: German troop deployments in, 107; Soviet invasion of, 113, 115; U.S. invasion of, 136

Albanian option, 45

American identity, 18–19

American imperialism, 117–18

anti-Americanism: in India, 139; in post–World War II Britain, 20; in post–World War II France, 26; as recurring phenomenon in Europe, 76

anti-Semitism, French, 23

antieventism, 137

Aragon, Louis, 31

Arrogance of the French, The, 22

Atlantic Alliance. *See* North Atlantic Treaty Organization

axis of evil, 27, 35–36

Aznar, José María, 35, 65, 110, 120

Baker, James: coalition building by, 29–30; on French antipathy, 13, 21; on Iraq war, 135

Baker-Hamilton Report, 122, 135

Ball, George, 85

Bay of Pigs, 64, 130

Bellow, Saul, 36

Berlin blockade, 128

Berlusconi, Silvio, 120

bipolar world: Germany in, 82; versus multipolar, 137; multipolarity as expected outcome of, 115. *See also* Cold War

Blair, Tony, 28; in coalition building, 29; on de Gaulle's attitude toward Britain, 52; followership goals of, 57–58; on importance of EU, 56–57, 94; on influencing the United States, 59–60; on Iraq war, 114; in Iraq war debates, 120, 121; leadership failure of, 7–8, 68–69; political abilities of, 52–53; relationship with Clinton, 57–58; UN as political cover for, 42; on war in Iraq, 4–5, 75–76

Bosnia, 107

Brandt, Willy, 98, 108

Braudel, Fernand, 137

Bremer, Paul, 130

Britain: economic relationship with EU countries, 78, 126; on German rehabilitation, 83–84, 94; leadership style of, 47–48; post–World War II anti-Americanism in, 20; public opinion on EU in, 79; public opinion on Germany in, 94; public opinion on U.S. leadership in, 78–79; resistance to European integration by, 93; in Suez crisis, 50–51

British-French relationship: de Gaulle on, 7; in EU's future development, 79; Iraq strategy in straining of, 66–67; as source of European strength, 55

British-U.S. relationship: British ambivalence concerning, 8; Churchill in creating, 48–49; de Gaulle on, 86; as at expense of EU, 74; Kennedy in building, 85–86; lack of parity in, 56; post-Suez study on, 51; public opinion on, 78–79; reassessment of utility of, 75–77; Thatcher on, 46

Brown, Gordon, 75, 77

Brzezinsky, Zbigniew, 116

Bulgaria, 110

Bush, George H. W.: coalition building by, 29–30, 63–64; on European security order,

ACKNOWLEDGMENTS

For this book, as for any other that came before—or any more that might come later—acknowledgments go first to my students, currently in the Graduate Program in International Studies at Old Dominion University, in Norfolk, Virginia, and previously at the Paul H. Nitze School of Advanced International Studies of the Johns Hopkins University and at the University of California in Los Angeles. What I write grows out of what I say, rather than the other way around, and what I say is often first said in the challenging context of a classroom where students keep me intellectually alert and personally renewed. To see so many of the students I have had the pleasure of having in my classes now hold positions of influence and power in and beyond the United States is cause for enormous satisfaction. It is to them that this book is dedicated.

I would also like to thank, most generally, the community of think tankers that has been a constant source of ideas and challenges over the years, first through the Johns Hopkins Foreign Policy Institute and more recently through the Center for Strategic and International Studies (CSIS). Such institutions are more than think tanks: they are action tanks that strive to combine scholarly rigor with nonpartisan policy relevance. They are in Washington and all over the country, and they have spread throughout Europe and elsewhere. In each of them are many people of quality I have met and with whom I have exchanged ideas, and I have gained immensely from these exchanges. They are too numerous to mention individually, with the exception of CSIS counselor Zbigniew Brzezinski, who did me the honor of having me be the first to hold the chair named after him at CSIS, where he is a constant provider of intellect, integrity, and friendship.

At CSIS, I also want to thank my younger colleague Derek Mix, who provided me with invaluable support on this and many other related projects; Derek has a bright future ahead of him. Thanks also go to Professor Michael

Brenner, a friend of many years, a scholar's scholar, at the University of Pittsburgh. He read the manuscript and offered valuable suggestions. Thanks, too, to Bill Finan, who guided me through the final phases of getting this work into print shortly after he joined the University of Pennsylvania Press after his many years as editor of the journal *Current History*.

Finally, and as always, my wife, Gail, and my son, Alexis, provided affection, comfort, and encouragement. They were, they are, the architects of our collective well-being, but, to be sure, they are architects without delusions.